SEEING
THINGS

SEEING THINGS

TECHNOLOGIES OF VISION
AND THE
MAKING OF MORMONISM

MASON KAMANA ALLRED

THE UNIVERSITY OF NORTH CAROLINA PRESS

Chapel Hill

Set in Arno, Scala Sans, Golden, Irby, and Lightburn
by codeMantra

Manufactured in the United States of America

A version of chapter 1 originally appeared as Mason Kamana Allred,
"Circulating Specters: Mormon Reading Networks, Vision, and Optical
Media," *Journal of the American Academy of Religion* 85, no. 2 (2017):
527–48. Published with permission of Oxford University Press.

A version of chapter 2 originally appeared as Mason Kamana Allred, "Panoramic
Vision: Consolidating the Early Mormon Gaze," *Material Religion* 16, no.
5 (2020): 639–64. Published with permission of Taylor and Francis.

Cover illustration by Jack Soren.

LIBRARY OF CONGRESS CATALOGING-IN-PUBLICATION DATA
Names: Allred, Mason Kamana, author.
Title: Seeing things : technologies of vision and the making of Mormonism /
Mason Kamana Allred.
Description: Chapel Hill : The University of North Carolina Press, [2023] |
Includes bibliographical references and index.
Identifiers: LCCN 2022027348 | ISBN 9781469672571 (cloth : alk. paper) |
ISBN 9781469672588 (paperback : alk. paper) | ISBN 9781469672595 (ebook)
Subjects: LCSH: Technology—Religious aspects—Mormon Church. |
Communication—Religious aspects—Mormon Church. | Mass media—Religious
aspects—Mormon Church. | Mormon Church—History. | Visions—History.
Classification: LCC BX8643.T38 A45 2023 | DDC 246/.95893—dc23/eng/20220809
LC record available at https://lccn.loc.gov/2022027348

CONTENTS

ILLUSTRATIONS

ACKNOWLEDGMENTS

I remember being told as a child that spirits were all around us. I felt amazed and paranoid, then somewhat ashamed when I never saw them. As a practicing Latter-day Saint, these kinds of ideas, along with the images, smells, and sounds of American Mormonism powerfully suffused my youth. Yet, as an adult, analyzing the ways Mormonism's interactions with the dead and visionary media practices shaped the church's own development often felt quite foreign. At every turn I was surprised by the appearance of strange specters from its technological past. Capturing these flashes of history and integrating them into a coherent study would have been impossible to pull off on my own. In fact, this book required a multitude of insights, suggestions, guidance, and support from living and dead sources. Aside from the fascinating archival discoveries, I was stimulated, inspired, and encouraged by numerous individuals who graciously helped usher this work along.

Much of the book began taking shape while I was employed as a historian and editor at the Joseph Smith Papers (JSP) project. I benefited from funding there and access to the Church History Library's immense archive. Special thanks go to my colleagues Chris Blythe and Jordan Watkins, for reading several drafts of early chapters and pointing me toward ever more sources. The book found its initial sparks in the lively conversations of the JSP project's notorious walking group, whose members covered as much intellectual ground—discussing historiography and developments within religious studies and Mormon studies—as they did physical ground strolling around Salt Lake City.

I am gratefully indebted to Jenny Reeder for introducing me to Elfie Huntington's work and reading early versions of several chapters. Thank you also to Kate Holbrook and Lisa Olsen Tait for their guidance and patience with my interest in Latter-day Saint women's history. Feedback from John Durham Peters and Ben Peters on a short essay included in their guest edited issue of *Mormon Studies Review* in 2018 provided formative kindling for the project. I wish also to express my gratitude to a long list of kind friends and supportive colleagues who read drafts and offered input, including Brent Rogers, David Grua, Spencer McBride, Robin Jensen, Jeffrey Mahas, Jeff Cannon, Christian Heimburger, and Matt Godfrey in Salt Lake City, as well as Tyler Gardner and Spencer Fluhman at Brigham Young University, Provo. The list continues with Scott Muhlestein, Becky Strain, Charles Bradshaw, and Joe Plicka in Hawaii. And dispersed across the world, Amanda Beardsley, Ben Bigelow, Mary Campbell, Randy Astle, and David Walker also generously offered feedback and direction.

I am indebted to my diligent research assistant Hadley Wurtz. Thanks to Jeff Thompson and Ben Harry at the Church History Library, as well as Cindy Brightenburg at Brigham Young University's special collections for archival assistance in finding and securing the accompanying images. I want to express my gratitude to Elaine Maisner, Andreina Fernandez, and the team at University of North Carolina Press for their marvelous guidance and professionalism. I thank them also for finding what were perhaps the most insightful and generous readers possible for the manuscript. Their perceptive challenges and praise masterfully discerned the book's potential and helped coax its ideas forward into fruition.

Finally, I thank Erika, my best friend and loving partner. While she is always down to join me looking into any strange or distant subject, she also reminds me to never lose sight of what is right in front of me.

SEEING THINGS

INTRODUCTION

O Lord when will the time come when . . . we may stand together
and gaze upon eternal wisdom engraven upon the heavens
while the majesty of our God holdeth up the dark curtain.

Joseph Smith, 1832

Moroni . . . being dead, and raised again therefrom,
appeared unto me, and told me where [the gold plates]
were; and gave me directions how to obtain them.

Joseph Smith, 1838

Mormonism began with visions of the dead. The ripples set off by those visions shaped much of the distinctive media practices that have suffused Mormonism's vitality. Joseph Smith, the founder of the movement, asked big questions and claimed even bigger answers in the form of the formerly dead.[1] Smith recounted how the resurrected Lord appeared to him in the woods; how the once-dead Book of Mormon prophet Moroni materialized as an angel in his parent's log home; and how he was directed to translate and publish the words of deceased ancient American prophets, several of whom would visit him in turn.[2] For Smith, seeing these things was not just believing them. It was productive. Seeing was a form of becoming. Mormonism was, then, born from visions of the dead, but its development was equally shaped by the media taken up by the living to see in extraordinary ways.

When the angel Moroni suddenly appeared in Smith's bedroom in September 1823 he told of some remarkable media, including a book of gold plates and "two stones in silver bows" buried nearby but completely unknown.

This foundational piece of the origin story of Mormonism also reveals its founding visionary media practices. For, as Moroni further explained, the gold plates should be unearthed along with the stones, which would allow Smith to see the translation of the plates as visions on the stone's surface.

Smith's eventual translation of the plates accentuated his sight and the interplay between the material and the discursive. Smith looked at stones, most often placed in his hat, to translate and dictate the contents of the Book of Mormon. Although the plates' physical presence was apparently crucial to the translation process, Smith looked in a hat. In other words, Smith dug up the dead material but brought it to life by looking away from the artifact and directly into the light of stones, by the "gift and power of god," as he described it.[3] This practice made words and matter do strange things. Indecipherable engravings on gold became visions on a stone, then words from Smith's mouth, and finally ink on paper. All the materials involved made the publication of the Book of Mormon in 1830 possible, but the seer stone was particularly integral to this process and productive in another important sense.

As Smith learned to master the technology of the stones by excluding light, peering into them, and dictating what he saw (all techniques dictated by the medium), he *became* a seer. This was not his first experience experimenting with this technology, as Smith was known to possess "certain means, by which he could discern things, that could not be seen by the natural eye."[4] But the process of somehow looking in stones—"Urim and Thummim," as they would be called—was consistent.[5] Just as Smith was not a seer until he used the medium of the seer stones, the loss of media could impede his abilities. After offending God early in the translation of the plates, Smith said his interpreters were taken away by Moroni, and Smith's gift (and identity) hung in the balance.[6] The stones did as much as Smith in enacting seership. Similar stones had made more than a few Americans into seers and treasure diggers, but Smith's use was also unique. No one had become a seer by turning gold into scripture. To put it simply, Smith looked at a stone but saw sacred text. In puzzling and provocative ways, Smith was seeing things.

Despite the folk magical flare, the defiant collapsing of the spiritual and the material marks this origin story as exceptionally Mormon. Latter-day Saints' use of technologies would largely follow Smith's lead with visionary adaptations that scrambled prevalent ideas about media and religion. Unlike the classical materialism of their contemporaries that described matter as "inert and purely mechanical," early Latter-day Saints understood matter to be coeternal with God, to be dynamic, and to have some form of agency.[7]

In new Mormon scripture, "the Gods" created the world not out of nothing but by organizing existing matter. In fact, they ordered the world, including light, the earth, and the planets and "watched those things which they had ordered until they obeyed."[8] Divine vision was met with material agency. The Gods saw everything into creation by watching intelligent matter choose to obey their command.

Mormonism's unique metaphysics held that anything that exists—including spirits and intelligence—is material and in a process of becoming.[9] And everything that exists has both material and spiritual dimensions in the Mormon worldview. "There is no such thing as immaterial matter," taught Smith. He elaborated further, explaining that "spirit is matter but it is more fine or pure and can only be discerned by purer eyes."[10] Seeing in and with media was itself a material-spiritual practice and always held the possibility of unleashing vision's creative ordering power.

Because of Mormonism's imaginative theology, Latter-day Saint media practices provide a telling case study to explore issues inherent to the fields of media and religious studies, especially around notions of materiality and agency. Although early Mormonism's unique materialist doctrines were only gradually articulated and not always clearly defined, in my reading they offer theological and often inchoate analogues to our modern conceptions of quantum entanglement and distributed agency. Initially these strange Latter-day Saint ideas contradicted many of their contemporaries, especially within Christianity.[11] But today they nestle in nicely with current theory and even nudge the wider study of media and religion forward. Critically engaging the organizing force of Mormon vision that orders their world into existence can advance our understanding of media's role in religious culture.

Mormons see in and through media the opportunity to process and produce. In fact, it is only through media that Latter-day Saints can achieve their greatest goals: to come to God and become gods. Religious experience and knowledge are not just facilitated by the primary medium of language and the sensory media of ears, hands, noses, and eyes. For Mormons, these and other media truly are the message—the message that the process of becoming through material experience is congruent before and after death. To become like God, Latter-day Saints need to see, feel, and know him in their bones. Catholic scholar of religion Stephen Webb reveled in Joseph Smith's wild theological claim that "we can know God through our senses."[12] And indeed, according to Smith we can know God as a material embodied being *only* through our own bodies. Emerging from this worldview, Latter-day Saints couldn't help but use media in ways that refused the separation of medium and message, natural and spiritual, and—perhaps most scandalously—of God and humans.

Media enable Mormons to see things into existence. They don't do this ex nihilo, but by interacting with media and the horizon of possibilities the material world offers. In this manner, the largest developments, shifts, and concepts of Mormonism were inseparable from media. In both hopeful and haunted ways, Mormonism was configured out of material practices of looking, charged with spiritual significance. Often this meant glimpsing what would otherwise be invisible to the natural eyes. Like mesmerism before and spiritualism after, Mormonism engaged the potential of managing belief in what was ordinarily unseen but understood to be physically real.[13] From gazing in stones to TV screens, Mormonism has been forged by managing visions in media. This book unearths the ways media encouraged certain visions and forestalled others, but also how they shaped the very identity and performance of Mormonism as a culture of seeing.

Media can be all kinds of productive things. Certainly stones, sticks, spirits, angels, and alphabets have had a role in determining and enabling Mormonism, since its very inception. But in this book the media of focus are technologies, including print, panorama, photography, typewriters, (micro)film, and television, that have all shaped Mormonism and its visionary practices. I take these technologies and their adoption as the skeletal and muscular core for the chapters herein, which together set up an orientation toward religion that emphasizes the role of visionary media in fleshing out religious culture and experience. Without insisting on technological determinism, I argue for the need to take the material media of Mormonism's past more seriously—to dig them up and see them with the light of a new lens.

The following chapters offer an archaeology of the role of media in the development of Mormonism. They tell the story of technologies enabling a new religion to interact with the dead, manage the flock, and gain acceptance in America. They reveal how Mormon vision generally transformed from radical to safe in the eyes of the nation. Despite disputes and discipline within the religion, the gaze of the nation largely supervised Mormonism into submission, to the extent that Latter-day Saint visions after the early twentieth century would comport with national belonging. Modern Mormonism's complex relationship with American mainstream, especially conservative, ideology became a key feature of its culture, and this is reflected in its media visions. At times Latter-day Saints tempered the radically expansive visions of Joseph Smith and early Mormonism with prevailing cultural ways of seeing and being seen. I am specifically interested in how media enable and showcase such developments and opportunities to see things in ways that direct culture and belief and how the faith tradition, which is now a global religion with more members outside the United States than within, might see itself forward beyond that national and political relationship. Part of the answer to this precarious situation is certainly to be located in technologies that are understood to be at once spiritual and material.

From the outset Mormonism was quite amenable to media, with early adopters and adept users of emergent technologies. Latter-day Saints used media, as spiritual technologies, to seek salvation for themselves and their dead, by refining religious understanding and performance through techniques of looking. In every case, these media practices maintained, drove, even pushed Mormonism certain directions to build the kingdom of God, as Latter-day Saints understood it. Media were vital actors in this process. Because of their ability to discipline behavior, recast the world, and even facilitate interaction with the dead, media enabled material-theological practices of beholding. They met users halfway and helped define Mormonism. Despite interacting with the same technologies as other religious Americans, materialist Mormons—sometimes deliberately—emerged somewhat differently. These differences came to matter through media practices of measuring, defining, and performing their religion. And this was accomplished by both users *and* the technology itself. From this entangled relationship of a distributed notion of agency, we must recognize just how much media practices have always enabled the very concept of Latter-day Saint.

Analysis of technologies and the techniques attending them offers glimpses into a process of "Mormonization," or the constitution of "Mormons" against the wider fabric of the world and others. In essence, media brought Mormonism to life by creating and processing boundaries and distinctions, often as repeatable bodily experiences. The way Mormons learned to use media—whether reading between the lines of print to see the dead, looking at panorama to see their dead prophet, or tuning a TV to gather the living—made them Mormons in the first place.

Bringing Mormonism to life meant a complex networks of things, including people, devices, and ideas.[14] This book is particularly interested in these hodgepodges and entanglements of the dead and the living, of media and things. A level of Mormonism has always been readily apparent in cultural texts through discourse analysis. After all, concepts such as revelation, truth, or spirit are talked about, written about, debated, and praised in words. Histories of the Latter-day Saint church have done well to investigate this discursive layer by consulting extant sources to narrate human actors and ecclesiastical developments. But that surface skin scarcely covers the significant work of media agency beneath. My aim here is to revive the Mormon media past by cobbling together its different parts and acknowledging these layers—not so much to isolate each component (as if they had any life on their own) but rather to illuminate their productive interplay. Peering through the textuality of the religion's past to discern its technological musculature better fits the theology of Mormonism and helps reveal the entangled relationship of matter and meaning.[15] Not only do both skin and muscle work within a network of veins, reflexes, electric charges, and techniques; they are even enmeshed and enabled on a molecular level. Likewise, language and expression were always inseparable from the material media that have too often been sequestered or simply forgotten. This book wants to electrify and reanimate the inseparability of both discourse and devices; ideas and individuals; skin and muscle.

The following chapters use technologies as the material "muscle" of entry points into past discourse networks, by employing a media archaeological approach to dig up the dead and trace the constitution of assemblages that have sought to make Mormonism endure. Analysis of these technologies brings the entanglement of media and discourse into relief on the distinctive terms of that period—especially how they enabled Mormon identity and practice. I am particularly interested in the Mormon structuring of vision: what is seen, how, and what is excluded through material-discursive practices.[16] For, more than we have realized, it was through their media practices that Latter-day Saints were able to enact the monumental shift from American scoundrels to superpatriots across the nineteenth and twentieth centuries. Approaching a cultural history of this development by way of media, bodies, and discourse requires some theoretical setup, and this book is in conversation with and greatly indebted to recent work within media studies, new materialism, and religious studies.

I unearth the significance of several technologies of the Mormon past, by employing an adapted version of "media archaeology." As an orientation toward media that grew out of German media theory, media archaeology was inspired by Friedrich Kittler, who anchored the ideas of Michel Foucault in the materiality of technologies. Foucault's "historical a priori" began to look a lot like deterministic media in Kittler's work.[17] Later scholars extended the project of Kittler's technical a priori, by challenging the linear models of technological progress, seeking out the initial vitality of dead (obsolete) media, and considering the ways media shape logic. This approach to technology and epistemology often highlights the role of media as material technologies that make up a "discourse network" enabling thought and knowledge. In the words of Kittler, this is "the network of technologies and institutions that allow a given culture to select, store, and process relevant data" at any given point.[18] This book has a lot to gain by crafting an approach to religion that is sensitive to how technology enables and constrains "even our basic ways of being in the world: seeing, hearing, thinking, and feeling."[19]

While media archaeology invites us to take nonhuman actors of the past seriously by attuning us to the material dimension of networks, it has often done this at the dualistic exclusion of discourse or with a clear prioritization of matter as the determining factor. My focus on the materiality of the concepts of early Mormonism that might otherwise seem to defy perceptibility, such as revelation, spirit, and vision, seeks rather to highlight the networked interplay between matter and meaning. As John Durham Peters has argued, "Media are perhaps most interesting when they reveal what defies materialization."[20] And although efforts to materialize belief are often at the heart of religious media, these interactions are never purely material or discursive.[21] Hardware can't just be mined to reveal "the 'hard' base of the chimeras known as 'spirit' (Geist), understanding, or the public sphere."[22] But these same technologies do "act" on, with, and against other things within networks. Considering the agency of material things is important, especially since religious concepts seem to concretize and endure only through their interplay with techniques and technologies. This means media archaeology requires updating and reconsideration.

As they have advanced the insights of German media theory, John Durham Peters, Bernhard Siegert, and Jeremy Stolow have been crucial for this book.[23] Trailblazing scholarship like theirs highlights how technology "forms the gridwork of orientations, operations, and embedded and embodied knowledges and powers without which religious ideas, experiences, and actions could not exist."[24] They have all helped chart a course to reconsider media as networks of logistics, infrastructures, and techniques that exceed anthropocentrism. German media theory in their hands has benefited from the work of Bruno Latour and actor-network theory to recognize how the most fundamental media and practices create meaning and distinctions.

Latour and his French colleagues refocused the "social" as a "momentary association which is characterized by the way it gathers together into new shapes," including nonhuman actors.[25] Within networks, agency is understood to manifest only in and through relations of actors. Rather than the intentionality of a single subject, agency is a "force distributed across multiple, overlapping bodies, disseminated in degrees."[26] This European mixture of ideas has helped to theorize both media's role in reality (fact) and its representations (fetish).[27] The shared focus on the very construction of culture through processes, infrastructures, and practices can deepen technically oriented histories and help enrich our understanding of religion and the distinctions that make it meaningful. Rather than an anticultural studies, German media theory can provide a way into a robust posthuman cultural studies.

Media archaeology can benefit from incorporating not only the insights of actor-network theory and the cultural techniques of German media theory, but also the deep provocations of feminist new materialism. Only then might a media archaeological approach engage the entanglement of discourse and materiality to help "overcome the dualisms that haunt" it, as Mira Stolpe Törneman has suggested.[28] In order to treat angels, spirits, objects, practices, and humans my use of media archaeology as a method is inspired as much by early Mormonism's theology of matter as it is by recent materialist work in feminist science studies. From Judith Butler and Donna Haraway to Rosi Braidotti and Karen Barad there has been a flourishing of intellectual advancement made in reconfiguring our understanding of the entangled nature of materiality and discourse.[29]

While there exist many "new materialisms," the feminist strands are often supported by the insights of quantum physics to show how matter itself "acts, creates, destroys, and transforms," behaving more as a process than a static thing.[30] Based on this recognition, these scholars urge us to take the agency of matter seriously in its intra-action with discourse. As Barad boldly puts it, "Neither discursive practices nor material phenomena are ontologically or epistemologically prior. Neither can be explained in terms of the other. . . . Matter and meaning are mutually articulated."[31] Once we realize the coconstitutive entanglement of matter and meaning we can better attend to the surprising swerves of history across intra-acting phenomena.

An archaeology of media inspired by this kind of accounting for "matter's dynamism, the nature of causality, and the space of agency, as well as a *posthumanist* elaboration of the notion of performativity," is much better suited for analyzing the complex assemblages of things and practices through which categories and boundaries coalesce.[32] This is true down to a microscopic, even atomic level.[33] Whether through "agential realism" for Barad, "cultural techniques" for Siegert, "logistical media" for Peters, or "actor networks" for Latour, distinctions are created through dynamic networks of matter and discourse that go beyond human agents but enact the very possibilities for meaning.[34] Concepts are created through their doing. And this iterative performativity includes the doing of all manner of things.

Because doing is connected to creation, the focus on the agency of media and cultural techniques needs some clarification. When we consider media and users, we might simplify Harold Lasswell's classic chain of questions in communications research, "Who? Says what? In which Channel? To whom? With what effect?" to first simply ask, "Who is doing what to whom?"[35] This is because that ambiguity is precisely the point. The doing comes out of the interactions between adopters of media and the preestablished possibilities, the operations governed by the medium. For this reason, I am most interested in the early moments of adoption of new technologies, where old habits face new technical standards in the first 150 years of the Latter-day Saint tradition. Here we can glimpse webs of actors temporarily coalescing and shaping the performance and definition of Mormonism. This also tends to foreground the nexus of symbolic meaning and matter, before it conceals itself into normalcy or morphs into a different assemblage.

My approach here extends Cornelia Vismann's articulation of cultural techniques. Vismann problematizes the "sovereignty" of a subject taking up and learning to "master" a medium. This sense of cultural techniques as media competence—the mastery and utilization of technology—reveals the productive power of technologies. Because, as Vismann formulates it, media "supply their own rules of execution," which "steer processes in different directions, toward different opportunities, and different persons," their integral doing must be acknowledged.[36] This kind of technique can be learned and passed on but is performed by the interaction of agencies—both user and medium—and this performative power is key. It is precisely this key that is turned with spiritual technologies, where human actors engage matter and symbolic meaning through their technological know-how, which also dictates its own use. The creationary process is neither merely media "determining" humans as objects, nor it is purely the actions of human actors, since these are already set to some degree. Both are enmeshed in becoming. This productive interplay must be methodologically dug up and analyzed to better understand media's role in enabling the creation of Latter-day Saint subjects in different ways within different discourse networks.

Combining media theory and new materialism, this book then contributes to the recent turn to material, lived religion, and postsecular critiques of the formation of spirituality in religious studies. In a broad sense, the material turn in the study of religion focuses attention on "interactions between human bodies and physical objects," often as sense perception in space and time to orient communities and individuals toward religious traditions.[37] This emphasis has attuned religious studies to the power of media as well as the embodied experience of religion, beyond objects as mere material expressions.[38] Considering the human senses and the relationship they have to material culture and meaning has greatly expanded the purview of religious studies and opened the door for media studies to further inform that rich focus. However, where some follow S. Brent Plate's assertion that "ideas, beliefs, and doctrines begin in material reality," I stress their enactment through practices that are always already both material and discursive.[39] Recognizing the entanglement of discourse and materiality and refusing to prioritize one over the other renders a fuller picture of religious identity, experience, and practices.

Another helpful development has been the recent efforts to pronounce the death of the secularization thesis in favor of a more complex arrangement of secularism and religiosity. Often inspired by readings of Foucault, scholars such as Talal Asad, Kathryn Lofton, John Lardas Modern, Jared Hickman, Emily Ogden, and Peter Coviello have all helped theorize the regime of secularism in American history. Where John Modern has especially revealed how secularism's metaphysics "assumed an almost biological presence" through a form of incorporeal materiality, Peter Coviello brings this insight to bear on religious studies itself.[40] Coviello insists that "'secularism' names the ideology that, in an occluded way, operates the secularization thesis." For secularism is now understood to be a means of ordering and distributing terms, of propagating an "interlinked series of binarized distinctions."[41] Taken together, work on postsecular critique gets at the machinery of secularism, as a disciplinary force that thrives in creating distinctions, ever enfolding in tomorrow what is excluded today.

These recent intellectual developments can help us appreciate the role of technologies in defining Mormonism, even as its public image shifted from that of scandalous outcast in the nineteenth century to quintessential American religion in the twentieth. So much of Mormon media history has to do with modes of performing distinctions, ways of beholding to engender radical visions, or standardizing vision to effect assimilation. Whether to perform their difference or enact their national belonging, technologies accomplished the composition of the religion as much as human actors. The performativity of Mormonism is thus located somewhere beyond mere members of the organization.

Certainly, performing has been a staple in Mormon history. Whether for and with the dead through pageants, as Megan Jones has argued, or pretending and playacting, as Jake Johnson has argued, performance and theatricality exercise a strong animating presence in Mormon culture.[42] But here I mean a distinctly nuanced form of performativity, of human and nonhuman actors creating by doing through a distributed sense of agency. This combined effect of techniques, practices, and technologies rendered difference and demarcations visible. Rather than a hollow performance or simply "acting as if," I mean that the performance of Mormonism, or the ability to be a Latter-day Saint, was to some degree the mastery and use of media that could create the distinction, and thereby performance, of Mormon and non-Mormon—parallel and entangled with such distinctions in discourse. And here I am most interested in how this was worked out as the management of visions in media.

WORD AND WORLD

Seeing Things analyzes networks of media by attending to their production and reception, but also their inseparability from discourse. As Nietzsche admonished, "Unspeakably more depends upon *what things are called*, than on what they are."[43] Words are not hollow signifiers, and language should not be conflated with discourse. As Barad reminds us, "Discourse is not what is said; it is that which constrains and enables what can be said," which includes the work of media.[44] Despite our long Cartesian tradition of separating material and discourse, it is through their entanglement that the world comes to matter. More than mere Freudian slips or clumsy catchphrases, articulating religious messages through media metaphors stresses the power of those very media to shape religious experience and understanding by constraining the material basis for its becoming.[45]

Expressions in words, then, act on while diffracting material media. The additive interference of these networks provides rich insights into religion's constitution and maintenance within words *and* the world. Following Barad's lead, I shift the focus away from the "representationalist" investigation of "correspondences between descriptions and reality" and toward "matters of practices/doings/actions."[46] Discursive practices and material phenomena are inseparable, thus "material-discursive" practice gets at the power of Mormon media to reconfigure the world and enact "boundaries, properties, and meanings."[47] Jumping between media, messages, agents, and networks, this book attempts to account for the practices through which differences are produced, are circulated, and intra-act with a host of other human and nonhuman things.

My attention to discourse then is a critical reorientation of early Mormon understandings of language, undertaken by shifting from their focus on overcoming its "fallen state" to matters of materiality. This aligns better with their own theology, namely that all spiritual knowledge and progress comes through matter not by transcending it. At times Joseph Smith yearned for God to deliver all his children from "the little narrow prison almost as it were totel [*sic*] darkness of paper pen and ink and a crooked broken scattered and imperfect language."[48] Because of the perceived mediating missteps of language, revelatory understanding could be contested, and language remained fraught in the Mormon worldview. This, of course, was not unusual. If conceived of as a mandatory but imperfect packaging of some otherwise pristine phenomenon, language could be seen as a degradation. A governing principle taught by Smith was the concept that God speaks to humans "in their weakness, after the manner of their own language."[49] However, and just as important, Smith's fellow church members were also told they were to receive God's word from Smith, "as if from [God's] own mouth, in all patience and faith."[50] Smith's vocal cords, tongue, and teeth—not to mention his material scriptural records—could become God's own mouth. And revelation was often realized or worked out in the materiality of words on paper, from edits to translations.

Words provoked passionate responses. Because human language was always arbitrary, and often shifting, sexist, and insufficient, it could be understood to require compensatory technologies. Machines and techniques were expected to fill up the hollow gaps between human and the spirit (while also creating and stabilizing such categories) by producing a secondary presence and spiritual experience. Yet, in my reading, they were in actuality revealing the inherent entanglement of matter and meaning. Latter-day Saint media practices unveil their materialist bend. They make clear there never was a message without a medium by stressing the "absurdities of immaterialism."[51] Within Latter-day Saint theology, God and data are both always found only in media, and Mormon visions seem to know this better than Mormon words.

For Latter-day Saints intent on getting more messages from heaven, media held the additional promise of capturing—perhaps even enhancing—religious senses, by training them. The spiritual was to be found in the technologies and through the physical body. As Amanda Beardsley's work has shown, this also played out on a distinctly sonic level, where hearing the word of God entailed controlling variables, purifying channels, and enhancing the corporeal senses.[52] It was a matter of expelling noise and imbuing the thing with spirit. Jake Johnson has also located the vibratory resonance of Mormon doctrine and practice in sound and vocal performance. From Joseph Smith's vocal translation as the ur-performance to American musicals, Johnson hears Mormonism as a religion of mimicry, vicarious voicing, and learning to listen to the word of God through others.[53] In the vein of Mormon sound studies Sharon Harris and Peter McMurry have also offered provocative insights. Rather than analyze songs or sounds, Harris and McMurry maintain that sonic objects in the history of Mormonism "shape what Mormonism as a medium and accretion of audiovisual mediums and techniques has been and may yet become."[54] There is clearly much promise in extending Leigh Eric Schmidt's brilliant work on the instability of aural spiritual data in nineteenth-century American Christianity into the entire history of Mormonism and listening.[55]

Whether hearkening through the ears or eyes, Latter-day Saints sometimes deemed media content "of the world" suspect. In Chiung Hwang Chen's account, Mormonism has always used media to effectively "promote and defend its faith," but media also constitute a threat to ecclesiastical authority as technologies enable participation and amplify the voice of dissenters.[56] Content was suspect, yet channels could be improved and elevated. This unique "compromise" is how the Latter-day Saint church approached media technologies, specifically radio, TV, and the internet in Gavin Feller's telling of Mormon media history.[57] Above all, Feller is interested in early adoptions of new media and the ways Latter-day Saints adjust and seek to build Zion through theologically driven adaptations. His work explores the synthetic processes of the Mormon media imagination, or how "Mormonism has imagined media and used media to imagine."[58] From the get-go Latter-day Saints thought with and worked out their religion in media. As Ben Peters and John Durham Peters have claimed, Mormonism is a media religion through and through, especially in the more elemental sense of the term. As they emphasize, "a medium is not only about the storage or transmission of meaning." It is just as much about "the ordering of time, space, and relationships"—the very projects over which the Latter-day Saint religion obsesses with eternal consequences.[59]

My work is in conversation with these scholars and seeks to further plumb the depths of a peculiar new religious movement to enhance our understanding of media and religion in general. Rather than seeing media as a negotiation—as external objects that are adopted from neutral to negative or positive ends—in my analysis Mormonism and the Latter-day Saint body are always already technologized. That is to say, there is no Mormonism before media, and there is no message of Mormonism without media. These technologies don't just disseminate Mormonism; they equally construct it, hence, my emphasis on media interactions as distributed agency. They might not have been baptized or registered on the rolls of the church, but media made Mormonism as much as humans did. Taking Mormon materialist theology seriously and fusing it with German media theory and feminist new materialism opens our eyes to the dynamic spiritual nature of matter and the agency of media in creating religious understanding and experience.

SPIRIT AND BODY

While media networks may indeed facilitate the creation of Mormonism to a great degree, this should not be understood as one-way street of technological determinism. Nor should it excise the experience of humans. In an effort to move beyond Friedrich Kittler's antihumanism, more recent German media theory has "readmit[ted] human actors" and agency into their scholarly purview.[60] This warm welcome appropriately ignites my view of a religious tradition that includes many human actors. For religious individuals, the very "wetware" of human flesh, blood, and guts that make media significant as technologies to help them connect with their fellow beings and commune with their gods cannot be ignored. Especially in Mormonism, with its deep roots in a positive theology of embodiment and materialism, analyzing hardware reveals just how central wetware remains in these networks.

Attending to the poetics of this embodied aspect of media interactions here owes a great deal to the work of Vivian Sobchack, Birgit Meyer, David Morgan, Erhard Schüttpelz, Thomas Elsaesser, Wendy Chun, and Bernadette Wegenstein, as is apparent throughout the book. Adding the insights of "bodily techniques" and experience to the media archaeological work of Wolfgang Ernst, Jussi Parikka, and Erkki Huhtamo serves to temper a posthumanist tendency that might all too quickly become mired in machines alone.[61] I too allow technologies to lead in the following chapters, but I never want to simply "indulge in ever more detailed readings of ever more arcane technologies" for the sake of trying to "out-Kittler Kittler."[62] This book wants to learn from the insights of the heyday of Kittler-inspired histories from twenty years ago, but never just party like it's 1999. In seeking to reveal the religious potential and historical uses of media networks for Mormonism, the carnal aspect of the body must be in play, especially because within Mormonism comprehension and experience—whether seen as spiritual or secular by outsiders—is the same and inseparable from the physical body.

Embodiment might breed "deep-seated cultural desires for spiritual transcendence," but it also refutes them.[63] And the following chapters reveal ways technologies called on and shaped a variety of unique modes of attention through focusing and visualizing. These were constructed for specific individual bodily senses, but also for collective bodies of viewers, readers, and users. Media were often acting on others to get them to listen, look, or behave in certain ways and to make these new assemblages endure. I want, then, to attend to the ways the body as "the indispensable medium" and "pivot of articulating materiality and virtuality" is "joined" with technologies, as a sort of coconstitutive meeting of old and new media, as Marwan Kraidy has suggested.[64] After all, in David Morgan's formulation, "to see is to see from the circumstance of a body."[65] This recognition is particularly resonant for Mormon bodies. In a new religious movement that elevated the human body to matter that is also the means of true happiness and eternal life, embodiment became central to spirituality and everyday devotion.[66] This book's chapters, therefore, focus on both the ways death (disembodiment) generated robust media practices, as well as the ways media were employed to discipline and enhance the embodied vision of the living.

Because of its theological prominence and divine provenance, the Mormon body was to be cared for, appreciated, and disciplined. Mormons then avoided idle hands, stiff necks, immodesty, and wanton eyes. But they also sang, danced, reconfigured celestial and romantic relations in polygamous households and yearned for perfected flesh in the next life. Their bodies could bridge the two worlds. Birthing spirits into this life as much as feeling a body come to terms with feeling the Holy Ghost were seen as direct blessings of embodiment. Media projects could help realize this. Religion could be made alive and animated if it addressed and appealed to the fleshly media of eyes, ears, noses, mouths, and hands.

This emphasis shows up throughout several chapters in the book that highlight how media were employed to discipline, train, and maintain Mormons as individual bodies and a community. Attention to medium specificity and bodily response also sharpens our understanding of how much these have intra-acted with doctrinal development in its representation and disciplined practice. Media technologies could be taken up to improve, unify, critique, or even reshape Mormonism, not only as a religion and corporation, but as a cluster of thoughts and practices that were always already entwined with corporeality.

Although this book attempts to, at times, "flesh out" the lived experience of religion in a physical body, it also summons the spectral core of spirituality and technology. This is crucial because bodily and material networks were often aimed at harnessing (the) spirit(s). And matter is deeply entangled with the meaning and recording of such liminal experiences with the dead across the veil of the living. This is particularly significant for Mormon theology. As Rosalynde Welch has put it, "Joseph Smith's declaration that 'all spirit is matter'" dissolved "Platonic dualism in a stroke and open[ed] the door to a metaphysics of pure matter."[67] Spirits are agential beings in Mormon accounts, and though they generally go unseen, they dwell here among the living. Excavating Mormon media networks then helps emphasize the ghost—or even host—in Holy Ghost. This aspect is not a mere curiosity or hollow nod to the spectral turn.[68] The ghosts throughout this book always haunt or help other agents, both mechanical and human. They also intra-act with thought and intention.

The media projects detailed herein can also be seen as Mormon attempts to deal with these and various other specters. This realization helps foreground the spiritual and visionary vitality of Mormonism. For a religion that was, from its very beginnings, focused on overcoming death, ghosts are both important and present, often under the tempered terms of "spirits" and "angels."[69] This proclivity for the spectral became enhanced and refracted through technologies, even if visions in media were increasingly attributed to science over time.

It would be tempting to chart a simplistic course of Mormons using machines to manage ghosts in reverse proportion to the frequency of visionary experiences—in other words a secularization narrative. Yet, as recent scholarship on secularity has helped reveal, these "enchanted" practices did not disappear but became the subject of people projecting their own desires to "*aim* at 'modernity.'"[70] And the very efforts at becoming modern subjects and citizens rooted in a prescriptive discourse of calculation, systematization, and the management of enchantment only haunted their creators.[71] Media technologies that could render specters controlled and (re)viewable as aesthetic products might even eclipse desires for extraordinary visions, but they certainly did not stamp them out.

The same technologies that made specters manageable, or even unnecessary, also seem to have multiplied spectral possibilities. As John Durham Peters noted, riffing on Kafka, "Every new medium is a machine for the production of ghosts."[72] Stored and replayable, media content always carries with it the haunting ability to outlast its mortal author. New technologies and powerful media could overcome the boundaries of "distance and death"; however, "the price of such conjuring soon became evident: a world of doppelgängers that had no flesh."[73] Jacques Derrida, too, remarked how "modern technology, contrary to appearances, although it is scientific, increases tenfold the power of ghosts."[74] Current work in hauntology—a playful term coined by Derrida to get at both ontology and haunting, presence and absence—has directed attention to the interactions between the dead and the living and helped underscore the power of that statement cribbed from Kafka.[75] Taking the matter of both body *and* spirit seriously, this book follows the lead of its various actors and respects the reports of hauntings and visions. It takes no stance as to the veracity of claims made by Mormons, Spiritualists, or other religious Americans. This tack foregrounds how, from the very beginning, Latter-day Saints always had to—indeed, expected to—wrestle with ghostly figures at the convergence of new media and practices of seeing things.

OVERVIEW OF CHAPTERS

The first two chapters trace webs of disciplining and shaping vision as repeatable practices. Print media rendered the electric shock and experience of spiritual visions into circulating texts that were both inspirational and instructional in the early church. After the death of Smith, panorama painting helped manage Smith's afterimage and get the body of saints on track toward a future rooted in a past of persecution. Both print and panorama warded off certain competing visions by effectively training and focusing users' attention. Paying attention meant drowning out and suspending perception of a bunch of alternative and threatening visions, or ways of seeing. The future of the church was intertwined with *which* visions of spirits were accepted and *how* they were seen.

The first chapter, "Circulating Specters," reveals this engagement with spectrality, whereby media helped Mormons come to terms with and provide terms for ghosts in Joseph Smith's taxonomy of supernatural beings (spirits, angels, demons, etc.) and print efforts to regulate and train vision.[76] If optical devices, like magic lanterns at phantasmagoria shows, could make spirits projected and visible, then the bounds of spiritual and biological vision were challenged in fundamental ways. The period's visual regime, which fashioned modern practices of vision and the possibilities of what could ostensibly be seen at all, underwent a crisis of sorts.[77] Ghost stories, both gothic fiction and visionary accounts of angelic visitations, provided texts for readers to work through this shift in the history of the experience and understanding of human vision.

In Smith's most polished account of his "first vision," where God and Jesus Christ appeared to him in the woods when he was a young man, Smith stressed over and again he had "actually seen" what was understood by others to be impossible. For Smith it was "actual" and material. Both stimulating and instructive, Smith's "ghost stories" also coincided with the founding Mormon media project of making visions material and repeatable through the reproduction of print media. In the wake of optical media's tricks and possibilities, trusting vision required new attention and training. From the publication of the Book of Mormon to sundry revelations, being Mormon meant learning and adopting specific techniques of reading (text) and seeing (visions), again looking at something to see something else. It meant becoming a visionary observer by turning natural vision into spiritual vision, or "hallucinating" between the lines.

The second chapter analyzes media rolled out to deal with the ghost of the dead prophet and Mormon past. Large painted panorama displays in the hands of Philo Dibble offered members ways of capturing the spirit of Smith, who was appearing to his followers immediately following his assassination in 1844. Caught and panoramarized, the image of Smith and the church's past could help consolidate power during a crisis of succession and provide a network of visual collective memories to be consumed in collective viewing. Panorama also provided a means to conceptualize and describe visionary experience itself. From the revelation of John to visions of revenant Joseph Smiths, panoramic vision was particularly suited to capturing visions in writing and visual display.

Unlike the individualized and imagined community of print, panorama displays literally brought the church members together to share a unique and standardized vision of Smith and church history. Members needed to focus on the image in the foreground to tune out a threating and chaotic background. In the 1840s, Dibble's panorama deployed medieval practices of observing religious images to get caught up in a spiritual experience and deeper theological understanding—all while suturing the community together. It is the argument of this chapter that—at least for the group that chose to follow Brigham Young as Smith's successor—being Mormon meant consolidating vision. It entailed specific techniques of avoiding schismatic breakoffs by coming together and sharing a vision enabled by the panorama.

This actually continued in a mutated form in the 1880s, when C. C. A. Christensen's panorama literally stitched together images built on oral histories he collected from surviving church members in order to stretch and roll the collective memory of the church into a shared experience. Dibble's images had helped support Brigham Young's vision of Smith, by providing images to fuel his succession. Over thirty years later, Christensen's panorama provided images *in* succession. Rolled along columns in sequence, Christensen's display updated the technology and capitalized on the connection to nineteenth-century attempts to simulate travel. Like trains and steamboats, panorama could also signal trajectory and narrative sequence. With a unified vision of the prophet and past, the medium of panorama experientially conveyed the sense that the church was headed somewhere.

The middle two chapters both concern themselves with representation and its material conditions of expression. This means both are also interested in content and images as visions or ways of seeing gender and race within Mormonism as it found its place within America. Chapter 3 follows the efforts of Mormon women expanding patriarchal visions through their work in photography and typewriting, just as gender ideals were narrowing within the religion to fit the national mainstream. Chapter 4 focuses on the first feature film backed by the church to highlight the precarious work of modernizing, as Mormons sought to visualize their whiteness and belonging on the silver screen.

In prevalent Mormon thought of the time, married women were celebrated as divine vessels employed in birthing spirits into mortal tabernacles. Problematically similar conceptions informed widespread cultural notions around gendered labor at new inscription technologies. Once employed, a woman could take down all her male employer said and write it out for him as a product of mechanical reproduction, much like Mina's mindset in Bram Stoker's *Dracula*—where she conflated being "married" with being "useful." If Mina could "stenograph well enough," she could "take down what he wants to say in this way and write it out for him on the typewriter."[78] Mina's fiancé would become her husband and boss, and the typewriter would prescribe the operations enabling the latter relationship. But typewriters also offered a promising space for cultural techniques that might highlight the incoherent process of policing gender. This all hinged on creative modes of reproduction, especially because notions of hollow vessels that don't leave their mark on their work—whether in spiritualist or workplace contexts—were always fallacies or worse, fantasies.

Women's roles were especially charged within Mormonism as the church turned from polygamy to a public image of modernizing monogamous families. New automatic writing machines, such as typewriters, and cameras created jobs for women to enter the workforce as assistants and secretaries. However, Brigham Young's nationally renowned daughter Susa Young Gates at the typewriter and the lesser-known deaf art photographer Elfie Huntington at the camera both found ways to use the machines without merely replicating ghostly or masculine dictation. By adapting cultural conceptions of the sensitive feminine touch into creative techniques, these women emphasized the role of agency, class, and skill in their work. This chapter argues that through interaction with typewriters and cameras, Huntington and Gates registered the complicated coconstruction of gender and technologies at the turn of the century. As a type of canny mimicry, they altered men's visions and gave them new meaning by channeling them through machines.

As machines could register creations without clear authors, the late nineteenth century also signaled the potential loss of the human touch. In its vampiric way the typewriter drained the blood of the author. As Kittler hyperbolically put it, on a technological level "man simply died around 1900."[79] Therefore, media projects and writings of Mormonism were not always clearly linked to any one human author. Determining authorship necessitated a reliance on contemporaneous sources, credits, and attributions, or metadata. This had profound consequences for visionary practices. Ann Taves argues that it was during this historical period that visions and trances under the new psychology were no longer spontaneous, but understood to be inducible and therefore able to be spread.[80] Instead of uniquely linked to a single charismatic individual, visions were somewhat homogenous and transferable. And it was during this same period that Latter-day Saints became largely assimilated and turned to the use of electronic screens to project and manage their visions. Mechanically reproduced visions on a screen addressed the masses and often eschewed the sense and importance of a single author.

In accordance with these technological advancements, the final three chapters each deal with dynamic screens. The foregoing media—print, canvas, glass plates, and type in the first half of the book—were all screens in the expanded definition of "surface[s] for retrieving and transmitting visual information," but film, microfilm readers, and television all utilized screens with dynamic data shifting in real time through projection.[81] This marked a qualitative change for embodied habits and a quantitative change for access and engagement with Mormon visions in the twentieth century.

The fourth chapter examines the representation of Mormons in mass media. It treats the use of film to share a positive vision of Mormonism and put the church in traffic with modern America. By cinematically staging the visionary experience of the angel Moroni appearing to Joseph Smith, the first official Latter-day Saint film, *One Hundred Years of Mormonism* (1913), combined modern technology and devotional history for a projected wide audience as American history.

The film came in response to the powerful anti-Mormon silent film from Denmark *Victim of the Mormons* (1911), but it signaled a new possibility for the church. If Mormons were cinematically connected to hypnosis, seduction, and the illicit trafficking of women in popular films, then an intervention was needed. The first turn was to church history. Although the film is lost, one of the few extant scenes shows technical camera tricks at work to make the angel Moroni materialize in Smith's bedroom. Staging the specters of Smith's visions through double exposure literally modernized the Mormon past and submitted it to the public sphere and *commercial traffic* of cinema. Now involved in proper trafficking and commerce, Mormons were increasingly in step with modernity. This chapter argues that the interaction with film refashioned Mormon visibility and attention to their look, by warding off negative images and curating a wholesome public image that entailed techniques of performing cinematic whiteness and American belonging.

The final two chapters analyze the ways microfilm and then television provided inspiration and means to systematize and get a handle on work for the dead and on standardizing the postwar church, respectively. Whether to rescue records and the deceased through a system of microphotography and proxy work or to gather and correlate the expanding church membership under visual standards, these massive projects both required thinking in terms of management and control.

In "Micromanaging Death," the fifth chapter, I analyze the church's doctrinal directive to perform proxy rituals to save the dead at the nexus of microfilm technology and the rescue of daunting amounts of records around the Second World War. Mormon genealogists credited the advent of microphotography as divine intervention for providing the managerial techniques to save records through duplication and provide the necessary accounting for ordinances performed in temples by the living for the dead. The technology was connected to world projects that would bring together vast stores of records and knowledge to create a shared database—a world brain—for the betterment of humanity.

In Latter-day Saint use, microfilm even allowed for instances of spiritual feedback, wherein spirits from beyond the veil could visit, guide, or instant message living genealogists to notify them their proxy work was valid. Good genealogist Mormons had to learn techniques of scanning, recording, zooming, and seeing with spiritual eyes. Visions of dead ancestors were tamed into feedback loops supporting a system that facilitated temple work, while also bolstering racial lineages and American belonging.

The sixth chapter shows how broadcast media could correlate the look and image of the church through teletechnologies and especially against the specter of communism and countercultural movements from the 1950s to 1970s. It connects the standards and logic of broadcast technology with the concept and flavor of Mormon Correlation, which was a sweeping reform that sought to standardize curriculum, doctrine, and practice beginning in the 1960s. During the age of television Mormons enjoyed an unprecedented public acceptance as patriotic, family-oriented, model Americans. Conforming to the 1950s ideal of these labels, especially through broadcast technology, shaped the church in significant and lasting ways.

The necessity of standards and their discursive resonance permeated Mormon homes and practice and was entangled with TV. From technical and national standards of NTSC (National Television System Committee) to Mormon dress codes and unified instruction, standards—both U.S. living standards and church moral ones—were meant to be attained and maintained as a sign of strength, nationalism, and godliness. Following these standards meant being in tune and coming into perfect harmony with proper broadcasts. It meant receiving the church leaders' vision and their image on the TV set as a vision in one's own home. The technology allowed correlated and standardized members to be gathered from their very living rooms by receiving the logic and effect of broadcast, as well as interacting and acting on the content through bodily techniques. This technical and religious tuning-in created a vision of twentieth-century Latter-day Saints as American families and provided an expansive system for their governance and for gathering the Saints scattered abroad.

This collection of media visions—scenes of starts, stops, dead ends, negotiations, developments, and revelations—all underscore the productive interactions with technology and death that have enabled and constrained Mormonism as a visionary religion. Far from the last word or *the* history of Mormon media practices, this book offers instead an archaeology of several strata from the religion's past. These interdisciplinary constellations underscore the agency of material media, the ways they acted to enable the performance and creation of a religious culture. Pushing the concept of media practices to combine materiality, cultural techniques, and posthuman performativity, the following chapters expand the methodological toolbox of cultural studies at the nexus of media studies and religious studies. It is my hope that a media archaeology that digs up dead and forgotten media contexts and questions current media practices might make communication with the dead mutually enlightening.

CIRCULATING
SPECTERS

I had seen a vision, I knew it, and I knew that
God knew it, and I could not deny it.

Joseph Smith, 1838

Hence it is, that when any vehement passion or emotion hinders the cool
application of judgment, we get no distinct notion of an object, even though
the sense be long directed to it. A man who is put into a panic, by thinking
he sees a ghost, may stare at it long, without having any distinct notion of it;
it is his understanding, and not his sense, that is disturbed by this horror.

Thomas Reid, 1785

J oseph Smith led a haunted life. Not only was he constantly shadowed
by enemies, but his thirty-eight years were also punctuated with a
series of appearances from spirits, angels, and demons. His preter-
natural ability to "discern things invisible to the natural eye" yielded such
spectral encounters, and Smith was adamant about their material veracity.[1]
He had "actually seen" these spectacular things.

Despite his initial hesitation in publishing the experience of his "first
vision," versions of the vision eventually circulated and recreated the scene
of theophany in countless readers' minds.[2] The 1838 account that circulated
most widely in print stressed the urgency that Smith's eyes had not deceived
him, almost to the point of obsession.[3] The narrative emphasized that it was
a "fact" that he "had beheld a vision" of God and repeated three times that he

had "actually seen" supernatural beings. The explanation continued that he "saw two personages" and, lastly, reiterated for good measure that he indeed, "had seen a vision." All that came in two paragraphs.

There was something extraordinary and perplexing about Smith's vision that prompted the desire to duplicate it through print. A later reminiscent and secondhand account recorded how Smith claimed "God touched his eyes" and "as soon as the Lord had touched his eyes with his finger he immediately saw the Savior."[4] Even decades later, records like this could inspire and instruct readers, igniting their imagination. And the "first vision" was not the only Smith vision committed to writing and circulated. Early accounts also published his visions of Book of Mormon prophets, deceased loved ones, and evil spirits, underscoring his uncanny ability to recognize them as such. Smith's accounts of witnessing specters conveyed his spiritual vision and, just as importantly, stored within them the data necessary to disseminate and recreate it, *to reproduce it*.

A seminal task of Mormonism's early years was to mediate the vision that brought about these kinds of experiences into a form that was shareable and manageable—one that could both package and provoke such vision. Participating in a booming print network trafficked the information and further circulated the specters, right into the hands and before the eyes of readers scattered abroad. This had particular import, for specters were in texts as much as attending their reception, since modern visions could come in the context of new technological deceptions and reports of false spirits.

Print was quite fitting to reproduce spectral appearances and manage their deceptive potential. The medium itself had a haunted origin, as a mistrusted "dark art." Memento mori and "dances of Death" texts stood as emblems of the craft and adorned the ink-laden sheets floating out the doors of the early print shop.[5] Through the same magic of mechanical reproduction, foundational Mormon texts could translate subjective spiritual vision into objective textual vision and back, for an imagined or projected community of readers across the blossoming faith.[6] The medium could spirit information away to a larger network of readers, viewing the exact same texts across time and space, and thus disseminate a unique Mormon literacy. For Joseph Smith challenged his followers to read scriptures in such a way as to "take away the veil so you may see," with an eye of faith and deeper understanding.[7] He maintained the material basis for this, explaining that visions were to be trusted only by "what you see by the seeing of the eye."[8]

This chapter argues that Mormon print practices provided spiritual vision *through* natural vision. By instructing readers how to see with spiritual eyes through reading with biological eyes, Latter-day Saints used print to store and reproduce the powerful electric shock of Smith's visions to help readers experience their own. Print helped Mormon readers conjure extraordinary vision beyond the page, even as it helped their leaders discipline it within the coalescing ecclesiastical hierarchy.

Managing spiritual vision in an age of sophisticated deceptions peppered both early Mormon texts and the contemporaneous and hugely popular ghost stories of gothic literature. In media theorist Friedrich Kittler's formulation, "the passion of reading" during this period in the early nineteenth century "consisted of hallucinating a meaning between letters and lines."[9] This suggestive and romanticist realization of the medium illuminates the significance of textual productions around the reliability of eyes in the face of ghostly apparitions. Texts from both Mormon and gothic traditions often sought to transfer the vision of narrators and creators to the reader, inviting them to try on the author's perspective and "hallucinate" with them between the lines. Smith's extraordinary vision, which materialized his beliefs and aspirations of "what *could be*," in Ann Taves's estimation, might be shared through textual production.[10] And the superior vision of America's father of gothic writing, Charles Brockden Brown, might also be experienced through the thrills of the text. Brown even reportedly gained his creative ability in the genre from his own impaired biological vision. Suffering from myopia, "he, therefore, felicitated himself on the thought that he had not the optics of ordinary men," but rather a "vision superior" to them.[11] Smith and Brown both offered sight through and beyond the natural eyes.

To be sure, the tension between the physical and the spiritual was not new. For instance, the ministerial edits to visionary accounts among American revivalists in the eighteenth century strategically attributed "miraculous sights to the meditative eyes of the mind, to what they called again and again 'the eye of faith,'" because of the editors' opposition to "visions seen with the 'bodily eyes,'" as Leigh Eric Schmidt has shown.[12] Nineteenth-century stories of spectral appearances pushed back against this logic. They further probed the tension between romantic reading and enlightenment rationality, by textually reproducing glimpses of the inexplicable and extraordinary. Literary productions and intellectual explanations for visions were simultaneously problematized and galvanized by spirit-conjuring phantasmagoria shows, which popularized the optical medium of the magic lantern, which projected objectively visible spectral images for audiences. Thus, to understand Mormon visionary accounts and gothic ghost stories, we must first turn to the thrilling technology that dazzled audiences by making images of specters visible.

PHANTASMAGORIA

Beginning in the late eighteenth century phantasmagoria shows would become something of an international sensation. By the second decade of the nineteenth century the shows had spread throughout New York, Boston, Philadelphia, and other urban centers, often utilizing educational halls for their demonstrations. The enclosed architectural space colored the experience and its transgressive connotations. For example, when Martin Aubee used the New York Lyceum for his phantasmagoria show a local newspaper decried his debasement of the religious into the popular, claiming the room had been "converted from a church into a place of amusement, for vulgar minds, such as tricks of legerdemain, and where the devil dances on stilts to the tune of a hand organ."[13] The rousing spectacle still had no fitting home. Like other folk practices, whose meaning and effect were yet undecided, the phantasmagoria was equal parts entertainment, science, and magic.

To provide their spectacles, the phantasmagoria shows used glass slides in the magic lantern device with an oil lamp or candle to illuminate and project images on smoke or screens. The space often featured strategically placed candles that were stifled or masked in order to suddenly darken or illuminate the room for effect. With the lantern projector in place and the eyes of the attending spectators dilated, the lighting effects were followed by projections of "ghosts appearing in different directions" and "the phantoms of celebrities."[14] The shows enacted the strange relationship between rationality and supernatural phenomena by combining technology and spectral appearances. As Terry Castle put it, "The specter-shows of the late eighteenth and early nineteenth centuries . . . mediated oddly between rational and irrational imperatives." In fact, the producers of the displays claimed, "the new entertainment would serve the cause of public enlightenment by exposing the frauds of charlatans and supposed ghost-seers."[15] Being tricked, or at least confronted with the possibility, could train rationality through visions of manufactured spirits.

Ghost seeing was the expectation. The phantasmagoria's magic lantern was embedded in an intrinsic "equivalence between the technology of illusion and supernatural phenomena," as the practitioner would often project "souls in hell, leering devils, the resurrection of Christ," and other spectacular apparitions.[16] Since their inception the preferred content of the shows was gothic images: revenants, ghosts, and goblins. A show offered all the apparitions one might fear or hope to see in real life, outside the entertaining context. Phantasmagoria haunted and thrilled both scientists and paying customers as technology popularized the capacity to create new deceptions. An 1802 article in the *Journal of Natural Philosophy, Chemistry, and the Arts* detailed the phantasmagoria's conjuring of "figures of departed men, ghosts, skeletons, transmutations, &c." to both enjoy and help explain how the shows worked.[17] Its use of optical media for spectacles was one of many devices that "organized inspection, pleasure, and analysis" and brought it from "the exhibition room into the everyday world."[18] The experience of the phantasmagoria—technical, urban, and exhilarating—was perhaps even mirrored in the low-tech, rural, hands-on thrill of Smith's money digging, with descriptions anticipating visions of treasure and guardian spirits. Participants in both activities utilized optical media—one a concave mirror, the other a seer stone—and both expected to see spirits.

Phantasmagoria was a productive medium to see with, but also to think with. It provided an experiential model to describe uncanny visions and deception in rational terms. Immanuel Kant made just such a connection in the 1760s, by forcing specters into a rational schema. In his text "Dreams of a Spirit-Seer," Kant addressed apparitions as mental phantoms, but actual possibilities through optical media. He defined spirits as simple beings possessed of reason, but with no spatial properties.[19] For Kant spirits were departed immaterial beings, who "may indeed act upon the spirit of man." Kant even conceded that visions of apparitions were based in a real "spirit-impression" and that the senses could actually perceive some of this, especially in those with heightened sensitivity, but his recourse to optical media to explain (away) the actual appearance of spirits was telling.[20] For Kant argued that spirit seers mistook the "mirage of [their] imagination" with the actual visible world, which "also happens for example when, by means of a concave mirror, the specter of a body is seen in mid air."[21]

The concave mirror was, of course, the core technology of the optical media used by Kant, including microscopes, telescopes, and in this case, magic lanterns. As Stefan Andriopoulos has revealed, Kant made numerous references to optical instruments throughout his writings to help explain mental processes and pitfalls. In "Dreams of a Spirit-Seer," Kant's critical philosophy, thus, "transforms the material apparatus of the magic lantern and its use in the visual medium of the phantasmagoria into an epistemic figure that highlights the limits and unreliability of philosophical knowledge."[22] Even within Kant's own writing the technology and material apparatus of script, *writing it out,* foregrounded the issues with knowing and seeing—trusting the eyes—as a metaphysical conundrum.

The technology also informed creative writing. Implying a potentially deceptive series of images changing before one's eyes, phantasmagoria surfaced as a metaphor for "modern reverie" in literary descriptions, as Terry Castle traced.[23] Nathaniel Hawthorne, the American gothic author, used the term in his writing to describe such shifting series of images seen but often illusory, like flickering reflections on water.[24] The effect of phantasmagoria too could be processed through text as it informed Thomas Carlyle's hugely influential history of the French Revolution (1837). Carlyle presented the potential carnage through the Jacobin leader Thuriot, writing: "Such vision (spectral yet real) thou, O Thuriot, as from thy Mount of Vision, beholdest in this moment: prophetic of what other Phantasmagories, and loud-gibbering Spectral Realities, which thou beholdest not, but shalt!"[25]

As a pejorative it could be leveled to insinuate another's credulity, as one Latter-day Saint, John E. Page, did to indict what he saw as the gullible nature of others, such as Rigdonites or Millerites. For "the old magicians, sorcerers, Priests of Baal, or modern nincompoops of Phantasmagoria, like Millerism" were ubiquitous, wrote Page.[26] Even while pointing the finger at others, Page broached precisely what was at stake: the desire to utilize the technology of the day to spread visionary experiences, while overcoming the deceptive pitfalls inherent in any medium. And where some authors used it as a metaphor for deception, others brought its tricks right into the text.

OPTICAL MEDIA IN PRINT

Vision in the face of phantasmagoria playfully captured a profound religious dilemma. The force of this dilemma was played out and proliferated in ghost stories of gothic fiction and accounts of angelic visitations. The implicit project of these narratives was to both affect the audience and provide opportunities for discernment, ones that could be reproduced in parallel with the reproducing medium through which they circulated. Mormon adoptions of print, then, reveal a similar radical relationship to vision predicated on the inherent entanglement of material reality and spectral possibilities. For Latter-day Saints, print might not only store ghost stories, but it might also project them for receptive readers. This projection would require managing credulity, vision, and hierarchy precisely during the time when "looking [became] a more conscious and culturally inflected act, with a range of new practices and forms of representation," when "looking itself [became] visible."[27] If properly done, material practices of reading could enable reading "between letters and lines" to provoke spiritual vision.[28]

Because of the nature of print media and the influence of optical media, both Mormon and gothic ghost stories served as the textual analog to phantasmagoria shows. They served to present enlightenment concerns surrounding optics and rationality in a vernacular and popularly consumable form. The emergent regime of vision in early Mormonism was regulated, fostered, and enabled by the media, which circulated its very tenets. As a development in the throes of late romanticism and modern science, Mormonism was immediately infused with the spiritual and modern "necessity of coming to terms with and providing terms for ghosts."[29] Spectrality had to be acknowledged and dealt with, both religiously and rationally. As the introduction to *Accredited Ghost Stories* of 1823 put it, "That such tales are true may reasonably be doubted: but that they are false cannot with any degree of confidence be affirmed."[30] This ghostly presence was felt in the proliferation of supernatural experiences, in circulating stories, and in the power of optical technologies early Mormons encountered.

Friedrich Schiller's popular story *Ghost-Seer* was an early example of the thrilling pull between epistemology and visions. First published in German between 1787 and 1789, *Ghost-Seer* was almost immediately translated into English and published serially in America, where it found a captivated audience. *Ghost-Seer* seemed to "allegorize Hegel's battle between the Enlightenment and superstition ... the power of disillusionment and the power of creating even more powerful illusions."[31] The text even revealed its own diegetic apparition as a magic lantern projection explained by one character to another, effectively coupling ghost stories and the curious science of optical media. But where some stories, such as Schiller's, sought to debunk or explain specters away, Mormon texts wanted them to proliferate—to jump off the page and be "actually seen."

Although Mormon readers shared the conviction with their fellow American Protestants that reading could "save lives and souls—or destroy them," they took a slightly different tack in their focus on visions. As David Paul Nord argues, for agents of religious publishing, "reading lay not in a Pentecostal outpouring of the spirit but in careful, studious, intensive reading."[32] But Latter-day Saints wanted deep intensive reading to proliferate visions. And where Evangelical print culture, in Candy Gunther Brown's estimation was a sustained attempt to use the Word to transform the world, Mormon print wanted to see *through* the word into the spiritual realm that was material and ever present.[33] Latter-day Saints sought to accomplish this by cultivating spiritual seeing through print.

With unprecedented literacy rates and new optical devices for both amusement and ocular augmentation, eyes required direction and religious discipline. The appearance and ubiquity of pictorial pointer hands, or manicules, in print media from the eighteenth and nineteenth centuries marked a symptomatic response, where new techniques were invented to train vision generally among potential distractions. Beyond pointing fingers, religious print media could deploy narrative techniques to train the mind's eye as an extension of lived biological vision. Religious Americans, like Mormons, needed such ocular discipline to realize and literalize the directive to have one's "eye single to the glory of God."[34] Training of spiritual and biological vision expanded during the late romantic period, when looking itself became both conspicuous and generative. This was not only a reaction to the Enlightenment but especially the "coming into being of the visual culture of modernity, with the profound and at times perplexing paradigm shifts that it produced."[35] Stories with seemingly unbelievable visions were perfectly catered to test and try a reader's faith in sight.

But it is not just the representation of vision in texts that helps bring the shifting configuration of deception, truth, and vision into relief in the early nineteenth century. According to Jonathan Crary, the act of observing itself, the practices and "techniques of the observer" were integral to and indicative of the "crucial systemic shift, which was well under way by 1820," and marked a cultural development of modernizing "human vision into something measurable and thus exchangeable."[36] Modern vision became a matter of concern and critical examination in the wake of developments like the microscope, the stereoscope, and scientific inventions that also became amusements, such as the kaleidoscope, peep boxes, and the phantasmagoria shows—not to mention toys, such as thaumatropes and phenakistiscopes. As Robert Jütte has shown, by the "late 1820s, optical and sensory-physiological experiments with so-called retinal afterimages led to the development of a whole series of devices which exploited the familiar tendency of rapid sequences of sense impressions to merge into one."[37] All these optical media opened new possibilities for packaging and playing with subjective vision and shaped new cultural conceptions of the art of seeing and deception.

But where Crary's insightful study focused solely on intellectuals, scientists, and philosophers as the elite users of optical devices and models of modern "observers," this chapter trains its vision on the formation of observers among early Mormon readers. Likely unaware of the deeply philosophical and technological treatises on optics (both human eyes and optic media devices), Mormons nonetheless faced the issue of navigating spiritual vision through the media of the day. In this view, Smith's seer stones, used to translate the Book of Mormon, not only are dead media for today's Mormons but were low-tech equivalents to the mechanical optical gadgets of his day. The groundbreaking meditations on vision and rationality from Immanuel Kant, John Locke, Thomas Reid, and Thomas Paine were, in essence, being acted out on the ground level of everyday nineteenth-century life through peep stones or spiritual eyesight, often recorded in and provoked by print.

A methodological focus on the vernacular level of society resonates with Smith's own account of his "first vision," wherein he carefully represents himself as a lower-class, grassroots seer who was miraculously privileged to see beyond what the educated religious elite in the community had seen or could conceive. In medium-specific ways Smith's account wrested enhanced vision from the top and placed it squarely in the eyes of the sensitive and discerning commoner. For who was equipped to "try the spirits" and discern? "The learned, the eloquent, the philosopher, the sage, the divine, all are ignorant," stated an editorial under Smith's direction.[38] Smith's teachings on vision brought witnessing and discerning into material practice by teaching spectators how to become observers—how to "conform one's actions, to comply with" certain practices of reading and vision.[39]

Through publication his experience could even be emulated. For this reason, the visitation accounts addressed not just readers but especially "spectators," a more appropriate term for nineteenth-century American audiences, invoked by Wendy Bellion. Though spectators often witness a spectacle as passive onlookers, they could be "moved by or motivated to action by looking" and even become "participants in the mental work of understanding, invention, and discernment."[40] For clarity, I refer to this latter form of more involved beholding as "observing," rather than spectating. Merging Bellion and Crary, then, I maintain that spectators are more passive onlookers, whereas, observers *actively* discern and often utilize optic devices to enhance their visual experience. Turning passive reading spectators into active visionary observers was the early Mormon project.

The rise in apparitions and supernatural phenomena—from projected images, to figures in circulating stories and print, to the actual experience of many—necessitated a rational and reproducible response. As an article in the *Spectator* put it, "The person who is terrified with the imagination of ghosts and specters is much more reasonable than one, who, contrary to the reports of all historians, sacred or profane, ancient or modern, and to all traditions of all nations, thinks the appearance of spirits groundless."[41] Apparitions could not simply be dismissed. The acknowledgment of the possibility of specters meant that, in the context of optical media, religious revival, and a dispensation of spiritual practices, *vision itself had to be cultivated and trained*. The intellectual, patriotic, and religious valence of vision in the early nineteenth century was especially pressing for Latter-day Saints, who emerged from the inspiring and confounding story of a boy who claimed he saw God and looked in a stone to turn gold into a new American scripture.

REPRODUCIBLE VISION

Mormonism's first and most fundamental foray into print media was the publication of the Book of Mormon in 1830. With an initial run of 5,000 copies, it signaled the establishment and audacity of Mormonism. Aside from the scriptural content, the book came with a built-in and reproducible opportunity to consider modes of vision. This revelatory potential was packaged in the eyewitness testimonies to the plates included at the end of the book's first edition. The accounts echoed the various explanatory and prefatory materials inserted in the many competing Bible editions at the time to "allay the reliability of bibles as authorities."[42] However, they also bore a unique materialism that prefigured spiritualist convictions in balancing common sense of direct observation with technological possibilities to behold the spirit world and consider the space between "naturalist and supernaturalist interpretations."[43] The printed accounts of both the eight and the three witnesses to the gold plates may convey "relatively little physical detail," as Ann Taves has argued, yet they powerfully juxtaposed two different modes of beholding with implications for a burgeoning modern epistemology of vision.[44] One account was a radical vision of supernatural phenomena, the other an extraordinary vision born of empirical and biological sight along with tactile experience and a matter-of-fact tone: one of spectators and the other of observers.[45]

The three witnesses, as spectators, witnessed a supernatural display "through the grace of God" as "an angel of God came down from heaven, and he brought and laid before [their] eyes" the gold plates. A voice even confirmed the truthfulness of what they beheld, which was "marvelous in [their] eyes."[46] They were privileged to simply sit back in awe and absorb the heavenly demonstration as an unforgettable spectacle. The embodied experience was fundamentally rooted in the activation of sight. While this might be read as the superior experience, it was the account of the eight witnesses that captured the participatory and active element of getting visions with both rational thought and eyes of faith.

Circulating Specters

The text for the other occasion of visual corroboration portrays the eight witnesses more pragmatically observing the plates. They actively saw and "hefted" the artifact, interacted with it. As active and scrutinizing observers they were able to make detailed observations, more in the rational spirit of the time. Fittingly, their observations suggest affinities with nineteenth-century practices of observation and detection with "autoptic vision," or with one's own eyes. As Greg Siegel has shown, this mode of astute observers was eventually expressed through and identified with tactics of the literary detective.[47] From C. Auguste Dupin to Sherlock Holmes, the nineteenth century witnessed epistemic shifts in seeing, between romantic hermeneutical to more forensic and positivist methods. And the eight witnesses to the plates seem an extraordinary hybrid, yet closer to the attentive observations and reasoning of Holmes. To them, the plates seemed to "have the appearance of gold," and the engravings had "the appearance of ancient work, and of curious workmanship." Their own words to describe the event matched the tone of "soberness" employed in the techniques of the cool and collected observers.[48]

Despite the difference, the two modes might build on each other. In other words, one might get at the spectacular through the practical, as print media provided a technology to package and provoke spiritual visions through rational practices. Learning to read, touch, turn pages, interpret, and act on text could lead to visions beyond those material practices. Keen observers could potentially discern between truth and deception as much as acquire the rational literacy requisite to access and download the data of supernatural experiences stored in print. Observing was a surer path to extraordinary vision.

The amazing sights of the plates—both observed and spectated— circulated with traveling missionaries and printing establishments and implicitly taught about levels of vision. Playing off enhanced vision and the rampant delicate deceptions in the early nineteenth century, the two accounts of these eyewitnesses collected and disseminated practices of vision as models. If readers would follow the book's own admonition to pray, seek, and study perhaps they too might have a similar opportunity to move beyond merely spectating the material text, to become an observer of extraordinary material.

The accounts shared an event and record of media witnessing meant to multiply. Although John Durham Peters has explicated the "second-hand" "derivative form" of media witnessing, Paul Frosh emphasizes the possibility of "witnessing texts" to coconstruct experiences of witnessing with active readers.[49] In this sense, the witness accounts might then recuperate the singular event, the instant, for readers as new instances of witnessing rather than depreciate its ontology.[50] As Latter-day Saints circulated their founding witness accounts within the available discourse network of antebellum American life they made them repeatable. The distinctly Mormon inflection to the available "network of technologies and institutions" enabled them "to select, store, and process [the] relevant data" that could reproduce such vision.[51] At the time of the church's founding the technology best suited to the task was print.

AMERICAN GOTHIC

It would be misleading to label Mormon accounts of supernatural encounters as "gothic literature," but the textual proximity and shared project made them important intertexts. As was the case with much of the American folk fascination with magic and the occult, gothic literature originally hailed from Europe, but the stories, motifs, and fixations of the movement haunted the American continent in unique ways that included a landscape of ghostly Native bodies.[52] Gothic literature in America ushered a return of the repressed, "for the generation of Jefferson was pledged to be done with ghosts and shadows."[53] Although Jefferson and others literally excised miracles and revenants from the Bible, the Book of Mormon reinserted America's Native ghosts into scripture and its own history.[54]

The American gothic literature emerged from a distinct context, where "the past constantly inhabits the present, where progress generates an almost unbearable anxiety about its costs, and where an insatiable appetite for spectacles of grotesque violence is part of the texture of everyday reality."[55] In this light, the narrative of the Book of Mormon presented itself as a religious and bloody history of America. It was the backstory of the visually driven, spectacle-laden gothic literature that reflected the violent formation of a nation on top of a native people. Despite Indian removal, warring, and concealment, the ghosts of Native Americans were all over the newly reinscribed and stolen land. Fittingly, Charles Brockden Brown explicitly combined "incidents of Indian hostility, and the perils of the western wilderness" in his adaptation of the gothic.[56] These dead figures could appear as specters, and the memory of the landscape haunted the new "divine" and manifest destiny of the country. According to Renée Bergland, when American gothic authors speak of Native Americans, they always use the language of ghostliness, with the insistence that "Indians are able to appear and disappear suddenly and mysteriously, and also that they are ultimately doomed to vanish."[57] And

Joseph Smith's fellow New Yorker James Fenimore Cooper famously portrayed a vanishing race of Natives just four years before the publication of Book of Mormon.[58]

Smith's early visions of Moroni and other Book of Mormon figures, who were in fact Native American ghosts with unfinished business, fit this milieu while exploding it. His visions even foreshadowed spiritualist conjuring of Indian guides in the coming decades.[59] But before the séance table was the book, which was supposed to spread Smith's visions and shock readers into visions and action. In Jared Hickman's estimation, the Book of Mormon not only recounted a contrarian racial apocalypse but went so far as to foster a "resurgence of the Lamanites' Amerindian descendants in antebellum America, by more bloodshed if necessary," to fulfill prophesy that they would accomplish the Lord's work.[60] Even as that book folded the past into the present, it made its dead authors speak from the dust and, at times, appear to living readers. It was scriptural in form and gothic in effect.

Visions of Book of Mormon figures started with Smith but could be extended to others, reading new scripture in new ways, by borrowing another infectious element of gothic literature. Not only was gothic literature marked by a preoccupation with optical deception and the necessity or inability to discern truth, but its visions seemed to spread. Contemporary author and critic Samuel Taylor Coleridge recognized the connection between "beggarly day-dreaming" and gothic fiction, writing, "The whole *material* and imagery of the doze is supplied *ab extra* by a sort of mental *camera obscura* manufactured at the printing office, which *pro tempore* fixes, reflects and transmits the moving fantasms of one man's delirium," to afflict a hundred others with the same "trance."[61] Gothic fiction provided a print culture to cope with the technology of conjuring up spirits and provoking frights, as it was happening in the phantasmagoria shows. But at the same time, if print could package and transmit "one man's delirium" to a host of other readers, then it had exactly what Mormons needed to spread the kind of spectacular vision that seemed unique to Smith.

But print had also taught readers to be wary of deceptions and that their sense perceptions might be exploited. Like other Americans, Mormons wanted to trust their senses. From seer stones to print, they had to wonder if media were tricking the eyes or enhancing them to see beyond immediate reality. As elite scientists and theoreticians were rethinking vision and optical media through each other between 1810 and 1840—resulting in what Crary has called an "uprooting of vision" and its stability—common Americans were simply worried about delusion and deceit.[62] Even though vision seemed "stubbornly grounded in the empirical philosophy of the eighteenth century, which espoused that the sensory organs could be honed to ascertain truth and identify deception," it was also the most susceptible to trickery.[63] Locke had taught one to depend on sensory experience to fill up the blank slate of the mind and that visual experience could be trusted. And Reid's articulation of "common sense" portrayed a mind capable of discerning truth through sensation, conceptualization, and perception. Yet, Reid explicitly argued that one required familiarity with optical media to avoid deception.

The potential mix-up in interpretation or deception was particularly acute in *"fallacies in vision."* Reid clarified that "to a man unacquainted with the principles of optics, almost every experiment that is made with the prism, with the magic lanthorn, with the telescope, with the microscope, seems to produce some fallacy in vision."[64] These widely held notions were being tested against optical studies and amusements, just as scientific knowledge was "spreading to the population at large" through newspapers and lyceum lectures.[65] Along with natural philosophy and scientific tracts treating optics and new technological capacities of deception, gothic fiction—with its many floating specters—offered a popular and shared network of coming to terms with optical deception.

In equal measure, ghost stories—both gothic and religious—created an opportunity for a layered (scientific/spiritual/romantic) approach to eyewitness testimonies in the exploding print market. As the 1846 publication *Ghost Stories* suggested in its subtitle, *"Collected with a Particular View to Counteract the Vulgar Belief in Ghosts and Apparitions,"* the play was between believing what one saw and detecting deception, even if secondhand.[66] In this sense, stories of specters also served as a literary foil to life, a narrative form of "turning against superstition and credulity by telling a cautionary tale about the deceptive power of optical media and an enthusiastic imagination."[67] While being schooled in rational vision and thought, readers enjoyed the frights and shock of supernatural phenomena.[68] Readers could have their cake and eat it too. Mormons sought to equally manage rationality with spirituality, to have their Reid and read, too, themselves into extraordinary revelations.

SEEING LIKE A SEER

Accounts of the heavenly messengers in the early church were accordingly shot through with the elements and air of ghost stories, presenting doctrine in a form that was both familiar and affecting. Rather than the systematic delineation of doctrine and beliefs later compiled in the "Articles of Faith," stories of spiritual manifestations would, like the ghost stories, get into the reader's bones. To put it in Kittlerian terms, the printed word was the primary means of storing and conjuring up data: the images and sounds that technology was not yet capable of storing could be reproduced through print media. As a written text that should elicit a sensory response, the texts of Mormonism required readers to become active observers to access the stored data and let it affect them. These readers, like those of sentimental novels of the late eighteenth century and gothic literature, must be open to the affect and effect of the medium of print. It is no coincidence that an early convert to Mormonism recalled being struck "like a shock of electricity" upon first encountering the "Golden Bible."[69]

The effect of these printed stories stemmed from their engagement with modern issues of truth and experience vis-à-vis religion, magic, media, and technology. But the force of the narratives also radiated from their ability and intention to elicit a response in the reader. Stories of apparitions were said to chill, tingle the spine, provoke reading addiction, or make the reader shudder.[70] Gothic fiction and visions were written to store the information necessary to have an effect. The printed accounts and stories were not just entertainment but formalized and perfectly reproduced texts that were supposed to step beyond their bounds. Transgressing their formal borders, the stories were to enter the reader's lives and affect, enlighten, or even haunt them. The attending bodily response was then meant to instigate certain states, whether shock and fear, or conversion and epiphany.

Whether evoking shudders or profound peace, visionary accounts could move readers from making sense of serial data on the page to seeing what was otherwise invisible to natural eyes. In the Second Great Awakening the necessity to determine truth through personal experience and vision imbued the texts with important instructional potential that could be shared. In this sense, the appearance of specters in texts of both Mormon and gothic traditions were meant to multiply. Like the gothic vampire that bites its victim to replicate itself, those that come into contact with visions and their printed accounts could themselves become visionaries.[71] Proper techniques could transfer visions as serial data from reader to reader and convert reading spectators into observers with their own visions.

Reproduction also bred repetition, as was the case when Smith's angel kept returning. Like a good serial story, the angel Moroni returned, recapped, and added something new three times in one night. By the end of his life Smith was visited by the angel Moroni at least twenty times, and the experience was not only repetitious but repeatable. As this experience spread in printed form and was trafficked by word of mouth, the vision multiplied. One of the earliest witnesses was Mary Whitmer, who was related to many of the witnesses published in the Book of Mormon accounts but also saw and spoke with Moroni herself as he showed her the plates.[72] At least ten other times the exact same supernatural being appeared to other individuals.[73] Similar to the intellectual and entertaining project of ghost stories, reading the visions from Smith should elicit a sensory response in readers and *convert* them, make them into one of those who can *see* like Joseph the seer.

The potential of print media to help reproduce extraordinary vision can also be evinced in the report of Benjamin Brown, an early convert to Mormonism, who was so impressed that he was finding the truth in Mormonism that the "truth was stereotyped upon [him]." That is, the religious information was transferred to his body as an experience. The spirit manifested itself to him, and Brown felt his immediate conversion could be best conceptualized through the technology of print media. The experience of his conversion was so permanent, he described it like "the change made on a clean sheet of paper by a printing press, leaving an indelible impression behind."[74] Brown even duplicated Smith's vision when figures from the Book of Mormon appeared in his bedroom.[75] Aligning his conversion with media and enacting Smith's visionary posture yielded Brown his own ghost story, which he, in turn, published.

Enacting reproduction through capitalist print media, ghost stories married romantic and enlightenment concerns into cultural commodities that kept coming. The angel and ghost stories of spirits appearing to humans made enlightenment philosophy, from Locke, to Kant, to Reid, percolate into the popular imagination and reading practices. The sense of haunting and the necessity to discern between truth and fiction—to use reason—became repeatable and persistent in serialized and circulating ghost stories. In this context, Smith's visions translated deep theological conceptions into a culturally comprehensible and consumable form. Rather than present the doctrine as an afterthought upon reflection or merely represent the events, vision accounts enabled experiences through the very entanglement of material and discourse. The texts made both enlightenment issues and Great Awakening hopes into a vernacular form as a type of lived ghost story. Out of this potent mixture, readers were to emerge as keen observers, perhaps even seers.

The texts mediated Joseph Smith's vision and experiences and brought them to a literate public who should then read, understand, and hopefully experience something close to Smith's enhanced vision. Instead of peddling nationalism, the smaller Mormon print network helps reveal "what print meant outside of the coastal urban loop" and for a distinct minority group of coreligionists.[76] Diverging from John Modern's analysis of the national and highly systematic print operations of the American Bible Society and the American Tract Society to cultivate rational reading habits, early Mormon reading networks were less coordinated even as they doubled down on the visionary potential of reading.[77] Mormon readers wanted to see as Smith did.

Missionaries sent forth with copies of the Book of Mormon taught, testified, and invited new converts. As one should expect, after reading the Book of Mormon and asking God if it was true, Zera Pulsipher reported seeing "angels with the Book of Mormon in their hands" in a "vision . . . so open and plain" that he yelled out in delight.[78] Similarly, after reading the Book of Mormon and contemplating its veracity, Oliver Granger reportedly had a "heavenly vision" while he was at—of all places—Mr. Mott's Eye Infirmary. Granger even claimed the angel Moroni visited him and taught him as he had done with Smith.[79] Myriad others reported witnessing heavenly messengers after reading the Book of Mormon and accounts of Smith's visions.[80] They were able to personalize and reproduce the hallucinatory promise of the printed word, that one might learn how to read and see as others, as a type of spiritual literacy.

LIMITS OF EMULATION

Other contemporaries also claimed actual visitations from God or angels in deliberate contrast to the proliferating ghost stories, but equally embedded in the same culture of reading networks and optical anxieties.[81] Beyond theological objections, preachers and listeners were wary of dreams and visions because of increased anxieties around deception. In Mormonism, there was a need for corroborating witnesses, a shared communal vision of rationality and order. This intersubjective vision could then take on an air of respectability and trustworthiness as it should with the Book of Mormon witness accounts. But the democratization and spread of spiritual vision intensified problems of authority. Illusion invited various ways of looking and interpreting. Revelatory vision, or second sight, could not simply run amok. A supplemental task to disseminating Smith's vision was corralling efforts and quelling transgressive uses.

As was perhaps inevitable, some exceeded the intended parameters of emulation in reproducing Smith's vision. Some readers translated the texts back into bodily experience that was considered transgressive, just another deception. One year after the publication of the Book of Mormon, John

Whitmer related some of the enthusiastic activity of new converts in Ohio. He decried how "some would fancy to themselves that they had the sword of Laban, and would wield it as expert as a light dragoon, some would act like an Indian in the act of scalping, some would slide or scoot and [on] the floor, with the rapidity of a serpent, which the[y] termed sailing in the boat with the Lamanites."[82] These types of supernatural manifestations required deciphering and included ecstatic members having "visions and revelations,"[83] jumping around, falling, "baptiz[ing] ghosts," and witnessing "balls of fire . . . flying through the air."[84] The descriptions could have just as easily referred to a phantasmagoria show, but the consequences for falling prey to deception were only intensified. Some onlookers met the display of spiritual "operations" with disgust or confusion. John Whitmer made sense of the behavior and those who participated as a lack of discernment.

The misreading of the texts and the misbehavior of their translation back into action—into seeing them happen again—were the result of incorrect vision. The demonstrations of misled energy were said to be the result of the fact that "the devil blinded the eyes of some good and honest disciples."[85] The adversary "took a notion to blind the minds" of those susceptible. The visionaries were actually victims, for they "had not enough knowledge to detect [the enemy of all righteousness] in all his devices."[86] The devil had simply blinded their untrained undiscerning eyes. They had peddled spectacles rather than sought out reasoned observations and extraordinary vision.

In direct response to the deceptive displays, Smith pronounced a revelation directing members to train their senses to avoid being "seduced by evil spirits" or "deceived."[87] The witnesses to extraordinary displays needed to become competent observers, since visions and apparitions were increasing in frequency. Some even "had visions and could not tell what they saw."[88] Philo Dibble recalled witnessing Smith publicly rebuke the "variety of false spirits" in Ohio, when he said, "God has sent me here, and the devil must leave here, or I will."[89] Smith's revelation, dictated to address the matter, acknowledged the increased presence of spirits and sought to "reason" with the saints concerning them. He had told his brother Hyrum, just days earlier, that he came to Ohio to regulate the church, "as the devil had made many attempts to over throw" the members.[90] The revelation made clear that bishops and elders would be ordained as the "head," specifically to help discern which gifts were of God and which of Satan to ensure "order."[91] The appeal to rationality and ecclesiastical order in the face of specters and spiritual phenomena was the revelation's true intervention.

Perhaps the challenge most symptomatic of the cultural and religious milieu came with Hiram Page's case of transgressive vision through a seer stone. Page had been one of the eight witnesses to the gold plates—those that observed and interacted with them. He had been a successful observer. But only a year later Page was utilizing an optical medium, a seer stone, to see beyond what the naked eye could. This too seemed an affinity with Smith's use of a stone as an optical means of glimpsing the otherwise invisible. Since several followers of the new church were persuaded by Page's revelations from peering into the stone, Smith inquired of the Lord. Smith then dictated a revelation stating that Page's vision was clouded and that "Satan deceiveth him."[92] Not only could stones become "dangerous media" in the wrong hands, but there were limits to the desired reproducibility of the founding vision.[93]

By the late 1830s, as Mormonism spread, so did its community of readers, who were testing the limits of its literature and visionary models. The British Isles became a hotspot, and its distance from the church's hub required more control through instruction and printed texts. In England, where international Mormonism first took off, a band of women were having visions and dreams that exceeded the doctrinal limits of the church by foreseeing and prescribing marriage partners for people. Their matchmaking visions were deemed dangerous. The missionary Joseph Fielding cautioned one of the ladies "to be careful about her Dreams, and told her if her Eye were not single, her Dreams would be mixed with Error."[94] Yet Manchester convert Anne Booth's vision of a deceased apostle and baptism for the dead may have helped spur Joseph Smith's introduction of proxy baptism. Once Brigham Young committed Booth's vision to paper and sent it on to Nauvoo, it was shared among the members, and Smith "used it rhetorically as a means of clarifying" his teaching on baptism for the dead a few months later.[95] While Booth's revelation provided comfort and support for Smith's radical vision of work performed by the living for the dead, many other visions and practices were outside the realm of acceptance and required systematic, even revelatory debunking.

SYSTEMATIZING SPIRITS

Yearning for heavenly visions was admirable, but the urgency to develop and manage proper vision intensified with the looming potential to encounter evil spirits instead of angelic messengers. Increased frequency of spectral appearances called for continued instruction on discernment. Print media could best spread patterns of vision as an antidote to the scattering "false spirits" that had "gone abroad in the earth." As his revelation had suggested months earlier, Smith eventually spelled it out: "Let us reason together that ye may understand."[96]

The demand for discerning vision was revisited with a revelation from Smith, circulated in 1839, but not printed until 1843.[97] As a type of instruction manual, the revelation taught how to deal "rationally" with apparitions. What became section 129 of the Doctrine and Covenants was a veritable explication on what to do when specters appear, and the assurance that they likely will. Smith's delineation of specters was somewhat similar to the multiply-republished classification by Daniel Defoe, who had written, "The apparitions I am to speak of are these 1. The appearance of angels. 2. Of Devils. 3. Of the departed Souls of Men."[98] Smith's revelation similarly classified three types, including: (1) angels of flesh and bones, (2) disembodied spirits of men made perfect, and (3) devils as angels of light.[99] But Smith's version latched onto the materiality of each type and its importance for embodied seekers of truth.

The esoteric teaching came in the wake of the unfolding temple endowment ceremony, which should tap into the powers of heaven. The spiritual force of the ritual seemed to open the floodgates to both heaven and hell, implying increased spectral encounters. The beings at the ceremony could include supernatural visitors, thus "the mortals among them required the ability to tell angelic friend from demonic foe."[100] Because the beings that might appear could be of three different orders, Mormons would require keen discernment. As natural vision alone was too conditional, too vulnerable to human and technological deceptions, Smith taught corroboration in another sensory test.

Those witnessing a specter should attempt to shake hands with the ghostly being. In a discourse given during the summer of 1839 Smith admonished, "We may look for Angel[s] and receive their ministering but we are to try the Spirits & prove them for it is often the case that men make a mistake in regard to these things." Smith added, "No vision is to be taken but what you see by the seeing of the eye, or what you hear by the hearing of the ear—When you see a vision pray for the interpretation if you get not this, shut it up—There must be certainty. . . . Lying spirits are going forth in the Earth."[101] In the spring of 1841, Smith further clarified, "Be not deceived nor doubtful of this fact a spirit of a good man or an angel from heaven who has not a body will never undertake to shake hands with you." By the acceptance or rejection of their handclasp, the living could "detect the spirits who may come unto

[them]."[102] The litmus test was material connection, a transfer of data across clasped hands that intertwined logic, doctrine, and the (common) senses.

By the touch—as with sound—the eyes could be verified.[103] Although both Kant and Smith would have agreed that spirits had intelligence, Smith's reasonable "testing" of spirits could also communicate with spirits' reasonable essence to determine, rationally, how to classify them. Apparitions appeared almost unable to act according to will but appeared instead wholly subject to the rules of Smith's reason. The materiality of the test, repeatable like any good experiment, was a failsafe and irresistible means of communication with its own power—a power that employed rationality and codification to transcend the power of the transcendent. These corporeal tests were necessary for Mormons to detect "false spirits & personages," and, as Smith stressed, "no one can truly say he knows God until he has handled something."[104] In materialist ways, trusting in the natural senses was the lifeblood of Mormon seeing.

The religiously inflected conundrum informed Smith's vision texts, where readers were meant to see and feel. In Mormon media practices, beholding and handling specters was fraught but desirable. They sought to root extraordinary vision in rationality and feeling. For them, the effect of gothic ghost stories and optical media, rather than demonstrate or debunk visions, might actually suggest their productive proliferation as rational and believable. Seeking to manage and systemize extraordinary vision, Mormons positioned the solution in material-discursive practices of hallucinating between the lines. All this was meant to cast readers' eyes beyond themselves, linking the "somatic body" with the "social body" to construct a visionary community rising above deception and toward acquiring celestial knowledge.[105] Through their print practices Mormons were made into visionaries, but ones who could also see the necessity of rationality, knowledge, and submitting to governance.

CONCLUSION

Gothic literature and vision accounts did something similar in offering readers opportunities to become enlightened. Yet, Mormon teachings and visionary accounts ventured a step further: they promised to teach readers how to both become visionaries of their own and be led by a governing body. In this particular context the "evangelical imperative" to act rationally and calculate was folded into its apparent opposite: a proliferation of spiritual visions.[106] By learning to read with the natural eyes and see beyond the page with spiritual eyes, Latter-day Saints felt they were glimpsing what was materially real, yet invisible to others. This material act should also build a community, by getting readers' minds to the comprehension and conviction that submitting to ecclesiastical order was equally a sign of truth and progress, a reality on the horizon.

Recognizing the ambitious and problematic emulation of visual practices in early Mormonism reveals the important dialogue between media and materiality to get at the invisible and absent. These unseen elements could be made visible through technologies but required a novel type of perception and management. By 1843 Smith even taught that eventually everyone (in the "celestial kingdom" of heaven) would have a white stone, a "urim and thummim," whereupon all things would be made known.[107] But for now the power of vision and stones was fraught with a creative energy manageable through print. Instructions coalesced into disciplined practices.

From its very inception, Mormonism established itself as a community of media users who expected the spiritual through the rational. Particular techniques of vision could elevate the widespread medium of print into a spiritual technology. Translating the effects of optical media into circulating stories of spectral appearances provided the training in spiritual vision that closely aligned with, even when it was apparently at odds with, rational enlightenment ideas about and the scientific explanation of biological vision. In effect, Mormon print reverse engineered Smith's vision by putting it into texts to be read, in order to bring it right back out. This project entailed not only mechanically reproducing Smith's extraordinary vision, but then managing the ramifications for authority once it had been unleashed. A promise of extraordinary vision coursed through early Mormon print media, which offered models of sharpened observation in the context of specters and visual deception. Instead of being victims of delusion, disciplined spectators could become a community of observers, recognizing the truth to be had beyond the natural eyes.

PANORAMIC

VISIONS

We have hitherto walked by sight, and if a man wanted to know
anything he had only to go to Brother Joseph. Joseph has gone, but
he has not left us comfortless. I want to say that Brother Joseph
came and enlightened me two days after he was buried.

William W. Phelps, 1844

[Mormonism] exhibits fanaticism in its newest garb . . .
seeing visions in the age of railways.

Charles Dickens, 1851

Joseph Smith was dead, to begin with. There was no doubt about it.
Only fourteen years after establishing the new religion, the prophet's
massacred body gave up the ghost on June 27, 1844. But now—
shortly after his assassination—he was appearing to his followers. Reports
multiplied that his spirit was continuing his work through visitations and
instructions. Once again, practices of spiritual vision would be paramount
to the maintenance of Mormonism. Where early Mormon print had circulated and spread spectacular visions had by Smith and others, now panorama
paintings could consolidate and supersede visions of Smith's own spirit. The
technology of the panorama could convert Mormon visual practices into a
means of cementing identity and authority around a shared image of the dead
prophet, linked to a clear successor. But it was initially unclear just whose
vision of Smith would govern the church's future.

One of the many who saw the disembodied Smith was devoted Mormon convert Philo Dibble, who dreamt he saw Smith's ghost walking toward him with a "sheet of [rolled-up] paper in his hand." The prophet then threw the roll into a tree from which it tumbled down, ricocheting between branches. Although others were assembled at the tree's base the roll fell directly into Dibble's hands. The revelatory experiences continued. Within days Dibble also experienced a vision of the prophet's martyrdom.[1] Between a visit from Smith's ghost, a witness of his death, and a symbolic charge to utilize rolled paper, Dibble felt he had been called to depict and share the church's past to guide its future. Combining his revelations and the popular medium of panorama, Dibble would play a central role in converting the circulating visions of Smith into a singular and collective image.

Dibble put his revelation into action. In March 1845, just eight months after Smith's passing, Dibble filed an Illinois state copyright to exhibit eight proposed panorama paintings.[2] By April he was exhibiting the scene of the martyrdom of Joseph and Hyrum Smith.[3] Dibble's show—a candlelight panorama display of painted scenes accompanied by music and lecture—was the first known attempt to visually mediate the Latter-day Saint church's history for live audiences. Dibble's panoramic scenes of the prophet (unfortunately no longer extant), along with the eventual inclusion of Smith's death mask and phrenology chart, helped embolden Dibble's own lived continuity with Smith.[4] Building on his personal and revelatory connections to Smith, Dibble translated the recent past into panorama art for the public. The perceived aura of the relics and renderings indexed the past and prophet for the surviving membership of the splintered church. Combined with the panorama, the whole show evinced a powerful memory project aimed at socializing and "retrospective contemplativeness."[5]

The death of the prophet and the glaring question of succession seemed to necessitate the medium-specific viewing experience of the panorama. Because no precise or uniform succession protocol was in place, members were unsure where to direct their vision and whom to follow. Dibble's images memorialized Smith and constructed a usable past, but Mormon panoramas went beyond cultural memory projects. With Dibble's panorama, members of the church could collectively consume a standardized image of their past that would at once forge identity, inspire faith, and most importantly: control the image of Joseph Smith by *managing his afterimage* from myriad apparitional appearances. It wasn't just Dibble who saw Smith after his death. In fact, too many individuals were competing for Smith's legacy and claiming visions of his spirit. In the crisis of succession that detonated in the wake of the charismatic prophet's death, the ghostly appearance and memory of Smith required consolidation. Panoramic scenes provided a unique solution.

Smith's appearance in the Mormon panorama paintings of both Philo Dibble (1845) and then later of Danish convert C. C. A. Christensen (ca. 1880) made that prophet and the founding past present in a powerful and shared form. This stretched Smith's image into an all-encompassing sight, literalizing the Greek roots of "pan" and "orama." As Dibble once described them, the panorama images could "display at one glance the most striking likeness" of the pictured figures.[6] The broader nineteenth-century fascination with the technology of the panorama was also eventually connected to both the experience of train travel and enhanced vision. As will be detailed later, the sense of wonder the enlarged painted images facilitated was also connected to sublime visionary experience of spiritual revelation. Employing language entangled with unique media experience to capture and relate their visions, Latter-day Saints began understanding revelatory experience, itself, as "panoramas" placed before them.[7] By turning revelatory glimpses of the past into a shared experience of aesthetically externalized memory, the panorama was a fruitful medium.

Not only could the painted scenes expand a viewer's archive of experience, but the medium could "determine [the] situation," by shaping how a figure or scene was stored, accessed, and therefore remembered.[8] Stretching a vision of the past across a horizontal axis—into a communal experience—the Dibble panorama exhibitions became a popular glue between the traumatized members of the church after their leader's death. The medium enabled Mormons to work through their shared trauma by virtue of a material-discursive technique of vision. After all, as Robert Orsi reminds us, sometimes "religion is less about the making of meaning than about the creation of scar tissue."[9]

The ability of panorama images of the prophet to suture the community and its wounds was surprisingly effective. Panorama effectively rendered Dibble's subjective spiritual sight into an objectively shared sight geared toward solidarity.[10] Like Mormon media practices with print, a singular vision could be stored and shared, but this time the effect was different. History became image and was thereby converted into a collective memory through a collective practice. For Mormon audiences the panorama medium became a "vessel" of an idea, a "container of possibility," specifically for the floundering religious body in Nauvoo, Illinois.[11] In the absence of clear direction, church members were forced "to decide which of conflicting succession claimants was authorized by God."[12] Finding their way to the panorama and consuming an image in unison helped alleviate confusion and funnel visions of Smith into Brigham Young's leadership.

The present moment seemed to require a project of mediating grief and memory into a shared and affective experience. The limited scholarship on Dibble's panorama has been quick to gloss over this moment and highlight his efforts to establish a museum and collect artifacts.[13] But the precise context and mobilization of these early panorama require analysis to better appreciate their power. Although panorama is virtually a dead medium now, the early panorama displays were vital and connected to lived experience. They were meant to get eyes and bodies caught up in feeling something. Mormon panorama more closely fit James Carey's "ritual" view of communication.[14] Instead of just conveying messages across space, panorama could maintain a community in time.

Especially since oversized paintings called on increased peripheral stimulation the paintings were meant to fix and energize embodied experience. Their aesthetic realism came from eyes feeling the limits of perception. The size of the images was impressive and thrilling, but more importantly they should gesture toward the experience of real life. These virtual screens made other times and places feel somewhat real as sensory experiences presented to the viewer. Extending a painting's dimension into panorama actualized the fact that, whereas "focused vision makes us mere outside observers . . . peripheral perception transforms retinal images into a spatial and bodily involvement and encourages participation."[15] Since panoramas "invite a peculiarly embodied, and highly immersive form of spectatorship" the medium activated communal spectatorship in stimulating ways.[16] Wide-angle displays signaled experience and community. Attending together, and listening and responding to accompanying lectures, as well as walking between paintings while crying and mourning, all got the body to feel the paintings through the eyes. And unlike the reproducibility of print, where copies always haunted the "original," the panorama images were unique. A panorama image could be shared as *the* image of the past or prophet and draw the community together.

Of course, Dibble's innovative use of the panorama medium did not spring up in a vacuum. In the nineteenth century the concept of a "panorama" spread just as rapidly as the actual devices, but the first panoramas were exhibited in London in 1791, and the earliest known examples in New York have been dated to 1795.[17] Although terminology for precisely what kind of material device was employed was still fluid and shifting, generally three types of panoramas were exhibited: static, moving, and circular. Static panoramas were quite simply paintings on canvases of imposing dimensions. Like Dibble's, they were most often sequential art. Moving panoramas, however, conveyed the rolled paintings between two revolving columns behind a proscenium, and the shows were often sporadic events given by traveling showmen. These panorama displays centered on virtual travel, as if by rail, with images rolling by in succession. Circular panoramas (cyclorama), which completely surrounded a viewer and required more architectural apparatus, created a heightened sense of immersion.[18] Although popular in urban Europe, circular panoramas were less successful in America. Better suited to American audiences were oversized paintings and moving panorama, since their ability to stretch canvas images and push borders seemed to spatially approximate the expanding frontier and even encourage immigrants to move westward and "stake their claim."[19]

The technology of panorama offered the delight in simulation. As American panorama displays proliferated throughout the 1840s, many functioned like John Banvard's "Mississippi River Valley," which took the viewer down a visual tour of the river. By the 1850s even religious panorama began appearing, offering viewers historical illustrations of New Testament events or "Scenes in the Holy Land."[20] As more clergy sought "to couple word and image in their battle for the congregation's attention," they turned to panorama projects, displayed inside the walls of the church and across several states.[21] Beyond providing virtual tourism, panorama could be instrumentalized to specific ends. The hugely popular "Moving Panorama of Bunyan's Pilgrim's Progress" of 1850, for instance, adapted events from Bunyan's widely read book into a magnificent visual display in order to shore up faith during the fundamentalist-liberal controversy that threatened the Anglican Church.[22] Keen panorama artists recognized the opportunities afforded by patriotic and celebratory scenes toward political, economic, and religious ends. Although their invitation to roam around them would suggest freedom, "the panorama's integration of the commercial and artistic" seemed in Tim Barringer's estimation, "paradigmatically modern and contrived to interpellate (in Althusser's sense) the largest number of individuals."[23]

The panorama's significance could take on local flavor for different sites of reception, but it was conceived in the timely turn toward visual media, which experimented with, challenged, and distracted the eyes. The nineteenth-century craving for new visions and optical entertainments was in part stimulated by these oversized paintings. In fact, the panorama experience can be "identified with the modern attempt to contain everything within a single view or picture."[24] This general interest likely soaked into Mormon consciousness when Latter-day Saints in Nauvoo witnessed or at least read about Banvard's Mississippi panoramas.[25] They also visited other installments, such as when George A. Smith and John E. Page went to see Frederick Catherwood's traveling panorama display "A View of Jerusalem" in Philadelphia while proselytizing during the summer of 1841.[26] It just so happened that Page had been sent on a mission to the Holy Land, but instead of joining Orson Hyde and actually seeing Jerusalem, Page enjoyed the virtual mobility afforded by the medium of the panorama.[27]

But in Dibble's enterprising hands the panorama initiated the first program of mediating Latter-day Saint panoramic vision—literally Dibble's and now collectively the Mormons' in Nauvoo, Illinois. In the sense that "panoramic perception, in contrast to traditional perception, no longer belonged to the same space as the perceived object," the medium appropriately appealed to Mormon viewers who were cut off from their founding leader and needed an apparatus to facilitate his remembrance.[28] Even with Dibble's static images, Mormon vision could be mobilized and framed by the panorama that was, at once, a vision of the past and an affective site/sight in the present. For Mormons in Nauvoo the panorama and the communal perception it engendered signaled a break with the objects being viewed—a break that was shared and excruciatingly felt. Dibble's panorama helped guide the Mormon gaze toward a singular vision. Becoming a "self-disciplining" viewer was a milestone in what Jonathan Crary has described as "the formation of modern audiences" in the nineteenth century.[29] But here the disciplining of bodies and eyes was occurring among Mormons with a specific religious significance.

Although the originals are no longer extant, historical descriptions reveal that Dibble's initial panorama included an image of Smith's martyrdom and a triumphal portrayal of Smith addressing the city militia, the Nauvoo Legion.[30] As if to capture the most regal and commanding aspects of the prophet alongside his ultimate mortal demise, the paintings' visceral effect could work from stark juxtaposition. In a letter to the English mission presidency, Dibble described how each scene comprised "128 feet of canvas" and was painted by Robert Campbell, who was "engaged in visiting places, taking sketches, and making himself acquainted with all the essential matters and facts as they may connect themselves with historical painting."[31] Beyond popular appeal, the paintings needed input and accuracy. In fact, the fidelity to "times, places, buildings, &c." impressed the spectators enough they were said to "frequently" "exclaim, 'I was there.'" Dibble elaborated that this intended effect was "so that all, while they feel anxious to hand down to posterity our illustrious martyrs, and record these visions of the past events[,] embrace subjects connecting their own salvation and interests with these sceneries."[32] Looking *together* at a constructed and framed past was meant to enact mutual guidance and institutional salvation in the present.

In September 1845 the Nauvoo policeman Hosea Stout went to Robert Campbell's studio to pose for his inclusion in the panorama image of Smith addressing the Nauvoo Legion.[33] But Stout also recorded minutes from meetings wherein the composition of the painting was discussed. The men in council argued over historical accuracy, whom to exclude (because of apostasy), and their disdain to be portrayed in company with some of the officers on the canvas.[34] Figures, such as Wilson Law and Francis and Chauncey Higbee, who all served in the legion until they spoke out against Joseph Smith and were excommunicated, were absent.[35] But others who, since Smith's death, chose to follow Sidney Rigdon, James Strang, or Alpheus Cutler, or to leave altogether could also be excised from memory. Stout recorded the officers' dissatisfaction with "some men who were to be put in conspicuous places on the scenery who were not officers and moreover betrayed the prophet & patriarch to death." Stout himself refused to "be seen portrayed in a group of such men for it would be a disgrace to [his] children."[36] Clearly, not just who was there, but who *deserved to be remembered as having been there* was at stake.

As a surviving study for the final panorama evinces, a multitude of militiamen were depicted, and Nauvoo's landscape and architecture are clearly discernable. The final product might have even adjusted the proximity and composition of the scene to ensure that individuals were recognizable. Dibble's images shared the immersive scale of other popular panoramas that provided background scenery to simulate travel or depicted biblical scenes and visions.[37] Yet, Dibble's scenes were surprisingly unique in their emphasis on narrative and identifiable historical figures. By so doing he adapted the medium to Mormon needs. It was precisely the details and identifiable bodies that mattered in ironing out a historical narrative during crisis.

An emphasis on local memory meant information and eyewitness accounts were necessary to properly render the past. Soliciting information from church members, Campbell painted the scenes as they were, but also as Dibble had seen them in vision. The paintings were shaped by research and inspiration.[38] Visions and memories shaped the images on canvas and their particulars determined what kind of a past would be carried forward. As the

Joseph Smith Addressing the Nauvoo Legion, by Robert Campbell, 1845.
Courtesy of Alex Baugh.

Nauvoo Legion painting implied, how one's image and allegiance to Smith were immortalized in Dibble's display bore some measure of cultural capital.

Accordingly, the panorama was created and exhibited in a tense environment of debate and conflicting views of the martyred prophet. The need for consensus and shared vision fueled Dibble's controversial efforts to create a public image of Smith, which was shown while in progress and then put on display in the Masonic Hall in Nauvoo. The martyrdom image evoked not only tears and remorse, but intense feelings of anger. Emboldened by his viewing of the panorama during a secretive meeting in the Masonic Hall, William W. Phelps felt there was "fire enough" in its depiction of injustice to get Mormons and Indians alike to take action against the government and have "God provide the means."[39] Where thousands of Nauvoo citizens would have witnessed Smith addressing the Legion, virtually no one witnessed his death days later in Carthage. Although John Taylor and others would attempt to describe and memorialize the event with printed narrations, Dibble was the first member of the church with the audacity to have his vision of it graphically represented for audiences.[40]

Within a month of Dibble's first showings, however, an illustrated pamphlet titled *A Correct Account of the Murders of Generals Joseph and Hyrum Smith* was published in Nauvoo, in May 1845.

Also created and printed by a few Latter-day Saints, this pamphlet lacked the collective spectatorial draw of Dibble's work. Based on the eyewitness account given by Warsaw militia member William Daniels, which included a miraculous ray of light stopping ruffians from mutilating Smith's corpse, the pamphlet was meant to foment Mormon anger and draw the flock together. Unfortunately, it was more appealing to the attorneys defending those charged with murdering the Smith brothers as they used it to "destroy [Daniels's] credibility as a witness."[41] The pamphlet's approach was also more focused on villains than heroes. In fact, the very first image was a profile of a vocal critic of Smith, Thomas Sharp, labeled the "murderer" with a "corrupt heart."[42]

With only three illustrations included in the text, the pamphlet used them all to detail the blood stains, drawn weapons, and infamy of the perpetrators, set against the miraculous divine intervention of light. Its visual style and antagonistic use in the trial, as well as rumors that Daniels profited from his narrative, all seem to have turned Mormons off from the pamphlet's visceral appeal.[43] Primarily, it lacked the shared, colorful, and live aspects of Dibble's show. Print texts in private—even illustrated ones—simply did not function like emerging visual entertainments, where new modes of attention and collective spectatorship were being forged.

The panorama embodied Smith and captured Mormon efforts to bring viewers to the same vision—to standardize visions for communal consumption, whereas print media had been better suited to disseminate discerning vision to disparate readers. As the previous chapter detailed, the early printed visions of the church could teach and enable members to obtain their own visons, but also how to judge if their eyes were being deceived. This was an individualized process spread across printed texts and reading networks. Similar to early stereoscopes, which were often consumed privately and placed the effect in the eyes of the beholder, Mormon print media put the visionary elements in the hands and eyes of the individual to work out.[44] Stereoscopes could be isolating but flaunted vivid photographic detail to make objects seem present with depth. In contrast, Mormon panorama harnessed the blurry details of painting and brought the beholders together—out of their homes—into communal space to view scenes that were decidedly absent.

It's worth mentioning, as David Walker has argued, that some later uses of stereoscopy also sought to "foreground" specific Mormon religious

From *A Correct Account of the Murder of Generals Joseph and Hyrum Smith*, 1845. Depiction of interior and exterior of Carthage Jail.
L. Tom Perry Special Collections, Harold B. Lee Library, Brigham Young University, Provo, Utah.

sites as photographic sights that could be located and contextualized through viewing practices.[45] Viewed during travel by rail to Utah, these late nineteenth-century stereograms of sites along the path could be enjoyed even after the pictured location had been passed. Stereoscopy in this mode shared the panorama's connection to forward momentum and the creation of new rituals that "pictorially, discursively, and analytically" focused viewers' attention.[46] They both foregrounded a view *after the fact*. If Dibble's panorama foregrounded a vision of Smith to be focused on, it too was at the deliberate expense of lingering and conflicting visions of Smith circulating in the background. This was a new twist on the print program to circulate Smith's own vision in the years leading to his death, now that succession was left unanswered.

Efforts to regulate bodies before the panorama of historical *and* revelatory visions had specific value for the members of the Church of Jesus Christ of Latter-day Saints during the crisis of identity and succession that followed the assassination of their prophet. The need to mold the members together and shape a shared focus was pressing. With the charismatic leader gone, whose vision was meant to proliferate and provide the model for emulation, the church was reeling. Several claims for carrying the church forward competed for grieving and confused followers. The situation required a shared vision of the future by giving meaning and form to the past.

Through the technology of the panorama—in tandem with writing and other practices of historical representation—Mormons were able to technologize and sacralize the past. The construction and exhibition of the novel form of visual culture mediated a panoramic way of seeing and tapped into discourses and experiences of revelatory vision described in similar terms. By collectively viewing oversized paintings—both static and later rolled into motion on large rotating reels—Mormons were able to see each other seeing the same sight. This ricochet eyesight sutured viewers into a community. Certainly, Dibble's panoramic take on the prophet and recent past reflected Maurice Halbwachs's delineation of collective memory as structured by social frameworks.[47] The paintings even functioned within Aby Warburg's concept of "social memory."[48] Yet, their initial intervention was to harness and channel the diffuse and scattered energy of revenant Smiths and uncertain futures.

JOSEPH SMITH'S AFTERIMAGE

The Latter-day Saints were unclear how to proceed without Joseph Smith at the church's head. Confusion and debate loomed over the surviving flock.

As Mormons searched for sure footing, several figures proposed plans for succession and claimed connections to instructions or authorization from Smith's departed spirit. The painted and shared images of Smith and church history were created in this context of traumatic memory and lingering visions of Smith.

Some were convinced Smith would haunt and curse his murderers, but more often Smith appeared to his followers, offering specific counsel or general condolence.[49] Already eight years prior to Smith's gruesome death one of his followers foretold how "Smith would be the Sixth Angel."[50] And in a felicitous turn of phrasing, Smith reportedly suggested that after his own death he "would not be far away" and "would still be working with you, and with a power greatly increased, *to roll on* this kingdom" (emphasis mine).[51] By having Smith "appear" in the panoramas of rolled and often rolling paper, his reported statement could be inflected with an aesthetic dimension. In some form or another, Smith should be visibly involved with the succession of the church. His ghostly appearances were no shock. They were expected.

Christopher James Blythe has demonstrated how these Smith visitations helped members cope with the rupture of Smith's death and the transition into a new post-Joseph church. Like deceased family members appearing to their kin, the appearance of Smith's ghost could comfort and lead the group from beyond. These appearances also had significant consequences for the crisis of succession. As Blythe sees it, through the lens of Max Weber, Smith's charisma was "routinized and regulated" by his primary successor, Brigham Young, to ensure and legitimize the succession. The efforts to consolidate the apparition stories of Smith were only part of a larger project to combat "rival claimants," limit interpretations, and establish orthodoxy within the flock.[52] Some potential leaders, including James Strang, Lyman Wight, and Alpheus Cutler claimed to have received "secret ordinations or appointments" from Smith before his death.[53] But others, such as Sidney Rigdon, claimed revelation from and visions of Smith after his death. Reports of Smith appearing to diverse witnesses were a "threat, as the disembodied Smith could trump church leadership."[54] The image and memory of Smith had to be regulated and implicitly agreed on, and media practices could standardize the past and membership to ward off distracting visions.

There were other options by 1845. Strang's excavation of metal plates suggested prophetic ability in recovering additional scripture as Smith had.[55] And locks of Smith's hair or walking canes made from the wood of his coffin materially connected their owners with the prophet, as much as the death mask and phrenology chart did.[56] But none of these properly narrated and standardized the mythic afterimage of Smith as a repeatable show, where visitors like Hosea Stout would return on multiple occasions.[57] Relics, ritual, and reminiscing certainly facilitated the work of connecting Latter-day Saints to Smith, but the panorama projects arguably captured the process in a more lived experiential form. That Smith might even reveal himself in "rolled paper" in order to "roll on" the kingdom seemed to converge in Dibble's work and could potentially make other individual visions redundant.

In a patriarchal church, it is no surprise Wilford Woodruff, Amasa Lyman, Lorenzo Snow, and other leading men reported seeing Smith in visions and dreams after his death.[58] However, an additional dilemma for the church's successors was that Smith's ghost did not seem gender biased. Women, such as Mary Ellen Kimball, saw Smith immediately following the assassination.[59] Diantha Farr, Mary Lightner, and Lizzie Smith were also visited by Smith's ghost at some point.[60] The visitations persisted, and by 1857 the frequency caused Brigham Young to publicly ridicule the reports, effectively delegitimizing women's visions of Smith. Young wryly explained, "As quick as Joseph ascends to his Father and God, he will get a commission to this earth again, and I shall be the first woman that he will manifest himself to. I was going to say the first man, but there are so many women who profess to have seen him, that I thought I would say woman."[61] None of these women claimed presidential authority over the church, yet they all had a connection to Smith that suggested a vague sense of spiritual superiority. With visionary men it was even more threatening.

A private tie to the prophet could undermine the new coalescing leadership and conjure the precise and haunting threat of more than one image, ghost, or connection to Smith outside the church leadership.[62] In just such an appeal to authority through connection, Heber C. Kimball interpreted his dream of Smith as a providential reminder of his and his fellow apostles' claim to leadership. Kimball's dream supported Brigham Young as the potential successor because Young was president of the quorum of the twelve apostles. However, the apostles' primary rival, Sidney Rigdon, also claimed to have revelatory connections to Smith. It is perhaps not surprising that Rigdon's vision of the church's future as well as his communications with Smith from beyond the grave were readily dismissed as a "long story" and a "second Class vision" by Young and the other apostles.[63] The contest over visions of both Smith and the future of the church required consent and consolidation. Rigdon's vision was not only second class, but it also lacked the visual components of seeing Joseph, taking on Joseph's appearance, and being involved in a project of displaying his panoramic image for the members, all of which were connected to Young.

With visions of Smith unfettered and running amok, who possessed the authoritative connection to him for the church? Young experienced (needed) his own vision as an authentication. In 1846, Young reported seeing Smith and discussing the future and doctrine of the church with him in a dream.[64] It was essential that Young's experience was shared. John D. Lee reported hearing Young recount the vision, and Hosea Stout quoted Young, ending by saying, "I want you all to remember my dream for I [sic] it is a vision of God and was revea[l]ed through the spirit of Joseph."[65]

Stretching the returned presence of Smith to its limits, later recollections even described seeing Young be "transfigured," as he took on the manners, sound, and appearance of Smith within months of the martyrdom. In Jake Johnson's estimation Young exercised his talent as a showman and mimic: he *performed* Joseph the best."[66] However it was accomplished, Young's performance became a rallying point for Mormons. At the legendary church meeting on August 8, 1844, Rigdon first stood and for hours pleaded his case to be appointed "guardian of the church." Young, on the other hand, *became* a vision of Smith. Channeling the former leader, Young petitioned the church to follow him and the twelve and literally embodied a Joseph Smith appearance for a collective audience as he spoke.[67] This was something like a Smith vision in real time.

Woodruff later emphasized the pivotal nature of Young's speech and the medium-like quality. "There was a reason for this in the mind of God: it convinced people."[68] As a secondhand recipient of the news, Aurelia Spencer Rogers recalled, when Brigham Young began speaking, "the Mantle of Joseph fell upon him, and he was like one transformed; his countenance, voice and form were like those of the late Prophet. Many in the congregation, even children saw this miracle; it satisfied the people and decided the question who was to be the leader."[69] Without even having been present, Rogers's conviction attested to the power of the circulating news and the need for a unifying and decisive afterimage of Smith to galvanize the succession. Although most accounts were reminiscent, even within months of the original transfiguration Woodruff sent the news to England, stating, "It was evident to the Saints that the mantle of Joseph had fallen upon him, the road that he pointed out could be seen so plainly."[70] The majority in attendance voted against Rigdon. Their confidence in Young and the apostles to lead the church established the core "Brighamite" faction that continues to carry the name Church of Jesus Christ of Latter-day Saints into the present day.

The effort to panoramorize the deceased prophet then paralleled and supported the larger project of guiding the church and consolidating leadership around an image of Smith. This was also evidenced in another crucial painting project in 1845 involving the creation and display of Young's life-size, full-body portrait in the Nauvoo temple's celestial room. As Jeffrey Cannon has detailed, the painting featured Young "with his hand resting atop 'The Book of the Law of the Lord,'"—a volume containing records of revelations, events, and the financial contributions of faithful members—to make the message clear: "Those who hoped to enter heaven must do so with the consent of Brigham Young."[71] Young not only commissioned the portrait, but he also chose the title, *Delivering the Law of the Lord*.[72] The seven-foot-tall painting captured a material truth. The book had been initiated under Joseph Smith and now continued literally under the hand of Young.

Appropriately, Young was also the first financial backer of Dibble's panorama paintings, offering Dibble two dollars and telling him, "Go ahead and I will assist you."[73] Young was at the center of both the ecclesiastical and the cultural projects of consolidating Smith's image to ensure solidarity. By 1848 Dibble proudly reported how "the first presidency, and the leading authorities of the church were the willing supporters and the hearty co-operators in placing [the panorama paintings] before the Saints, on such a magnitude as to bring before the Saints scattered throughout all the world, the importance of uniting their interests with my labours in this department of the work of the building up of the kingdom of God." Dibble's language even evinced his intended aesthetic necromancy in making "a Joseph and a Hyrum appear and speak to the eye and heart of the thousands of Saints assembled at Nauvoo, Winter Quarters, and Council Bluffs."[74] Fittingly, Dibble's panoramic image of the martyrdom was first displayed in Nauvoo next to an image of Jesus raising Lazarus from the dead.[75] Dibble could provide the singular and uniting image the flock required and, with Young, provide the essential access to Smith as a noble, affective, and shared experience.

A dream recorded by Woodruff in April 1845 (the very month Dibble began exhibiting his paintings) nicely aligned with the project of shared vision taken up in the panorama. Woodruff dreamed the apostles were all together as they saw and conversed with Smith, who instructed and consoled them. "All seemed happy to see the prophet once more," reported Woodruff.[76] Collectively seeing the past in the present built the temporal bridge that could not only unite but also manufacture consent and trajectory amid a crisis of succession. By sharing the image of the undead Smith, the followers could be shaped into a single body with a clear direction forward.

Panorama helped visualize narrative progression. The expectation that one image led to the next in a narrative sequence provided the shared sense of forward direction. In this regard, panoramas could function as a "vehicle for homogenization" and were well catered to trafficking views, in both literal and abstract terms.[77] The Dibble panorama, in concert with other forms, insured that "early Mormons had clear, literal images of Smith orchestrating the work of the church from beyond the veil."[78]

Although panorama paintings could be reenactments, with an "interest in bringing back the dead and reconstructing an experience," Dibble's also functioned in the other direction.[79] In an aesthetic sense, Dibble's panoramas *caught* Smith's ghost for his viewers by providing a shared image of his death. Dibble even connected them to George Watt's "enscetching" or "phonographic outline of the trial of the murderers of the Smiths" as another medium of accurately capturing, storing, and representing Smith to his followers.[80] By outlining and shaping Smith and church history, these media worked to testify of and solidify a past. The represented prophet could aid the grieving process, while rendering the scattered and contested visitations from his ghost unnecessary. The form's means of directing shared vision was uniquely fit for the challenge, because the panorama functioned as a "school for the gaze; an optical simulator, where an initially extreme, or unusually 'sensational' sensory impression, could be experienced repeatedly and without risk, until it became a routine, everyday component of human seeing."[81] On a reduced scale, a similar process was required regarding the church's past and fallen leader. Oversized imagery and historical lecture could enact and fulfill the need for closure and continued prophetic guidance. As a near rite of passage, Patty Sessions recorded her visit "to the Hall to see the panorama of the massacre, as shown by Bro. Dibble." [82] The next day she packed to leave Nauvoo.

At once stabilizing the afterimage of Smith and providing a cathartic shared past, Dibble's panorama became a powerful coping mechanism and connective tissue between members. Wilford Woodruff astutely realized the potential of Dibble's memory work. Although he and the others in attendance had lived through the scenes on display, Woodruff remarked how their "children, future generations, & those who come to visit Zion will feel deeply interested in" the images, which "would present to the view at one glance All the seenes [sic] that this Church has passed through."[83] The scenes could provide cohesion and consent for survivors and prosthetic memories for their posterity.[84] By stitching newcomers and children into the shared panoramas of the past, members were equally acculturated into a community and its memory.

The effect of the exhibit was clear. The youth "were particularly quiet and listened with deep interest to all that was said, and doubtless a strong and lasting impression was made upon all present."[85] Amy Brown Lyman remembered being held "spellbound" as a youth witnessing Dibble's enormous panoramas accompanied by "dramatic descriptions." For Lyman the "scene of the martyrdom at Carthage Jail was so real and was so vividly stamped upon [her] mind" that she could "visualize" the "whole sad episode in all its details."[86] The panorama helped the affective and shared vision of Smith fuse the church membership and span generations. It is perhaps fitting that by 1848, as many Latter-day Saints were migrating west, Dibble solicited donations for the construction of a museum and offered a unique reward for submissions of at least five dollars. Those benefactors would receive their own portrait painted "on a separate scenery, connecting [them] with Brothers Joseph and Hyrum, and the twelve."[87] By subscribing to both Brighamite Mormonism and Dibble's artistic endeavor, members would have their image rendered and placed into the very sequence of panoramic scenes that helped get them behind Young and moving westward.

PANORAMIC EXPERIENCE

Dibble's panorama work was catalyzed through his own panoramic spiritual vision. Supporting Dibble's divine call, Woodruff concurred in 1848 that since "Dibble has been moved upon to set up these paintings I feel to bid him God Speed," and if Dibble would continue to represent scenes of church history in a "gallery in Zion," then "it will be the continuation of the rise and Progress of the Church & Kingdom of God."[88] Born of visionary experience, the efforts were meant to provoke further visions, ones that were controlled and shared. The power of mediation was made evident as memory and conviction were interwoven with an authoritative image of the prophet, seen "at one glance."

Although seemingly counterintuitive, the turn to imposing simulations of Smith carried a sense of monumental presence. His absence ensured the images' significance. As one of Smith's apostles had commented following the martyrdom, "while the testator lived, the testament was not of full power; all that was done was preparatory."[89] Cast onto canvas and controlled, the image had less of the paradoxes and rough edges of Smith's real-life persona. It could be readily accepted and revered.

In the impressive form, the communal image of Smith—literally expanded and exhibited—on the panorama resurrected important elements of medieval visual culture. In a romantic sense, earlier churchgoers collectively viewed images of Christ on the walls and windows of their places of worship and focused on this communal visual culture, rather than on individual study. Religious devotion was steeped in shared visual images. But ever since the printing press, some felt the words on the page increasingly became the "principal bridge joining human beings" together. Or even more exaggerated, "the printed word smashed the stone to smithereens and broke up the church into a thousand books."[90] While early Mormon print took advantage of this effect to store and disseminate its visionary techniques, panorama made the religious images and instructive potential visual, public, and shared. The experiential culture of a community of faithful members viewing shared visual culture in one designated place could be updated. Church members had to come to the panorama, as to church, to see the communal image.

The visibility of the shared vision was also significant. The phenomenological experience of seeing others seeing the same images surely helped foster a sense of community. The panorama viewing experience updated the insights of observational practices put to paper by the theologian and early humanist Nicholas of Cusa in the fifteenth century. In his tract *Vision of God*, Cusa recommended to monks that they each view an icon (in this case a painting of Christ) from three different points on an arc and then compare their results. Since the image appeared to look them in the eyes from each vantage point the monks could conclude that God's vision is truly omniscient.[91] However, equally important was the fact that the monks saw each other sharing the same viewing experience from different points. This lived spectatorship, shared in conversation and comparison, helped solidify that God's vision, and by extension his love, equally covered all. By seeing and being seen, all viewers were equal in God's sight and shared the same visual field. The embodied exercise translated an overwhelming concept into an experience.[92] If Dibble was lucky, his panorama could also accomplish something similar.

REVELATORY PANORAMA

The medium of panorama was also coconstitutive with revelatory experience in general. With its expansive images, panorama made Mormon viewing into a material-discursive technique that enacted the entanglement of seeing within word and world. Mormons used it to rethink revelatory experience

and language—to conceptualize second sight. As Kittler
"We knew nothing about our senses until media provided
aphors."[93] The material function of panorama being unrolled
of viewers offered connotations beyond magic lantern displ
netoscope. The unrolling and revealing of images, narrative
data in time as a visual experience nicely captured the material
visionary experience. Put another way, panorama's literal unfolding or visions
offered new ways of reading old texts and articulating revelation.

Not surprisingly, when Presbyterian minister William James Reid wrote
his 1878 treatise on John's vision in the book of Revelation, he described it
with the mentality of his time, using media to figure the apostle's experience.
Reid put John's apocalypse into motion and called it "a series of visions,
which the ministering angel unrolled before the eyes of the apostle like a
great panorama. Let us sketch the surroundings of the apostle when this
panorama was unrolled, and as they are revealed to us in verses 9–11."[94] It was
"as if [John] looked upon the successive pictures of a panorama."[95] As David
Morgan has skillfully traced, during the 1880s Arthur Butt traveled throughout the American south and displayed his "Book of Revelation" panorama
to great acclaim.[96] The medium of panoramas, especially those dealing with
specific content, welcomed the conception of revelation as panoramic in nature. By 1885 Latter-day Saint bishop Orson Whitney used the same language
to describe John's revelation. Whitney explained how "the world's temporal
existence passed before [John], like the scenes of a mighty panorama."[97]
The description of apocalyptic unfolding was neatly folded into the material
practice of panorama spectatorship.

A revelation from Joseph Smith in 1832 had employed biblical language
to describe the revelatory act of the "curtain of heaven" being "unfolded as
a scroll is unfolded, after it is rolled up," and how the result would be that
"the face, of the Lord, shall be unveiled."[98] Similarly, the panorama's ability
to be unrolled and unfold truths and visions lent it an almost archetypal
and apocalyptic flavor. A rolled-up piece of paper, such as the one caught by
Dibble in his dream, could have anything within. Only upon being unrolled
and revealed did it exercise its power and enlighten the viewer with visions
caught and mediated into repeatable and shareable sights. But the connection
between panorama and the visual element of revelation was more explicitly
coupled over time as the medium's reach extended.

In 1855, Woodruff explained how "in the vision of his mind [the Latter-day
Saint], sees displayed on the great panorama of the world all the scenes th
are to transpire in the present day, while the wicked are ignorant of

out to transpire."[99] Similarly, Orson Pratt spoke of Nebuchadnezzar's dream as scenes "in the grand panorama of kingdoms that passed before him."[100] George Q. Cannon even inflected the revelatory experience of near death with industrial hallmarks of rails, electricity, and the telegraph, saying how "every event of their lives passed before them like a panorama, with the rapidity of lightning."[101] Each of the visions was unrolled to roll a sequence forward. Spiritual visions were "panoramic" in their scale and ability to unfold/reveal their core connection to sequence. Time, events, and images always "transpire" or "pass by" in panoramic visions.

Often the unrolling of a panorama was accomplished by showmen and narrators. Echoing these traveling showmen who would accompany panoramas and provide explanatory and entertaining lectures, personages that appear to living members of the church could also present spiritual panoramas. These instructing supernatural beings assumed the role of lecturer and presenter, a function similarly fulfilled by Banvard, Dibble, and others, such as Artemus Ward. In 1896, Woodruff described how a messenger appeared to him as he was praying in Abraham Smoot's home one night. The "personage told me he had come to instruct me. He presented before me a panorama. He told me he wanted me to see with my eyes and understand." Woodruff explained how, if Woodruff were "an artist [he] could have painted the whole scene as it was impressed upon [his] mind."[102] Of course, Joseph Smith claimed he had been audience to numerous supernatural instructors during his lifetime, but now these spirits didn't just talk. They were understood to have shown him panoramas. In a church address also in 1896, John Henry Smith imagined Joseph Smith saying in reaction to his many visions, God you have "presented the panorama of the human race before my mind, and wrote upon that panorama that which was to be accomplished."[103] Although cinema had just been born, the best media-rich language to conceptualize Smith's visions was still the panorama display. Closer to the paper of scripture—where records of supernatural sights had been stored for centuries—panorama infused modern visions with its rolling and revelatory format.

CONTINUITY TO PROSTHESIS

Dibble's panoramic painting worked as a convergence point of Mormon vision and not only shaped a generation of memory for members of the church but also influenced future artists, including his primary successor, C. A. Christensen.[104] Although Christensen's panorama images came later were, therefore, less connected to the succession crisis, they updated and

eclipsed Dibble's and did their own cultural work. His creatio.
outside, prosthetic, borrowed fantasies of the events. These
even better suited for appropriation and came at a time when, t
mons, Young's ascension to leadership itself was merely histoi
cession essentially settled and forgotten, the second panorama ṭ
visual memory to reestablish specific lineages and institutional n
the church as it weathered increased cultural threats from the railway connections to the rest of the nation. They helped make early church history, along
with its geography, trauma, and deceased figures experiential and portable.
Just before the church began to purchase eastern lands to reconstruct its
past by "turning the American landscape into their scrapbook," Christensen
captured the scenes and populated them with important people, some dead,
some still living.[105] Through Christensen's panorama the lost elements could
be enjoyed and trafficked.

Christensen's use of the moving panorama also helped underscore Dibble's obsolescence. Dibble complained to church president John Taylor in
1879 that Christensen had "plainly manifested a disposition to entirely sup-
plant me in my business" and that Christensen had even "gone to my painter
and tried to stop him from painting for me and to join their company."[106]
Christensen himself was already an accomplished painter who was rapidly
establishing his name throughout Utah. The previous year he even completed
a series of paintings depicting events from the Book of Mormon and the
Bible, along with a scene of Joseph Smith receiving the gold plates. These
eleven small canvases were sewn together and rolled in vertical motion to
present to Native Americans by Dimick B. Huntington.[107] They represent
yet another project of rolling histories before an audience to suture them
into a larger shared past.

Although Christensen began exhibiting his panorama in 1878 and grew in
prominence, Dibble continued to exhibit his scenes and relics. As late as 1893,
two years before his death, Dibble posted a notice for an exhibit and concert
he was offering in Springville, Utah.[108] It is perhaps not inconsequential that
Dibble's static panorama paintings with lectures and artifacts were challenged
and largely eclipsed by Christensen's twenty-three moving panoramas in
an age when railroads were not only connecting people and ideas, but also
providing new experiences of panoramic vision.[109]

Christensen had even worked on the railroad in Echo Canyon in 1868, and
his moving displays reflected the integration of the locomotive into travel
and the Utah basin.[110] Unlike other urban centers, the train hadn't shaped
and modernized Utah until 1869.[111] The connection of the golden spike

ppled bilaterally into both Mormon paranoia and Gentile hopes of civilizing the Mormons. Logistically, the railway "made it harder to keep temptations at bay and easier for the federal army to send in troops."[112] Railroads into Utah also shifted vision from focusing on the past into "dreams of the future."[113] The rail, above all, symbolized the threat and promise of networks. Finally networked into schedules, destinations, and mechanical movement, Utah's Mormons joined the rest of the nation in novel experiences of time and space.

With industrialized travel on rails, the traditional experience of movement and sight attending the carriage or boat was outdated. Connected, locked on course, and faster than ever, the rail inevitably courted the passion for progress. After his travels in the United States, the French economist Michel Chevalier noted how "the American has a perfect passion for railroads; he loves them . . . as a lover loves his mistress." But the deep-seated appetite for the speed and connection of trains was not just because an American's "supreme happiness consists in that speed which annihilates time and space," but also because the "mode of communication is admirably adapted to the vast extent of his country."[114] Here the term "communication" meant the movement or "transportation" of humans and cargo, including letters and mail, yet the telegraph also lined the train tracks and further networked the nation.[115] In Chevalier's estimation, the vast American landscape seemed to necessitate "communication" by technologies, such as the train and telegraphy.

Train travel collapsed space while offering the passenger a scene through the window that approximated moving panorama shows, much like Christensen's update to Dibble's images. Robert Louis Stevenson's 1885 poem "From a Railway Carriage" captured the experience and coupled the painted form with the panoramic images whizzing by the train's window.

> All of the sights of the hill and the plain
> Fly as thick as driving rain,
> And ever again, in the wink of an eye,
> Painted stations whistle by.[116]

Straddling the shifts in mobility and embodied experience of the world whooshing by, contemporary travelers commented on and enjoyed the connection between vision and trains in the nineteenth century.

Riding the transcontinental rail, a passenger described how one could finally "enjoy this wonderful panoramic display" of the scenery if they sat in the correct cart. In her estimation the rail made the "utopian dream" to "view the grandeur of the Rocky Mountains" into a reality.[117] Similarly, a Mormon missionary in Europe instructed the readers of his scenic travelogue that "all this must be blended together in an ever varying panorama in order to give an idea of a railway trip through Switzerland."[118] It was a dialectical relationship between panoramic vision and travel by rail. As scholars Dolf Sternberger and Wolfgang Schivelbusch would agree, the "railroad first and foremost [was] the main cause for such panoramization of the world."[119]

Of course, this new form of travel made the virtual travel and experience of viewing panorama displays into a lived reality. With the proliferation of railroads and the eventual ubiquity of photography, panorama displays lost some of their novelty. Christensen's panoramas clamored for the special effect of motion and increased realism associated with train travel. But even the earliest Mormon panoramas from Dibble had another characteristic in common with the effect of trains on the world. Trains led to coordination, shared time, specific direction, and a newfound velocity that signaled resolution.

As a project of ensuring a trajectory for Brighamite Mormonism, the panorama too needed to "pick up speed." It needed to take its viewers on a ride into a shared image of their past, which would directly affect their future. As rival claimant for succession Sidney Rigdon had recognized after Smith's death, the church "lack[ed] a great leader." Rigdon perceived the need for unifying the church's direction, exclaiming, "You want a head, and unless you unite upon that head you're blown to the four winds."[120] Even Woodruff recorded in his journal upon returning to Nauvoo shortly after the assassination that the members "felt like sheep without a shepherd, as being without a father, as their head had been taken away."[121] Young boldly declared to the members, "Do you want President Rigdon to be the head or do the Saints want the Twelve to Stand as the head . . . Stand next to Joseph?"[122] What panorama had in common with trains went beyond sideways glances of landscapes. They shared the inherent sense of travel and trajectory.

By spanning and shrinking time and space, the train and the panorama display were both meant to take the viewing passenger *somewhere*. In fact, actual trains and other media, including stereographs, travel guides, or journals, were also used to get "travelers to pay attention to specific objects in the foreground of their voyage" with the specific intention of "attaching to them special significance, and weaving around them certain narratives."[123] Combining locomotion with disciplined vision of prepackaged sites worked in favor of sequencing and narrating a shared past. This forward momentum defined the steam engine and drove the Mormon community toward the production of a unified and unifying vision.

Christensen's capacity to build on Dibble's work by modernizing the technology while maintaining the focus on the martyrdom of Joseph Smith and the immediate aftermath proved powerful. Christensen joined forces with his brother Frederik, sewed their 6½ × 10 foot canvases together and began exhibiting in 1878. Although they shared their sense of direction and travel with trains, Christensen's canvases could also be rolled in vertical succession. Describing the reaction to his work, Christensen wrote, "Now the eye as well as the ear can receive correct ideas of the history of the church."[124] Many of the church's first generation reached out to Christensen to offer their input and transmit it to the next generation. Christensen knew he was shoring up the memory of the dying generation of members who personally interacted with the prophet Joseph Smith. "The Mormon Panorama," as Christensen's moving presentation came to be known, began with seven images and swelled to twenty-three over the course of three years. The new canvases would be sewn into the series and revisions could be made to fit the continued input and recollections given by individuals from the period who wished to consult Christensen. In historian Steven Harper's estimation this was a powerful "recursion" of memories, or adding of new elements to "consolidated memories."[125] The construction and exhibition of the panorama reanimated the Mormon past by stitching members and memories together and putting them in motion.

Smith's image was, once again, made central to the Mormon Panorama display. His assassination provided the climactic turning point in the show, and its depiction included the only banner of the panorama, along the bottom, announcing, "THE BLOOD OF THE MARTYRS IS THE SEED OF THE CHURCH." That image then rolled into canvas number 15, a chaotic tableau of mob members gathered around the fallen body of Smith. Image 15 perpetuated William Daniels's story of divine intervention stymying the efforts of an assailant who attempted to further harm—perhaps even decapitate—the slain body of Joseph Smith. Rays of light radiate from the top right of the painting and hold the menacing figure at bay. With knife drawn and face blackened, the would-be assailant stands with his left hand raised in response to the imposing light. Frozen in time, the assailant only serves now to provide the left margin of a frame of white around the martyred Smith's body. Flanked on the right by fleeing women in white, the fallen body lies in stark contrast to the preceding image of Smith in Carthage jail fully upright and alert, still immaculately portrayed. Framed and protected in the panorama's depiction, the prophet's martyrdom prefigured and visually paralleled the destruction of the Nauvoo temple. The display then rolled into an image of the glowing white Nauvoo temple. The architectural body—white, pure, and whole—commands attention. This is then displaced by an image of that same edifice ablaze, vandalized, destroyed, *martyred*. The Nauvoo temple and prophetic era are sealed to Smith, and the destruction of both flesh and edifice signal the portability of those connections into a new geography and succession. As the lost elements roll away, the audience is rolled forward into the great trek west.

Beginning with the "first vision" and ending with the saints entering the Salt Lake Valley, the Mormon Panorama emphasized persecution and deliverance during the life of Smith as the core components of the Latter-day Saints' legacy and identity.[126] Audiences were vividly introduced to the centrality—even fragility—of Smith in the church's memory. This ability to show the prophet's body in glory and destruction as the seed of the church could imply his direction from beyond for the continuation of the church body. The travel, or communication, undertaken between canvases and from Nauvoo into the Salt Lake Valley became a visual memory for Utah residents. The panorama took audiences across aestheticized space and time as initiation into the worldview and memory appropriate to bolster and illuminate the events after the martyrdom. In this regard, Dibble's and Christensen's panorama projects intersected in meaning and effect. Moving on and painting the past that led to the present was predicated on the stabilization and reverence for a unified vision of the founding prophet.

CONCLUSION

The Mormon panorama projects created not only canvases of memory but also unique visual experiences and a collective practice of observation from rank-and-file church members. With grassroots production, Dibble and Christensen might have been the proprietors, but the images felt like they belonged to all church members who were able to see *in unison*. With its ability to fold the recent past into the present, the panorama served the purpose of unifying and standardizing the Mormon gaze. By directing it toward a consolidated—painted and enlarged—image of Smith in communal settings, the future of the movement could be mapped onto a now controlled and singular past. The panorama helped comfort and rescue Smith's followers, whose vision in his absence was reeling and lacked definitive direction.

Nineteenth-century Mormon panorama translated ideas and desires into a manageable medium with connotations of enhanced and shared vision. These media practices signaled the development of new modes of Mormon authority through powerful didactic and gendered techniques of vision. Both

THE BLOOD OF THE MARTYRS IS THE SEED OF THE CHURC

Top left, "Mormon Panorama Fourteen / Interior of Carthage Jail"
(78 × 120 inches); *bottom left*, "Mormon Panorama Fifteen / Exterior
of Carthage Jail" (78 × 114½ inches); *top right*, "Mormon Panorama
Sixteen / The Nauvoo Temple" (77 × 113 inches); *bottom right*, "Mormon
Panorama Seventeen / Burning of the Temple" (78 × 114 inches).
*C. C. A. Christensen (1831–1912), ca. 1878, tempera on
muslin, Brigham Young University Museum of Art, gift of
the grandchildren of C. C. A. Christensen, 1970.*

print and panorama pushed for visions and an overarching shared vision of governance, but with panorama the direction was reversed. Its public vision could foreclose private ones. By getting Latter-day Saints to come together and take on a singular expanded vision as a shared official vision, panorama made the Mormon past hinge on the blood and spirit of the prophet Joseph Smith. With Smith gone, but resurfacing in both reassuring and threatening ways, the unifying vision of panoramas proved revelatory and timely. They sealed that bloody and tumultuous past to Brigham Young as successor and then to Utah as a manifest destination.

SENSITIVE

MACHINES

The typewriter, it is obviously a blessing to
mankind and especially to womankind.

Christopher Sholes, inventor of the typewriter, 1888

There is no more suitable work for woman than photography. . . . The light,
delicate touch of a woman, the eye for light and shade, together with their
artistic perception, render them peculiarly fitted to succeed in this work.

Richard Hines Jr., 1899

n Mormon culture, the ideal media practice of women was childbirth.
The organic and strained process of giving birth signaled the entrance of
women into the network between worlds. In Latter-day Saint teachings
maternal reproduction also suggested women's greatest—even divine—
potential "to be the medium through which a child of God shall come to
earth, to fulfil [*sic*] a wise and glorious purpose," by "giv[ing] temporal bodies to heavenly spirits."[1] Of course, such a vision of women's reproductive
capacity was as tyrannically constraining as it was intentionally exalting. But
it provides an important cultural backdrop to gendered visions of reproduction, agency, and automatic inscription technologies in Utah at the turn of
the twentieth century.

The emphasis on the mediating role of women as would-be wives and
mothers was a common misperception of the varieties of women's identities
and experiences and was by no means isolated to Latter-day Saint culture.

Often inspired by woman's corporeal connection to childbirth, public discourse around newly femininized vocations and a decades-long history of spiritualist mediumship described and fashioned women into the more sensitive sex—better suited to act as channels for transmitting information between two points, whether at the séance, telegraph, or switchboard. In both office work and channeling, "the trope of feminine passivity dovetailed neatly with the demand for an undistorted mediation of information," as well as with a shared "ambivalence about where to locate authoritative agency in the interface between humans and machines."[2] Issues around femininity, authority, and reproduction were heightened in the late nineteenth century when photography and typewriting, in particular, were marketed to women as ways to mechanically reproduce, most often as secretaries and assistants to male superiors. Much like notions of maternal instincts, problematic discourse around women's "sensitivity" and skill at these machines feigned praising a constructed sense of their nature while entrenching cheap labor and gendered hierarchies across home and the workplace.

While some scholars have shrewdly attempted to recover the hidden traces and intentions of female assistants, this chapter is interested in the coproduction of technology and gender through more explicit forms of self-expression made by two Mormon women.[3] First, I turn to the photographic work of Elfie Huntington, who never bore children, nor married until her late sixties. Instead, Huntington ran her own photography studio as a single deaf woman with a speech disability in Springville, Utah. Next, I turn to Huntington's much more prominent contemporary Susa Young Gates in Salt Lake City, who was the daughter of Brigham Young and an outspoken advocate for Mormonism and women's rights. Gates composed her prolific feminist literature through her typewriter and ultimately sacralized maternity. Although Huntington began as an assistant and Gates was first a stenographer, they both went on to create extensive bodies of personal work that functioned as technological and social practices to modify their sense of self through the mimicry and expansion of gendered visions in photographic images and type.[4]

These women's experiences with machines between 1890 and 1920 "offer transformative suggestions for the religious imaginary and the development of the woman subject."[5] As Grace Jantzen reminds us, it is the very "shaping of those experiences through material and discursive conditions" that we must account for when analyzing "the reciprocal construction of experience and subject-positions."[6] The insights of new materialism and technofeminism focus our attention on the entanglement of gender and technology, where neither category preexists the other and their properties are produced through techniques of use and performance.[7] Instead of tracing all the ways technology reproduced gendered labor, emphasizing the "contingency and heterogeneity of technological change" can reveal the agency and role of Huntington and Gates in "transforming technologies" away from mere mechanical reproduction toward feminist ends.[8]

As Huntington and Gates were transforming machines, gender in Mormonism was undergoing profound revision. Under pressure from the government, the Church of Jesus Christ of Latter-day Saints formally revoked plural marriage in a manifesto given by church president Wilford Woodruff in September 1890. As they unevenly sloughed off polygamy, Latter-day Saints increasingly fashioned themselves as good American citizens. While this meant they had to "re-make their men," they also began to narrow vocational options for women and direct them to "choose a worthy companion, get married, become trained in all things domestic and have children."[9] Initially, however, the "surplus girls" of a newly monogamous Utah had been encouraged to enter the workforce, including nursing, education, photography, or typewriting.[10] The unsettling shift in gender expectations coincided with technological innovations. Cameras and typewriters had been around, but after 1890 these machines suggested new possibilities for Mormon women. They also helped carve out a space to work through and problematize cultural notions of sensitivity and woman's sphere, just as church leadership increasingly sought to domesticate the same.

During this tumultuous turn of the twentieth century, Elfie Huntington and Susa Young Gates managed visions through media in ways that underscored the disjointed production of gender. While Huntington utilized photography as a material practice to critique oppressive norms of courtship, marriage, and gender, Gates utilized the typewriter to widen gendered visions inherited from her religion, including the "first vision" of Joseph Smith, without transgressing them. I argue that both Huntington and Gates were able to realize and register critical oversights in the patriarchal visions that informed the religious role of women at the time. Instead of reproducing men's visions wholesale—though their machines were uniquely capable of doing just that—they focused and critiqued them through their clever re-creations. As a feminist form of mimesis in the vein of Luce Irigaray, these were "playful repetitions" that made visible what otherwise went unseen.[11] They utilized machines in a manner like spiritualism but channeled patriarchal visions, through "canny mimicry," by deliberately reproducing gender stereotypes in imperfect and amplified ways, including as ideal machine operators.[12]

Their technical work foregrounded creative possibilities and provided evidence for an expanded image of Latter-day Saint women that ran counter to popular depictions. Rather than oppressed slaves of polygamous harems, these were active operators registering woman's subjectivity with the most modern machines.

DEVELOPING DESIRES

Although the invention of photography was dominated by men and came decades before Elfie Huntington's adoption of it, her work offers a unique interaction with photography and Mormon vision. Not only was she the "ghostphotographer," or uncredited camera operator and retoucher, for much of Latter-day Saint photographer George Edward Anderson's work in the 1890s, but Huntington was a prolific photographer outside of these secondary and operational roles. In 1903 she left Anderson and opened her own studio with fellow assistant Joseph Bagley. She remained in Springville, Utah, where she had lost her hearing to scarlet fever at the age of four and lost her parents only a couple years later. Raised by her extended family, Huntington was steeped in the local culture and became something of a beloved community figure. She was socially active, even as her identity as a deaf woman would seem to render her doubly marginalized.[13] Through her insider lens from the margins, Huntington critically examined the pervasive Mormon perspective on the world and gender.

Huntington's series of photographs titled *A Bachelor's Dream* manifests the convergence of photographic media and cultural critique with particular force through its staged visions of women. The series of three images portrays a seated man gazing at a different woman positioned behind a full-sized frame in each photograph. While the furniture, camera position, and frame all remain exactly the same throughout, the bachelor's "dream" of women shifts between different types, until at last he rises to approach a bride, who has miraculously appeared before him. The series' mixture of haunted congruence between reality and fantasy along gendered lines is packaged with a deceptive simplicity that belies its conceptual depth.

The Bachelor's Dream was a trope that circulated throughout the nineteenth century in a variety of texts, including Thomas Hood's poem "Bachelor's Dream," Donald Mitchell's book *Reveries of a Bachelor* (1850), popular sheet music, and illustrated books, and as a subject it was considered a "favorite recitation" by 1906.[14] A catalogue from 1899 described the Bachelor's Dream scene as: "Bachelor falls asleep and dreams of different fair ones. He awakes when a bride appears and takes her."[15] Bachelors in these texts were never meant to remain so; they were always portrayed desiring one thing: a wife to have and to hold.

Before Huntington adapted the Bachelor's Dream into a realist photographic fantasy with an emphasis on seeing as taking, the renowned art photographer Oscar Rejlander had already visualized the scene. His photograph from circa 1860 shows the bachelor reclining, asleep on a chaise lounge with his right hand cupping his groin, while a conical wire structure, like a crinoline, supports various women as miniature effigies acrobatically positioned along its tiers. This image played on the connotations of bachelor reveries and the channeling of sexual energy already thematized in Mitchell's *Reveries of a Bachelor*, where the author used "oxymoronic language" to try to "unite pleasure and law, activity and thought, within bachelor identity" as sexuality properly directed toward sentiment.[16] A commentator remarked in 1863 how Rejlander's single photograph showed "how a story could be told" through manipulation of the composition and the strategic use of figures.[17] With its loaded imagery and provocative sleepy touching, Rejlander's visual *Dream* manifested the scene's implications as a man's ostensibly instinctive bodily reaction to looking, even in a dream state. Whether she was familiar with the image or not, Huntington updated the sentiment. She added sequence and additional nuance to the cultural image recorded in the photograph.

With her deft use of the camera, Huntington employed what Daniel Novak has described as "the technology of realism" to create "what appears to be its opposite: the nonexistent, the fictional, and the abstract."[18] In fact, Huntington seems to have actualized Rejlander's own project by further developing its core premise and making the scene come to life. By representing "scenes and encounters that never occurred," art photographers like Rejlander or Huntington created images "both more realistic and more *photographic*."[19] Huntington's *Bachelor's Dream* series is more photographic in its self-reflexive play with mechanical vision, and it is more realistic in its critical deconstruction of cultural norms. The series of images thematize the issues and power relations structuring and inciting both the viewer and viewed into a photographic, and often gendered, process of taking and being taken.

Riffing on the earlier iterations of the Bachelor's Dream, Huntington's composition highlights what, since the pervasive influence of Laura Mulvey and Luce Irigaray, would be called the male gaze: the constructed nature of looking, pleasure, and control through gendered representation exercised across media. In Mulvey's well-worn account of Hollywood cinema, men

A Bachelor's Dream, series by Elfie Huntington, ca. 1900.
L. Tom Perry Special Collections, Harold B. Lee Library,
Brigham Young University, Provo, Utah.

generally advance the plot and are the active bearer of the gaze, whereas women provide narrative-arresting visual spectacle and are fashioned as objects to be looked at.[20] A similar politics of vision animates *A Bachelor's Dream.*

From the first photo in Huntington's series the power of sight is asymmetrical. A woman in common nineteenth-century dress stands behind a frame, as if she were a life-sized photographic image, and captures the attention of the man seated nearby. However, his attention seems to wane in the second photo in the series, after the woman has transformed into a New Woman, donning a combination of a long frock, a beekeeper's hat and thick leather gloves with motorcycle goggles in hand. This ostensibly liberated figure doesn't coax the man from his chair and more closely resembles Huntington herself, who rode a motorcycle and left behind a picture of her face swollen apparently from bee stings, likely from her business partner Joseph Bagley's family-owned apiary.

The shifts in clothing between shots recall the insistence of Irigaray, that a woman becomes such, or is considered a "normal woman," only by entering into "the masquerade of femininity," an oppressive "system of values that is not hers, and in which she can 'appear' and circulate only when enveloped in the needs/desires/fantasies of others, namely men."[21] Huntington's images pointedly visualized the very process of early twentieth-century Mormon women refashioning themselves for monogamous marriages and as a performance for the nation.

In the series, the man waits while images of different women cycle before him. Only when the female figure finally appears as a bride does the man jump from his seat and attempt to enter the frame of his vision on the wall. This is a Bachelor's Dream scene from the turn of the twentieth century, when the trope no longer denounced the sexual and monetary "dead ends" committed by bachelors and instead promulgated the "healthy" release of "pent up" sexual energy in marriage.[22] The play with the frame-within-the-frame has a multiplying effect and guides the viewer's vision to the bachelor's, thereby visualizing and enacting the fact that photography was now implicated in mechanically duplicating and "unifying all subjects within a single global network of valuation and desire."[23]

Huntington had dropped the dream, however. This was open-eyed fantasizing and a pictorial condensation of the editorials, both national and local, detailing what men want and what the "ideal woman" was.[24] An editorial to young Mormon women collected such opinions after a member of the church's first presidency, Joseph F. Smith, had suggested a "symposium of the views of some of [the] leading brethren, as to the perfect woman." It was intended to "present to the young girls a series of pictures which would be to them ideals to live up to, a model on which to mould their own characters."[25] While the Latter-day Saint leaders showed some variance in descriptions, they all saw women as ideally a supportive and pious wife. Anything else was preparation for just such a role.

In Huntington's series it is only a certain woman, whom the bachelor has conjured into photographic reality through fantasizing, that excites him. The series then powerfully replicates and toys with a simplistic view of gendered relations and an ideal "scene" of womanhood that *makes the man move*. In the desiring vision of the man now at full attention, the final woman is even positioned differently as if ready to exit the frame and come to life. As a beautiful precursor to the scene in Hitchcock's *Vertigo*, when Scotty awaits Judy's transformation into his idealized version of Madeleine, Huntington's series cuts to the core of a long history (and future) of gendered viewing, picturing women as a gesture of possession. And this was particularly cultivated in her own profession.

The privileged role of male spectatorship in the series was a more subtle suggestion of what contemporary Utah photographer Charles Ellis Johnson was secretly profiting from with his equally staged mail order erotica. By serving the Latter-day Saint church publicly, while privately peddling exotic shots of scantily clad women, Johnson also provides a particularly telling lens into Mormon engagements with photography—both institutional and scandalously personal.[26] Johnson was even able to tap into orientalist imagery of polygamous Mormons to color his erotic photography for export, as Mary Campbell has detailed.[27] He played on and profited from the public image of Mormon women as oppressed slaves in harems. Ironically, the same technology offered Johnson and others an unprecedented ability to immortalize church leaders by taking their likenesses and distributing them, literally putting them into the hands of members and customers. But he did the same with the seminude bodies of women models.

Beholding images by holding photographs was too often a material practice of taking the women by looking and touching. This asymmetrical gaze was even proposed in a letter from Pennsylvania to the Latter-day Saint church historian's office in 1880, while polygamy was still officially practiced. The letter's author, one J. P. Crowl, petitioned Orson Hyde and Orson Pratt to furnish him with photographs of several women he would then like to take as wives upon his arrival in Salt Lake City. Not only was he requesting mail order polygamy, but the author specified the women should be posed as "perfectly naked as nature made them."[28] The written request serves as both an antecedent to Johnson's erotic photo business and a textual index to the gendered politics of looking in the photographic era. By 1901 Salt Lake City police were even cracking down on "vice" and "lewd" pictures of girls peddled at local saloons through kinetoscopes and photographic media. For it was "well known that boys have been for long time past visiting the saloons for the sole purpose of viewing the obscene pictures in the slot machines."[29] With astounding realism, photography could frame and capture the female body as an object for consumption—further highlighting a much more common arrangement of gender around the technology of the camera and efforts to gaze on women in scientific, artistic, and pornographic ways. Huntington critiqued the basis of this beholding and gendered power that was ubiquitous and bolstered by, while shaping, photographic practices.

Huntington's work pushed the medium's boundaries to make a single spatial continuum suggest a temporal continuum, in order to tell a story. Just a decade or two after Eadweard Muybridge was working on "animal locomotion" to photographically capture the human body, undressed and in measured motion, Huntington was suggesting motion and time in still photos to get at what *moved* viewers in their carnal density.[30] In this sense, Huntington's version of the Bachelor's Dream can also be seen to invite qualification of the often ahistorical and seemingly monolithic accounts of the male gaze. For she highlights the ways the viewing body is susceptible to sensations and the connection between vision and haptics. Beyond woman as passive image, it is different types of viewing devices, configurations, and effects that made looking into a form of (be)holding. Unlike magic lantern projections or panorama paintings, photographs were often tactile and mobile, touched and touching. Photographs were often possessions one handled and kept. They emphasized the embodied nature of vision, by offering experiences of looking at images in one's hands brought close to the eyes. As her series exemplified—in sequential form when the man jumps up and suggested to its viewers, who might also handle the images—photographic vision got viewers to feel, touch, and act in certain ways. It was deeply implicated in norms around gender performance and expectations, both social and sexual.

Inspired by the camera, Huntington seems to have captured the cultural narrowing of women's roles, even as she lived outside of them. With a wink, her series framed not only the supposedly most desirable path for women to take but the very implication that photography and visions of ideal femininity were in cahoots. Huntington clarified just how constructed, limiting, and framed the ideal picture of a woman was, especially as she never fit that image in her own life. Her insightful *Bachelor's Dream* series is nothing less than a majestic collapsing of gender norms through projecting and exposing a male vision as wholly confining and constructed. Itself a joking mimicry—recycling a well-known trope—Huntington's *A Bachelor's Dream* suggests what might be for so many its own reversal, a photographic nightmare.

SPIRITED PHOTOGRAPHY

By turning a lens to society's marginalized and forgotten, some of Huntington's work prefigures that of Diane Arbus, who also helped normalize such outsiders through photography decades later.[31] Mary Campbell has also compared Huntington's penchant for "broad swaths of awkwardness, strangeness, and sheer vulnerability" to the later work of Lisette Model and Robert Frank.[32] However her work is categorized, Huntington's images stand out for their insistence on critiquing normative vision by widening its purview. Huntington's photos of a man with no feet, supporting his arm on one of his prosthetic legs, or of an unconscious drunk man prostrate on the ground, capture alienation and society's downtrodden in ways that few male photographers seemed to offer. Localized, the photos present scathing alternatives to the "portraits of leading men" marketed by local male photographers Charles Savage and George Ottinger.[33] Images of an incomplete body or one steeped in inebriation complicated the Mormon culture that reverenced the physical body by emphasizing its eventual perfection and increasingly denigrating the consumption of alcohol in the early twentieth century. The photos, while stunning, have no apparent purpose or commission. Huntington's insightful images seem to work against the capitalist tendency toward economic practicality and ecclesiastical propaganda that drove much of the photography around her.

Huntington also created highly staged photos, closer to her *Bachelor's Dream* series, that were much more playful but just as critical as her images of individuals on the margins. Although she left no commentary, Huntington's timely images of herself and others cross-dressing, playing cards, or drinking alcohol from empty prop bottles had strong critical resonance for the local Mormon culture. She seemed to revel in costumes and performance. After all, she hosted theatrical shows for a local woman's club and appeared annually as "the Goddess of Liberty" in Springville's Independence Day parades.[34] As if to deliberately queer Utah Mormon photography, Huntington shuffled surface appearances and conventions. In one photo Huntington's business partner, Joe Bagley, holds a bottle to her lips as two men lying next to them cuddle under a blanket. In another photo Huntington and three other women dressed as men wearing hats encircle a lone man dressed as a woman with a long cotton dress, a broach, and a large bow in his hair. All five are looking straight at the camera, perfectly posed and playful, but only Huntington, the author of the scene, has a sly smirk on her face.

By gender-bending and breaking strong taboos Huntington realized the photo as a framed, demarcated area for creation and performance. Huntington's gallery seems to have provided her a space where she felt comfortable transgressing social norms. Like mediumship in the séance of spiritualism— where "the mechanics of power inherent in the Victorian codification of gender difference" could be sabotaged, bent, and reversed—technology for Huntington served as a site for the construction and subversion of gendered norms and subjectivity.[35] She channeled patriarchal visions by technically reproducing them through her camera, but she punctured them with critical changes. Although there is no indication that Huntington subscribed to spiritualism, the movement's long tradition of women managing and interacting with patriarchal visions provides important context for her media practices.

During the second half of the nineteenth century, spiritualism and its provocative use of technology spread, just as cameras and typewriters entered the commercial market. Often said to originate with the Fox sisters' reports of spirits communicating through raps on a wall in upstate New York in 1848, spiritualism eventually "generated an entire theology around . . . the utter connectivity of earthly existence and its relationship with the spirit-world."[36] From its beginning, the movement was also particularly suited to women, who were characterized as generally more sensitive than men and, therefore, more effective at communicating with the dead. By the late nineteenth century, women spiritualist mediums, including Victoria Claflin Woodhull, Cora Tappan-Richmond, Emma Hardinge Britten, C. Fanny Allyn, W. H. King, and H. T. Stearns, were performing in Utah and throughout the nation, often inspiring and inspired by women's rights activism.[37] These women, like the devices used in spiritualist displays, were described as sensitive and more in tune with the otherworldly.

Spiritualism's fecund mixture of ideas piqued passionate devotion and vehement dismissal across the nation. And that evocative ambiguity was precisely the pocket where spiritualism thrived. For spiritualism was also a heterogenous and adaptive movement that walked the tightrope between rational and supernatural modes. As David Walker has skillfully traced, spiritualism flourished in open-ended demonstrations that invited doubt and urged individuals to decide for themselves, often by providing the very "technologies of disenchantment and the tools of ritual critique."[38] It embraced uncertainty and even found productive use for the many delays and disruptions in modern infrastructures, by offering a "means to scale between" these gaps.[39] Spiritualism was particularly powerful in blurring the rigidity of cultural boundaries and empowering what was often understood to be weak, negative, or even meaningless.

Tinkering with spiritualism's emphasis on feminine sensitivity also suggested productive possibilities to push boundaries in acceptable ways. For spiritualism held that the unique "'electrical' constitution of women," based on their stereotype as "weak in will and intelligence," yet strong in "chastity, passivity, and impressionability," enabled them to be mediums and authoritatively comment on topics such as "marital equality, reproductive rights, and universal suffrage."[40] As Ann Braude has noted, "Not all feminists were Spiritualists, but all Spiritualists advocated woman's rights, and women were in fact equal to men within Spiritualist practice, policy, and ideology." This meant "the very qualities that rendered women incompetent when judged against norms for masculine behavior rendered them capable of mediumship," where they could surpass "limitations on women's role without questioning accepted ideas about woman's nature."[41] Their very sensitivity could be productive and liberating, because as spiritualist mediums, women were able to ventriloquize and express bodily "what could not be vocalized by the rational, speaking, and implicitly male self."[42] Spiritualist women, in Jeremy Stolow's account, were then able to make "artful use of widespread nineteenth-century tropes of moral purity and assumptions about the sensitive nature of 'the weaker sex'" in complicated ways. They could "speak out while avoiding the responsibilities of authorship, proclaiming merely to convey the judgments of the world of spirit upon the world of the living."[43] Combined with new technologies, this power of channeling another person's words bore a prescient urgency. It inspired skillful ways of both exposing the constructed nature of gender and its accompanying stereotypes, while enabling women to work within these social confines to express transgressive ideas through various forms of ventriloquy.

In a technical and aesthetic way, Huntington's work channeled and reproduced existing cultural ideas as loaded images. But her reproductions were inflected with important exaggerations, distortions, or transgressions to highlight her own perspective on the social construction of reality. Just as gender was a disjointed process that was shored up and turned into social reality, Huntington developed images as clever constructs that troubled those existing practices. Importantly, her automatic work with the camera was infused with her agency and creativity to underscore construction itself. Her photographs performed and displayed the performative nature and ever-shifting development of gender.

Huntington's staged transgressions were radically opposed to the more institutional Latter-day Saint forays into photography, which reflected a widespread nineteenth-century sense that the photograph relates to, reproduces, perpetuates, even proves a "solid reality."[44] The alleged indexicality inherent to photography made the medium ideal for the church to assert authority and bolster truth claims. George Edward Anderson traveled east and captured the founding church sites with his camera, in order to—much like Christensen's Mormon Panorama—anchor and archive a lost time and place.[45] Photos of church leadership in chart form disseminated the figures' likenesses as well as their hierarchical position. The photos of wives of Joseph Smith even helped the church support its claim that the practice of polygamy had originated with the founder, when the reorganized Latter-day Saint church argued it was a subsequent invention of Brigham Young.[46] These attempts to reclaim early church history through photography or embalm leaders through portraiture reinforced a belief in the ontological realism of an apparatus that doesn't lie.

But this was just one side of the story. As Huntington explored in her work, photography also had a critical, even spiritual component. It inspired tricks, magic, and wonder for some practitioners and astute observers, including Charles Baudelaire, Oliver Wendell Holmes Sr., and Edgar Allan Poe. As the pictorialist photographer Henry Peach Robinson saw it, "It is not the copying of nature that gives artistic delight, so much as the intellectual pleasure to be derived from getting the best effect out of any given materials." The most inspired practitioners elevated realism to a higher realm, emancipating viewers from "the trammels of rigid fact" toward the "finer regions of artistic truth." Put succinctly, Robinson stated, "in aiming at truth we must not forget the spirit."[47]

The limits of artistic tricks and a more straightforward faith in the photographic image were crystallized in the medium-specific phenomenon of spirit photography, which appeared as miraculous double exposures and suggested the ability of sensitive plates and operators to capture and store the otherwise invisible. William Mumler's widely publicized trial for fraud in New York quickly spread the hope and humbug around seeing the dead in photos. The trial and the many responses it elicited "quite literally positioned the Bible and the camera as competing mechanisms of religious authority in modern America."[48] Mumler believed that photography was able to write scripture with light, that it "offered truths unknown to earlier divine revelations."[49] Photography just might function like a seer stone by displaying the otherwise invisible as divine truth, if practiced with proper sensitivity and techniques. As ever more photographers conjured spectral images through multiple exposure or some unexplained force, the rage for photographs of dead ancestors or anonymous specters spread.

But Latter-day Saints didn't have much interest in spirit photographs. While viewers were searching in photos, as "secondary manifestations of the supernatural—the visible, residual and physical imprint of their" loved ones, Mormons were baptizing their deceased ancestors in temples.[50] Both Latter-day Saint and spiritualist rituals required a second body, one to act on behalf of the material yet disembodied spirit. They both required actions and attention of the living to register and index the dead. However, Latter-day Saints generally dismissed spirit photographs, because of their implicit connection to the Godbeite schism from Mormonism in 1870 and the images' lack of discernible messages. Latter-day Saints took issue with spirit photography's framing of spirits. Instead of allowing for learning and advancement through sense and signal, "the dead were made static—truly dead, and worst of all *silent*."[51] Rather than give life to the dead through capturing light, spirit photographs didn't make the dead alive enough in the Mormon view. As described in the church periodical the *Deseret News*, for Mormonism spirit photography was "utterly useless, nonsensical, dumb."[52]

But as a photographic effect, multiple exposures could be utilized to critique culture by shuffling and haunting reality. In just such a spoof-spiritualist mode, Huntington staged highly constructed scenes that foregrounded the technology of the camera and its ability to challenge verisimilitude with special effects—the very issues at stake in spirit photography.

In one photo a man reaches out to embrace a ghostly woman, who appears as a second exposure and translucent. Huntington had to carefully render the addition of the woman so that the couple's hands would line up. Likely with tongue in cheek, she had constructed a spirit photograph of the new Mormon norm: a monogamous—and certainly, as ever, a heterosexual—couple. In another image of a couple seated in a parlor, Huntington imposed double-exposed figures of a second couple sitting adjacent. But at least one of the women even appears to be Huntington herself (possibly doubled). The layers of exposures make the details blurry, but if it is indeed Huntington in both pairings, then she appears with two different men, completely engaged with both at the same time.

Huntington injected spectral doppelgängers, who haunt the ideal social and religious marital configuration, even after the multiplication of marriages through polygamy had recently been disavowed. Her double-exposed images used the very form of humbug hope (to see a spirit in a photograph) in order to mock the false hope of a social convention she never quite fit. Marriage and courtship seem either a ghostly ideal just beyond reach or a hollow image intensely promoted but never living up to its hype. Huntington's work carved out an aesthetic space, where such critique is technologically possible and ostensibly safer.

Huntington's spectral images partook in the belief that the camera's sensitive plates could reveal potential truths otherwise invisible to the naked eye. But not in the precise way Spiritualists claimed. Her plates were not giving "objective form" to real "immaterial phantasms that the optical revolution had exorcized."[53] Instead, her work foregrounds the tension between photography as a scientific apparatus based in "mechanical objectivity" and the unique inflection given by "issues of skill, gender, class, and taste" that left its use open to both spiritualist enterprises as well as imaginative feminist ones.[54] Creative "artistic," or "pictorial" practitioners, like Huntington could produce manipulated views of reality by exercising an increased sensitivity to otherwise neglected or unsensed compositions. If photographers were sensitive enough—as women, spiritualist mediums, and the photographic plates were culturally understood to be—they could work along the edge of "objective reality" to reveal deeper, otherwise unseen, truths. These truths might expose the exclusive or oppressive nature of social norms. They might also reveal certain individuals, who are otherwise ignored and neglected—those who are rendered culturally invisible.

Unlike the bachelor in her version of the Bachelor's Dream trope, Huntington directed her gaze to those outside the idealized standards. She photographed disabled, drunk, non-Mormon, transgressive, and costumed bodies (Halloween images seemed to be a favorite). She both acknowledged the realities photographers often excluded and constructed alternative and critical versions of reality by playing with surface appearances. She crafted images with double exposures and gender-bending performances to mimic the construction of reality as a haunting critique. But her work also reminds us of the variety of experiences women had during this time. Instead of essentializing all women as wives or mothers, Huntington's photography evinces the formative role disability and alterity might have played in her particular experience of the world, suggesting a more nuanced understanding of gender as it comes to matter through technology. Huntington exposed the standard and well-known visions of men by creating layered and critical new versions. Her photographic work reveals the potential role of the technology in teaching a magnified form of vision toward inclusion and understanding rather than framing and possessing.

TYPING VISIONS

Elfie Huntington was not alone in tinkering with gendered visions through technology. In true modern fashion, Susa Young Gates purchased her very own Hammond typewriter on April 12, 1890.[55] At this point in her life, she had no intention of using it to work as a man's amanuensis. Like Huntington, Gates too could navigate the conceptualization and performance of gender by interacting with technology. Where Huntington had to work against the intrinsic reproduction of reality enacted by the camera, Gates merely had to work against standardized type and cultural practices that often reduced the typewriter to rote reproduction of another's words. Yet, the differences between the two women went beyond specific characteristics of their media.

Gates came from status and privilege, and despite her hardships she enjoyed an unusual degree of support and freedom to develop her craft. As a daughter of a polygamous wife to second church president Brigham Young,

Gates was trained in music and ballet, and able to obtain a university education. As Huntington's senior by twelve years, Gates embodied class and gen-
erational aspects of adopting machines in the 1890s. Gates's voice in printed
works, such as the *Young Woman's Journal*—she conceived of it while on an
ecclesiastical mission in Hawaii and founded it in 1889 upon her return to
Utah—took on a decidedly didactic and maternal tone.[56]

And unlike Huntington's photographic interventions, Gates and her work
had wider influence on Latter-day Saint culture and the nation and can be
characterized as a creative doubling down on essentializing and sacralizing
women as mothers. She helped fashion woman's independence and representation within the church through several periodicals and in managing auxiliary organizations. Her influence was so pervasive that she was sometimes
even referred to as the "thirteenth apostle."[57] Her work was also instrumental
in helping to change the public image of Mormon women. As a well-known
representative and defender of her faith, she managed to forge ties across
party and religious lines. Gates fulfilled national appointments, published
widely, and was "closely acquainted with popular suffragists such as Susan
B. Anthony, Clara Barton and Charlotte Perkins Gilman."[58] She repeatedly
traveled to Washington, D.C., as a representative and served in both the International and National Council of Women.

Through all her work in woman's rights, education, health care, and fostering the next generation of women authors, Gates just kept writing. Her
prolific feminist content gave expression to her command of the typewriter
and echoed her editorial position of authority. Printing presses and typewriters helped with the rapidity and reach of her labor, but she also worked to
deliberately overcome the perception of cold machinery with life. Much of
this was due to Gates's efforts to imbue her creations with vivacity in contrast
to rote, memo-like, transcription. Gates was said to "have a natural power
of giving herself to humanity through her writings; they glow with life and
on that account kindle fires in other minds and other hearts."[59] When Gates
reached back into the past to write her histories of prominent Latter-day
Saint women, she was very aware she was doing so from the "present modern
machinerized day," as she characterized it, in contrast to the romanticized
days of the early church.[60]

As some writers feared, the typewriter could efface humanity and provenance in the same way the camera upheld an authority of objectivity. As Bram
Stoker's 1897 novel *Dracula* thematized, in its vampiric way, the typewriter
drained the blood of the author.[61] Or as Friedrich Kittler put it, with the
typewriter's "standardized text, paper and body, writing and soul fall apart."[62]

The perceived loss of individuality with the new inscription technology also worried Gates's friend and coreligionist Emmeline Wells, who lamented the novel concern that "if we must write a letter it must be done on the typewriter (to save time), and all the individuality is taken out of it; it's machine work only, and lacks the touch of fine tone that letter-writing once had."[63] Typewriters were double-edged swords that seemed to render writing efficient, yet gothically severed from its author's humanity.

But writing by any means was also surviving. As Gates realized, "Unless some one fixes the pen-stroke, tools the metal or marble, all that is now me will soon have gone into the silence of unutterable forgetfulness."[64] Her preserved creative output in archived and published forms forcefully captures the adoption of the typewriter and its effect. Her handwriting fades as she eventually adopted typing for all her correspondence. With most of her literary creations the typed drafts clearly evince the active mind of an author at work with the insertions, corrections, and deletions made in graphite guiding the next typed iteration. Despite connotations of mechanizing creativity, the machine seemed to meet her halfway in expediting her output and characterizing her autonomy.

Early on, Gates's work is focused on gender equality and elevating women's doctrinal role as mothers. Rather than critique the tyranny of this role, Gates praised marriage and motherhood as thorny material training grounds for eternal progression that connected women across time. A typed draft of her poem "To My Mother's Mothers" captures her deep-seated conviction in the sanctity and power of motherhood. Although it was "inspired by" a talk a male priesthood leader gave on Mother's Day, in typical fashion Gates magnified and deepened the vision of motherhood.[65] Her version was an expansion, stemming from personal experience shot through with Latter-day Saint doctrine.

The poem's five quatrain stanzas utilize an *abcb* rhyme scheme and provide a visual "ladder," just as Gates described the rungs on a maternal ladder rising upward, "one by one, to Eve, to heaven, to God," in the poem's final line. The first stanza addresses the dead. Gates speaks to her mother and grandmothers, acknowledging that they enjoyed love, youth, and motherhood in life, but that death itself only brings "a fuller sense of truth." Then the poem moves to Gates's own daughters and their daughters, in whom Gates sees the spark of those departed spirits. From the title, which plays on a suggestive homophonic effect of the possessive and the plural, the poem considers the linking of motherhood across deep time. Whereas very few church leaders spoke about specific mothers or heavenly mother, aside from extolling the virtues of motherhood in the home, Gates poetically multiplied their central and infinite presence.

The poem envisions a "glory" in the "heavenly-lit eyes" of children that sparkle with gratitude and a debt to mothers, *plural*, who "bravely, nobly see use That ladder in earth's sod," to bring spirits into fleshly tabernacles in this life and then direct them upward to "Eve, to heaven, and God." Her hand-written edits coax the thoughts further and toward the poem's next iteration, where heavenly eyes become lit by heaven and a "brave" mother becomes a "just" mother. But perhaps the most telling shift is Gates's decision to change mothers from "seeing" that ladder of motherhood to "using" it. Vision shifts to performance.

As was typical of Gates, she combined the deep contemplation of what she considered a spiritual truth with activity. Writing, speaking out, advocating women's rights, traveling, and raising children were all the dynamic expression of an eternal principle in her mind. Departed mothers, from Eve to her own, were with the living through maternal bonds. Although Gates's vision of motherhood often confined and excluded many women, motherhood for her was brave creation full of personal sacrifice and material realization. As an expression through the rapid impression of keys and the follow-up technique of pencil to paper, she pursued the potential of motherhood into its logical extension, a chain of mothers into eternity—a ladder with no beginning or end. And like the editorial work on paper, Gates saw her maternal work in this life as the location and situation where her development of divine nature was worked out and refined.

TOUCH TYPING

Even as she took from men's words Gates amplified them, refusing rote mimesis for expansion and revision. Gates typed her own creative perspective into her work, which was not the most common use of the typewriter by women at the time. As Pamela Thurschwell and Leah Price have pointed out, the "feminists' perennial hope" that writing machines such as typewriters and cameras would allow women to "assert or find themselves clashes with the grim statistics" that women most often adopted the machines in the capacity of secretaries and assistants to men.[66] Gates's ability to turn the typewriter on its inventors and use it to personal and creative ends was the much rarer exception. Rather than liberated and creative, women typists were often alienated and reproducing the work of others. Employers could easily rationalize the entrance of woman workers into the field of typing with gendered and condescending logic. In Christopher Keep's estimation, it was precisely the "fit between the culturally accepted sense of women as nonsubjects and the typist as absent which allowed the gendering of the typewriter as a specifically feminine attribute."[67] Hence it is often the case when studying women typists that "the extensive archives they leave behind usually refer to others."[68]

Both workplace and spiritualist conceptions of women at machines could efface the operator. They might render her (crucially) a sensitive medium to use the technology efficiently, yet otherwise incidental in the process of rote reproduction. Just as the perceived extrasensory capacity of women qualified them for work as telegraph operators and spiritualist mediums, it also suggested their aptitude in typewriting—to facilitate the flow of information, rather than get in its way. As the prolific spiritualist author Andrew Jackson Davis put it, the female medium could determine the "strength of the communications," but if the control from the dictating spirit is "perfect, the medium is annihilated, so to speak, as far as individualism of character is concerned."[69]

Spiritualist séances welcomed the typewriter's suggestive functions. Because typewriting "effaced the personality of the writer" it "encouraged spiritualists to imagine that the texts generated during séances were dictated by disembodied spirits."[70] Automatic writing in séances showcased "touch typing" or typing "blind" (without looking at the keys) to emphasize the uncanny nature of the new mechanical form of writing. In this way, spiritualism extended the inner logic of Isaac Pitman's shorthand method that already urged the blind, absent, and self-effacing quality of typists.[71] At times, spiritualist dictations even radically reversed the common gender roles found in workplace typewriting. For within the context of mediumship, spiritualists could "openly and flagrantly" transgress gender norms.[72] In 1892 William Thomas Stead typed up the words of the deceased woman Julia A. Ames.[73] He professed to be able to communicate with her and other spirits through his "spook machine" typewriter, which worked "upon the table-turning or spirit-rapping principle."[74] Four years later Joseph M. Wade published a memoir for the deceased theosophist Helena Blavatsky, which was "dictated from the Spirit-World, upon the typewriter, independent of all human contact," and was supervised by the ghost of the typewriter's inventor G. W. N. Yost.[75] And John Ballou Newbrough produced over 1,000 pages of scripture at a typewriter. His hands were controlled by spirits as a "line of light" shone on them and extended "heavenward like a telegraph wire." Newbrough described the text typed through his body and machine as clerical labor. He simply copied a series of "transcripts from the libraries in the heavens."[76]

Because connections to the spirit world had been forged through typewriters, it was fitting and somewhat ironic that Latter-day Saint church president Joseph F. Smith expressed his revelatory vision to the church in 1918 by dictating it and having it recorded through a typewriter.[77] It was equally fitting that the revelation dealt with the afterlife and the administration of spirits. But this important communication and its dictated reproduction in type occurred between President Smith and his son, likely because they both held the gender-specific priesthood authority to manage visions and revelatory matters for the church. The priesthood was considered by Latter-day Saints to be the true means of communicating with spirits, not "such uncertain means as tappings and mutterings, but by direct revelation."[78]

Susa Young Gates subscribed to the same differentiation. As a close friend of President Smith, she was even invited to read the typed text of the vision two weeks before the church body did. Lisa Olsen Tait has shown just how much it meant to Gates when she noticed the vision's mention of Mother Eve and her daughters in the spirit world.[79] Gates published the vision in the *Relief Society Magazine*, noting its inclusion of "women's labors on the Other Side." She felt it would become a "clarion call for [Latter-day Saints] to awake to the immediate necessity of looking after their dead."[80] Gates loved the idea of spiritual visions still being enjoyed in the modern world and inspiring the Latter-day Saints to work.

While Gates focused on developing genealogy and temple work in her later years, decades earlier she remembered her excitement reading stories of spirit rappings as a young woman, citing in particular Hawthorne's *The House of Seven Gables*, "which sent ugly shivers of fear rippling down [her] spine at each perusal but which possessed a morbid fascination for [her] unwilling opening mind."[81] In the *Young Woman's Journal*, Gates confessed her childhood fascination for stories of "fortune-telling and magic," and how "weird literature" meant more to her than playing.[82] But she recalled her enchantment only to discredit it for young Mormon readers of the 1890s. Now she had to take a stand against fantastic literature and the pitfalls of spiritualism to help cultivate the future and face of Mormon femininity.

In 1900 Gates wrote sternly to her readers, "Many of our young people ask the question, even today: Don't you believe there is anything in witchcraft or modern spiritualism? Why, most certainly we do! There is a terrible and awful power in it!" Just as stories printed in her journal or discourses from church leaders explained, for Gates too, spiritualism could be "evil" and a "perversion of the priesthood." She even noted how in many spiritualist traditions, "singularly enough, it is women who have originated" the "spiritual errors."[83] Mormons welcomed visions but expected them to echo those of male church leaders. As Gates exemplified, for Latter-day Saints spiritualism was a slippery slope and often understood to be a counterfeit version of their own interactions and management of the dead. It also helped serve as a foil to focus the authority of Latter-day Saint priesthood holders.

Revelations for the entire church required priesthood authority, but they also required secretarial work to transcribe and disseminate the governing visions. Amanuenses, scribes, and clerks, like President Smith's son at the typewriter, had provided the religion with a notation network from its very inception. To facilitate the translation of the Book of Mormon, Emma Smith, Martin Harris, and Oliver Cowdery took turns transcribing Joseph Smith's dictation. After relocating to Utah, Brigham Young first had men providing phonography and stenography for church leaders. Young even temporarily implemented an entirely new alphabet, the "Deseret Alphabet," to bring immigrants and a diverse people under one word-processing practice. According to Amanda Beardsley, the alphabet was an attempt to eliminate confusion precisely between sound and symbol, by constructing unique letters for each phoneme rather than merely reforming spelling.[84] This could foster universal communication, while cleaning up and standardizing the work of recorders.

A former secretary for Brigham Young, George Watt, who had been a major advocate of Pitman shorthand, brought the first typewriter (an 1873 Remington Sholes and Glidden) to Utah, and the machines were gradually adopted across the church, signaling the new order of bureaucratization, beginning in the mid-1880s.[85] By 1883 John Whitaker was teaching typewriting (along with phonetics and shorthand) at the University of Deseret, later renamed the University of Utah. Shortly thereafter the apostle Franklin D. Richards reached out to Whitaker and hired him in the church historian's office as an "amanuensis and typewriter."[86] There the work of male historians and managers was soon facilitated by the newly feminized workforce of women at machines, including the unsung female typists Minerva Jenson, Bertha Emery, Lois Roberts, and Eva Jenson.[87] The typewriter also aided the efficient organization of Latter-day Saint auxiliary groups, including the Relief Society and Young Ladies Mutual Improvement Association.[88]

By the first decade of the twentieth century Susa Young Gates reported to women "in all the world" that in contrast to the image of "supposedly 'enslaved' 'Mormon' women. . . . The girls of the church have imbibed the modern monetary independence, and thousands of them are typewriters, clerks, artists, and school teachers."[89] An article on the typewriter included in the *Contributor*, a periodical aimed at Latter-day Saint youth, emphasized how as the "invention has proven an inestimable blessing to the whole world it has marked an epoch in the history of woman's work." The author went so far as to suggest that "to nothing more appropriately could women erect a shrine than to this little clattering instrument, which has been the most effective means not only of educating men to a true appreciation of the value of woman's work but of opening *her* eyes to the true dignity of labor."[90] But the majority of Mormon women at typewriters were still filling the expansion of the new workplace structure and continuing the amanuensis tradition by typing up the words of male superiors. This arrangement mirrored a general sense across the country that rather than dictate women should "limit themselves to anonymous passive transcription."[91] It also paralleled Mormon women's recuperative defenses of the then-defunct plural marriage when they simply "reproduced the voice of their male leaders."[92] But the story of Mormon women and agency is much more complex.

Oddly enough, polygamy and then its eradication might have even bolstered the ability of some Latter-day Saint women to enter the new technological opportunities with a distinct self-sufficiency. The practice of polygamy had allowed, even forced, many women to band together, fend for themselves, and take on increased responsibilities.[93] The practice had fostered a sense of subordinate autonomy, where "many of the most active and influential women in late-nineteenth century Utah were wives of polygamists."[94] For a time, gender roles were more flexible, and women worked in various vocations alongside men or in their absence. Some women even traveled to the eastern United States or Europe to gain education and experience or further develop their craft.[95] But Gates and an increasing number of Latter-day Saints adopted the typewriter just as the specter of polygamy was waning and its memory was being recast.[96]

Just months before the disavowal of polygamy Lizzie Smith wrote to the young Latter-day Saint women that "to exclude woman from active occupations and confine her to the cares of the household is to attempt an impossibility—to close the way to progress."[97] A year later the sentiment took on a new urgency. In 1891 Mary Howe wrote in the same periodical, the "order of things [polygamy] has vanished, owing to the determined efforts of a paternal government. The question now arises, what is to become of our surplus girls?" Howe answered by encouraging young women—"whether [they] expect to marry or dread the coming years of single life"—to take up a vocation, such as medicine or education, but also photography or typewriting.[98]

Women working through machines was seen as a feminine and permissible media practice, for a time. As much as the discontinuation of polygamy meant Latter-day Saints "initiated a series of profound self-revisions," their adoption of typewriters often aligned with the gendered workflow of their fellow Americans, signaling a modernization of the church in technical and embodied practices.[99] From the nexus of this ecclesiastical identity crisis and the media landscape, a new generation of women emerged. Many studied typing and negotiated the workplace and aspirations for an expanded sense of careers for women by reproducing dictation. Others, like Gates, typed up original works in women's magazines and national papers directly treating marriage, motherhood, religion, equal rights, and careers.

TURNING THE TYPEWRITING TABLES

To effectively use her typewriter, Susa Young Gates needed to develop a new form of attention. Where the focus on touch and the machine's sensitive feedback worked well within spiritualism, it was also a technique, a practical skill that forged new experiences of mental exertion and repetitive focus. One principal shift was the disruption of eye-hand coordination. According to Mark Seltzer, handwriting was the organic link between hand and eye that translated "the inward and invisible and spiritual to the outward and visible and physical." But the typewriter changed this. The mechanization of writing in the typewriter is what Seltzer notes led to a "dislocation of where the hands work, where the letters strike and appear, where the eyes look, if they look at all."[100] The typewriter fashioned a new vision of writing, one that "severs the link between the eye, the hand and the text."[101] This trained a new sensitivity to the simultaneous, but dislocated, application of the eyes and hands. Women as typists could wield this disjointed sensitivity for more efficient typing, but also as a cultural technique for creative operations. In so doing, they had to learn to manage a new split form of attention, which was for some operators, like Gates, a crystallization in minute practice of their divided care across home and work.

Gates expected her work at the typewriter to affect others and to be synergetic with her work as a mother. On August 19, 1895, she typed a characteristic to-do list for the day, including practicing riding her bicycle and a healthy dose of writing, along with completing some household chores.[102] Although she often bemoaned her inability to find the energy or time to write in the face of housework and she struggled with debilitating mental health issues in 1902 that lasted for a few years, Gates was incredibly productive.[103]

Sensitive Machines

She cherished her roles as mother and wife, but "because writing seemed as natural as breathing," her creative efforts at writing—amid domestic work—inspired a generation of Mormon authors and still provide an important moment for women's work through different inscription technologies.[104] Typing her way through the potential dilemma of parsing "woman's work," Gates must have felt the truth in apostle George Q. Cannon's singular statement in 1892, when he suggested that women cannot "confine themselves entirely to household affairs" or it will lead to "drudgery," "unhappiness and melancholy."[105] Gates had conceded in an article in 1894 that she was "one of the most dissatisfied members of [her] sex," but writing evidently mitigated some of this dissatisfaction.[106]

Gates sought to forge a model of motherhood in both literal and literary senses that clearly reflected her own experience. Despite her struggles, she saw no mutual exclusion in the difficult demarcation between motherhood in the home and womanhood out in the world. Because her focus on gendered roles, even if expanded or exalted, never eclipsed the primary role of motherhood for women, she was also likely shielded from any direct censorship from male leaders. Ultimately, she contributed to the further development of Mormonism's emphasis on women as mothers. Where Huntington focused on marginalized individuals and the powers structuring gender and courtship through photography, Gates magnified the role of women in learning, working, and especially motherhood. She found ways to envision women as wholly equal to men in her mind, even if they were locked into roles that were so often hierarchical.

In her typed ruminations "Women's Place in the Plan of Salvation," Gates wrote, "[Woman] stands side by side with him, not above him and not below him. Her opportunities, responsibilities, and duties lie parallel with that of her male companion."[107] Gates continued by typing out her own reinterpretation of the Virgin Mary's maternal role as the medium that brought Christ into the world. In her draft notes she wrote, "No mortal man, perhaps, could have lived the perfect unselfish law of life eternal so as to become the father of Jesus; could it be that only a woman could thus qualify for that one-sided earthly parentage?"[108] This was innovative without quite espousing Christian Scientist Mary Baker Eddy's description of Jesus being "the offspring of Mary's self-conscious" and created by her thought alone, which she actualized because of woman's "more spiritual nature."[109]

Gates clung to an essentialist view of reproduction and gender roles in her personal meditations with the expectation they would be published, read, and lasting. In fact, Kathryn Shirts has argued that it was Gates's understanding of motherhood as a parallel and integral supplement to the patriarchal priesthood power that shaped a century of Mormon belief and practice.[110] Gates and several other prominent Latter-day Saint women "encouraged young women to pursue educational and professional opportunities" but never seemed "to imagine a future for their daughters other than marriage and motherhood."[111] Gates's firm insistence on motherhood as part and parcel with her own creative output also shaped her depiction of Mormon women. Gates never characterized raising children as unequal servitude, even though so many of her contemporaries experienced it as such. She argued that, "contrary to the image portrayed by the national press, Mormon women enjoyed more rights than most women."[112] Gates's writings and embodied media practices helped counter that public image. She performed and espoused a liberated Mormon woman, with rights, influence, and a passion for motherhood, even if the tension of balancing one's attention persisted.

Gates recalled her father, Brigham Young, teaching her early, "If you were to become a woman in the world + fail as wife + mother, you will have failed in everything."[113] This graphic equation of symbols and its dogmatic message informed Gates's behavior. Explaining her prolific career, Gates proudly stated, "As I wrote I rocked the cradle with my foot." Hands writing and feet tending to the family, Gates's body matched the seemingly split but somehow unified mentality of a professional and attentive mother. Self-stylized as a medium to life, Gates poetically described her baby son as holding in his "tiny hands a chain from [mother] to heaven."[114] Having dealt with the stigma of divorce at a young age and endured six miscarriages and several early deaths of her children, Gates wrote from a position of experience often neglected in patriarchal prose.[115] Whenever her children asked a question, Gates recounted how she would pause the writing and answer them, because, as she noted, "my children were first!"[116] And Gates self-identified as one exploring and fulfilling "woman's role and abilities—both in the home + out." It was written of Gates that she, in particular, found the secret to success in "motherhood with a varied and distinguished career," by matching her "aggressive characteristics" with the "tenderness and self-sacrifice" of a successful mother.[117] At the time "it was thought absolutely impossible to combine the two," but Gates was determined to create and thrive in both arenas, the one inflecting the other.[118]

Gates's experience and personal vision of motherhood informed one of her most radical writerly explorations. She had the courage to interpret Joseph Smith's "first vision" to be a declaration of the equality of men and women. Beginning in the 1880s, after the church canonized an account of fourteen-year-old Smith seeing God the father and Jesus Christ as embodied beings in 1820, Latter-day Saints increasingly credited Smith's "first vision" as the origin story of Mormonism.[119] Now, 100 years after the time of the theophany, the church wanted to emphasize and celebrate it as a unique and groundbreaking feature of their religious tradition. Out of eighteen invited contributors, Gates was the only woman author in the special issue of the church's official periodical the *Improvement Era* dedicated to the 1920 centennial of Smith's vision.

Without voicing heresy, Gates's essay "The Vision Beautiful" shifted the focus of that vision to the feminine. In her short retelling, she interpreted the vision to mean there was a heavenly mother and to signal "woman's free agency" in "civil, religious, social and finally, financial matters." Gates understood one declaration Smith reported from God—"They were all wrong! They draw near to me with their lips, but their hearts are far from me"— as referencing more than denominations. For her, it denounced in one fell swoop all Christian interpretations of woman's role and the ways men had misled and "shackled" woman "because of her very virtue, tender sympathy, and patient desire for peace." Scraping off any domination or denigration of woman based on her sensitivity allowed Gates to widen Smith's vision to a global pronouncement that was especially resonant for first-wave feminism's desire for equal rights. Through her typewriter once more, Gates had made a male prophet's (now) founding vision foreshadow the entire "liberation of [woman's] long-chained will and purpose."[120]

Beyond what Smith reported seeing—and this is a crucial intervention— Gates saw "the divine Mother, side by side with the divine Father, equal sharing of equal rights, privileges and responsibilities, in heaven and on earth."[121] She not only re-created but also expanded Smith's vision to retrofit women into the prophetic past and enact their equality in the present. And she apparently pulled this off without ruffling feathers or facing church discipline.[122] Like her personal work with the standardized constraints of the typewriter, Gates found a way to explore and push within orthodox ideas about gender. Through just such a process she found a feminine divine—a Heavenly Mother—by typing her into the founding prophetic vision of Mormonism. In effect, Gates's intervention was arguably even more "spiritualist" than Huntington's production of double exposures and alternate visions in photographs. Of course, this was an epistemological intervention, rather than a supernatural one. But by putting the equality of the sexes and the presence of the heavenly mother in the mouth and eyes of the deceased prophet Joseph Smith, Gates respectfully but cleverly ventriloquized the dead.

By the time of the essay's publication women's roles in Mormonism had been effectively narrowed. Gates sounded a vision of gender equality just after women's autonomy had been thoroughly subsumed by the priesthood. Between 1908 and 1918, her dear friend President Joseph F. Smith had formally centralized all church activity and standardized curriculum under the priesthood line of authority.[123] These conceptual and organizational shifts were even reflected in the auxiliary periodicals. Thomas Alexander describes how "the semi-autonomous *Woman's Exponent* magazine was replaced by the church-owned *Relief Society Magazine*," and the magazine Gates had founded, the *Young Woman's Journal*, had been "combined with the [church-owned] *Improvement Era*" by the end of the 1920s.[124] As Amy Hoyt and Sara Patterson have shown, even the content of the periodicals shifted toward training men to specialize in successful careers and women to stay home and have children.[125] The words typed up by women formerly under full control of female authors, editors, and printers were brought under the control of the priesthood-holding male leaders.[126]

The notion of priesthood itself had changed. According to Jonathan Stapley, whereas previous understandings of priesthood "required the incorporation of women to be coherent," the new "priesthood cosmology" of the early twentieth century "was based on the entirely male ecclesiastical priesthood" and "excluded women to maintain coherence."[127] If "typewriter" had conflated woman with the authority granted to a machine, "priesthood" now clearly conflated man with governing and revelatory power. And the priesthood leaders' vision of the ideal Mormon woman was that of excellent homemaker and birthing mother as medium to life.

As Gates navigated the narrowing roles attributed to her gender, she seemed to see things others did not. Her vision was translated into insightful and activist writings that helped elevate the standing of women in Mormonism and suggest futures pregnant with possibility. In this context, Gates enacted a feminine subjectivity that was pioneering for her sisters in the church and readers of national papers, even if her vision's theological implications were left unexplored and ultimately essentialized all women as mothers complementary with governing fathers.

Men such as Mark Twain and Friedrich Nietzsche recorded their interaction with the typewriter, but theirs lacked the encumbered, or for Gates *enhanced*, overlap of labor that shaped Gates's life experience.[128] For she navigated a divided attention and body. And it was precisely in this difficult embodied labor that Gates felt she would find and become like God, even

God the mother. Her vision split between hands typing and pages being written, attention split between home and work, and efforts split between sustaining the narrowing of women's roles in the church and simultaneously seeking to endow them with additional breadth and depth all refracted a period of transition, full of threat and promise.

CONCLUSION

The technical visions of Susa Young Gates and Elfie Huntington came just as Mormonism was revising its relationship to the nation, gender, and visionary experience. Around the turn of the twentieth century, church leaders emphasized the importance of members *feeling* the Holy Ghost rather than *seeing* spirits.[129] Visionary experience was now more of a confirming sense to conform with the visions of leaders. As Christopher James Blythe has traced, visions from rank-and-file members were increasingly met with suspicion, as priesthood leaders taught that only they "could be trusted to discern whether a revelation is legitimate."[130] Accordingly, Mormon women at machines during this transitional period primarily found ways to replicate and praise the well-known visions of men, rather than record and disseminate new ones.

Huntington and Gates used media in creative and destabilizing ways to channel and challenge gendered visions, as spiritualism had done for decades. Even though spiritualism was often perceived as another threat to Mormonism, it helped suggest the radical potential of photography and typewriting to bolster women's rights and modify women's roles. Spiritualist applications helped the machines open doors, to the spirit world, as well as to new creative possibilities outside of common gender configurations. And this creative work focused the significance and power of women as uniquely suited operators of the devices. It even suggested ways of pushing back against social norms within parameters that made it safe to do so.

By exercising their creative power and shooting it through the rapid-fire keys or the dilation of the aperture, Huntington and Gates registered their own perspective and the complicated coconstruction of gender and technologies at the turn of the century. Their media practices were Mormon in purpose but spiritualist in effect. For they both altered men's visions and gave them new meaning by channeling them through machines. By so doing, Huntington and Gates reproduced patriarchal visions without *reproducing* them. That is to say, they addressed gender by re-creating but critically expanding visions in type and photography. And their expansions often drastically transformed the possible meanings and significance of those visions. Although they utilized machines of reproduction to do so, they found a fecund space between pure mimesis and disconnected novelty.

Whereas Huntington developed views of suggestive transgressions and exposed the problematic patriarchal gaze through photography, Gates typed out her efforts to conceptualize womanhood *alongside* the priesthood and within patriarchal visions. Despite all her ambitions for radical new ways of understanding and performing womanhood, Gates ultimately helped solidify women's roles as ideally mothers, locked into a binary system of governance under the priesthood power. This compatibility with mainstream American gender roles together with Gates's prominent position ensured that visions of femininity within Mormonism would appear closer to Gates's version rather than to Huntington's. Although church leaders would repeatedly cast women as maternal media to life throughout the twentieth century and urge women to avoid workplace machines and remain at home, Huntington and Gates offer potential models for unscrambling the fractured and frustrating processes of policing gender. They used media to open eyes to new ways of seeing old visions. As their work exposed, reproducing reality as it is will never change it. It must be tinkered with and expanded, in short mediated.

CINEMATIC

TRAFFIC

Moving Pictures bring to everyone an absolutely clear idea of foreign
peoples through their customs and through scenes of the world and through
the industries and pursuits of man. They have a tremendous educational effect.

Thomas Edison, 1911

Motion pictures are defaming the character of
the people of the Mormon Church.

David O. McKay, 1912

At a climactic moment in one of the very few surviving scenes of the
Latter-day Saint church's first film, *One Hundred Years of Mormonism* (1913), a heavenly being enters the frame.[1] He doesn't need a
door or a window. The angel Moroni simply materializes in Joseph Smith's
staged bedroom, magically fading in and out of visibility. The fantastic effect
was achieved through the technique of double exposure and brought a thoroughly modern element to the visual presentation of the church's foundational narrative.

By employing double exposure, *One Hundred Years* produced supernatural beings that were perceptually real—present, but not quite whole.
Although cinematic, the representations seemed to conform to the cultural
optics of the nineteenth century, when Smith had his visions and ghosts were
understood to be transparent.[2] The use of trick photography also drew on a
long history of optical illusions, often related to the supernatural. By echoing

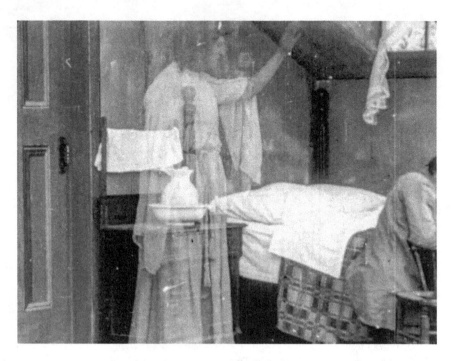

The angel Moroni appears in Joseph Smith's bedroom in an early scene
and surviving fragment from *One Hundred Years of Mormonism*, 1913.
Church History Library, Salt Lake City, Utah.

the earlier forms of phantasmagoria and spirit photography to represent the
spectral, much of early cinema—like this scene—was equally experienced as
"a kind of magic show."[3] But in *One Hundred Years* the special effect pulled off
another trick. It technologized Smith's vision and integrated it into cinema,
as just another scene in the history of America.

The peculiar fusion of modern technology and Smith's spiritual vision
in *One Hundred Years* formally enacted in miniature the larger project of as-
similating Mormonism into modernity. In other words, the first feature film
from Latter-day Saints was a "history film"—an ostensibly true story—that
used special effects and cinematic specters to tell its tale of religious frontier
Americans. The scene literalized the incorporation of Mormon experience
into modern technological conditions through the medium of cinema. It
simultaneously invited skeptical viewers to try on Smith's vision and see as
he did. This remarkable fact foregrounds the persistent struggle of fitting
early twentieth-century Latter-day Saints into modernity and stands as an
emblem of this chapter's larger argument. By sharing an "authentic" vision
of Latter-day Saints, *One Hundred Years of Mormonism* taught viewers to see

Mormons differently. It reversed connotations around Mormon vision from hypnotic and controlling to pious and miraculous. Most importantly, the film made Latter-day Saints modern and coded as cinematically white Americans to emphasize their national belonging.

The shift in Latter-day Saint optics was made possible by film, which could store and replay serial sensory data to animate and update the church's supernatural history for modern audiences.[4] As a storage technology, film seemed to ward off death but also created a slew of undead images, haunting possibilities, and threatening representations on-screen. This by-product of media technologies around 1900 renewed old concerns about image control and privacy rights and birthed altogether new ones. The appearance of likenesses connected to—but equally severed from—specific beings enabled sensational representations, which were easily exploited. Prominent examples of such representations were the scandalous portrayals of Mormons in early silent films that made entertainment out of a religion under transformation. The degrading copies and imitations were threatening but served an important cultural function for audiences, as Mormon doppelgängers often thematized the precarious prospect of the religion's assimilation into modernity.

Most films were clearly unsure of this possibility. Whether commercially opportunist or sincerely meant as social education, early Mormon-themed films sought to work out the seemingly inherent inability of Mormonism to keep pace and become incorporated into the modernizing and progressive world—to enter the traffic and network of modern life. This chapter, then, reenvisions the cultural intervention of Mormonsploitation films (from 1905 to 1922) as cinematically working through the ominous assimilation of Mormons by staging the lawless and unmodern integration of "victims" into Mormon trafficking. It was against this backdrop that Latter-day Saints made their first film. If anti-Mormon depictions were "contraceptive" in their attempt to keep Mormons out of the circle of modern life, then I argue that the first Mormon film was apotropaic in its attempt to ward off libelous doubles and replace them with an American image of Latter-day Saint citizens. This meant medium and content were inseparable in their ability to signal the entrance of Mormons into modern traffic and to put the cultural conventions of belonging into motion.

One Hundred Years enacted the modernization of Mormonism by displacing doppelgängers and trafficking in mass media. The film integrated an acceptable image of the church's past—as both legally copyrighted and a part of American history—into the modern media network of cinema. This intervention also reflected Utah's infrastructural connection to the larger nation. In both the material-discursive media practices of fashioning their public image and the concrete condition of technological infrastructures, Mormons were increasingly plugged into modernity and *seen* as good American citizens.

POLYGAMY IN THE AGE OF MECHANICAL REPRODUCIBILITY

Unlike the angelic specters and sympathetic actors put forward by *One Hundred Years*, the early twentieth-century representations of Mormons were shaped by antagonistic perceptions of Mormon marriage practices. This view of Mormons had for decades mixed their sexuality and race into a potential threat to the entire nation. Popular perceptions from the late nineteenth century rendered Mormons as less than white and as debased in the public sphere. In the eyes of the nation, Mormons did sex and religion *wrong*, and this made them racially suspect. Cast as underground miscreants, Mormon doppelgängers in film were accordingly evil and perverse predators who thwarted modern progress with their backward networks of human trafficking. Improving Mormon optics would require intense revision of these public displays.

Latter-day Saints' remarkable efforts to shift from nineteenth-century outsiders to twentieth-century ideal Americans made them prime candidates to translate into cinematic figures, which would in turn provide an opportunity to work through anxieties surrounding the new media landscape of interconnection and exchange. On-screen, Latter-day Saints were dangerously caught in the processes of nations determining good and bad religion. In this sense, Mormonsploitation films engaged the kinds of secularizing narratives that sought to order, distribute, and propagate an "interlinked series of binarized distinctions."[5] Latter-day Saints provided the cautionary foil to the seamless integration of religion and modernity. And while there existed any number of obstacles to the modernization of Mormonism, polygamy was particularly ripe for visual critique.[6]

Some of the renewed anxiety around polygamy was sparked by the hearings to debate the seating of Latter-day Saint apostle Reed Smoot as a U.S. senator between 1904 and 1907.[7] The sensational affair inspired numerous cartoons and films that built humor and critique on the visual gag of hyperbolic reproduction. In these satirical images of Mormons, cars lengthened, like stretch limousines, and were filled to the brim with wives and children.

Pocket watches had extended photograph lockets, which would accordion out to depict countless wives. Multitudes of women were portrayed encircling a single male figure, either as the henpecked husband or as the supreme sultan. And perhaps most telling, an image that combined Mormon modernity with traditional tropes of courtship and love featured cupid with a machine gun.[8]

As it did in political cartoons, the figure of polygamy in motion pictures effectively concentrated anxieties and hopes around the social project of modernity. Polygamy in film was the means by which one could filter out Mormons as un-American, "Turks," or otherwise foreign elements.[9] By the early twentieth century polygamy's specter seemed to preclude Latter-day Saints' ability to modernize and identify as upstanding white citizens, because, stretched to its humorous limit, polygamy signaled both factory-like sexual reproduction as well as an unmodern backward practice of strange religionists that might infect others.

If modern rationality and technology provided the means to combat the alien practice of polygamy, then film as the most modern of media could likely best represent and thematize this process as a narrative and visual entertainment. Disseminating and screening films should even instruct viewers how to recognize and prevent illicit trafficking. The medium of film was especially effective at conveying the modern significance of traffic, as the "accelerated circulation" of goods, peoples, technologies, and information, as Kristen Whissell has argued. Whissell has emphasized how "particularly modern" the "experience of being absorbed into traffic" was and how silent films, such as *Traffic in Souls* (1913), responded to and featured the same in the early twentieth century.[10] Because the figure of traffic "could simultaneously accommodate and bring into relief the old and the new, the modern and everything displaced by it," it was a loaded crystallization of modernity.[11] Extending Whissell's argument to consider Mormon-themed silent films reveals the power of cinema—as both material visual practice and moving narrative images—to sensationalize Mormon assimilation as a modern dilemma.

Mormonsploitation films engaged this salient feature of traffic by appropriating the conventions of white slave trade films and augmenting them with fears of being trafficked into a supposed Mormon system. The Mormon underground was represented as a counterfeit to the technological landscape of modern traffic that included automobiles, telegraphs, cinemas, trains, and commerce. This configuration allowed the films to play with notions of being forced into traffic with Mormons, as a conflation of modernity and cinema. This means the films' suspense often hinged on the promise and threat of becoming modern, which entailed living "within and by means of infrastructures" of connectivity.[12] Being connected always meant that malevolent users could hack those same networks to harm others. Conspiracy theories of a Mormon underground borrowed from and further developed the lexicon of white slave trade films to visualize the dangers of connectivity and being trafficked against one's will.

Like white slave trade films, the subgenre of Mormonsploitation films invited audiences to vicariously feel the thrill of abduction and incorporation into Mormon polygamous networks. Yet, the films also engaged a metaproject. They provided a screen to play out anxieties around Mormons and their perceived inability to fit into or become absorbed into modern traffic, as a national flow toward capitalist Christian ideals. In actuality, the films were thematizing the incompatibility of Mormonism just as Latter-day Saints were increasingly aligning themselves with mainstream Protestant American culture. As Thomas Simpson has traced, after the end of polygamy and "the dissolution of [the communal economic system], Mormons would gradually embrace capitalism, becoming more integrated into national markets and muting their separatism" beginning in the late nineteenth century.[13] Amy Hoyt and Sara Patterson have also shown how Latter-day Saints embraced the Boy Scouts of America and ramped up their patriotism around 1913, as they sought to fashion an ideal model of American masculinity. In fact, aside from their emphasis on priesthood power, Latter-day Saint men now "had much in common with the ideals of their white, middle-class, Protestant contemporaries."[14] However, the films often staged the nightmarish reverse. Rather than modernize and conform, screen Mormons would capture sympathetic protagonists and bring them into illicit systems of traffic—their alternative network of reproduction through polygamous marriages and multiplied childbirths.

In the films, polygamous traffic and reproduction were not represented as isolated perversions disconnected from modern life. They could be enabled by the very connectivity of the modern world and exploitation of its infrastructures. The practice of polygamy was understood to defy national laws and siphon from the gendered flow of information and goods. In this mode, Mormons were cast as vampires sucking the blood out of modern systems of exchange.[15] The bloodsucking effect—humanized in the motif of stolen daughters—was primarily the perceived inability of Mormons to work within the machine of modernity for the common good. Clearly taboo in its disavowal of traditional monogamous practices, polygamy was also represented as a network issue. The neoromantic vilification of Mormons was a means of capturing the dangerous flow of bodies and commerce, as a form of immoral and ethnically exotic traffic in the logic of modern systems. Because of this dilemma and film's inherent connections to modernity, the battle over the image of the Mormon Church was waged through the material distribution of film, as much as through images *on* film.

By casting the issue of "modern Mormonism" as an oxymoron, Mormonsploitation films probed the ramifications of a networked world in general and the place of Mormonism therein, in particular. Often with an alarmist tone, the films explored the communication technologies and practices connecting Mormons with the world by focusing on threatening fantasies of polygamists invading the entire world and preying on women. It is important to recognize, however, that the films were often just as interested in media and mobility as they were in religious rascals as glitches within the system. For this reason Mormonsploitation films made the connection between Mormons and modernity into a threatening dilemma by staging predators that dubiously interact with information storage and processing.

TRAFFIC AND INTEGRATION

With cinematic depictions of polygamy church leaders had to again disavow the flickering images and practices portrayed. In reshaping their public image church leaders were "striving by every possible means to work away from the old issue."[16] In business, politics, and cultural practices Latter-day Saints were ready to be in the world. Following Utah's statehood in 1896, the church dropped its emphasis on "group economic enterprise, sold most of its business properties, disbanded the People's party, and in general adopted a 'line' consistent with the dominant policies of the nation."[17] As Latter-day Saints negotiated mainstream America, they strove to maintain some sense of a distinct identity, but often in terms that would only enhance their sense of virile masculinity (through health codes, missionary work, and education) or feminine domesticity (through maternity and homemaking).[18] These emphases helped mold Mormons into ideal American citizens and tempered their perceived weirdness. Yet, the medium of cinema often brought the stranger elements back into distorted focus.

Most of the films engaging Mormonism "featured negative—often virulent—portrayals influenced by anti-Mormon traditions in stage melodrama, Victorian literature, and unsympathetic news accounts pandering to popular prejudices."[19] The films updated popular captivity narratives, only now Mormons were the captors, "in the place of the offending Indians and

Catholics" from earlier tales.[20] As Brian Q. Cannon and Jacob Olmstead have indicated, Latter-day Saints were increasingly troubled by the deleterious effect the "hostile depictions of the Church, its history, and its missionaries on the silver screen" had on their public image.[21] With the production of Mormon-themed silent films between 1911 and 1922, lifelike images of Mormonism were circulating without the church's approval or control.

Mormonsploitation films thematized the issue of assimilation by inhabiting their settings of exaggerated reproduction and networks of traffic, technology, and data with cinematic doubles of Mormons. Film images of Mormons spread their presence, but only to keep their assimilation at bay. In order to achieve this paradoxical effect, there is often a near geometric choreography of bodies and flows of information in the most popular examples of these films. Motion and traffic are captured in viciously seamless circuits, suggesting the dangerous but efficient nature of Mormon systems as eerie doubles to the traffic of modernity.

Technology in the hands of Mormons might mean strange but effective reproductions. The 1905 short film (possibly the earliest Mormonsploitation film) *A Trip to Salt Lake City* leveled comic critique at Latter-day Saint polygamy by playing with the "now you see it, now you don't" temporal epistemology of early cinema.[22] By choreographing the alternating appearance and disappearance of a multitude of wives and children from behind different curtains on a train, the film condensed the threat of perverse reproduction in a concise visual gag. The father arrives in the train cart and is soon bombarded with centripetal force from every direction by rambunctious children and busy wives. His eventual solution: installing a milk canister with multiple tubes to connect each wife's compartment. He networks them. A technological intervention tames the whole scene and updates the raucous familial arrangement. As if the sacred procreative powers of American monogamous marriage had run amok, the father's ability to reproduce on such a scale was a deliberate foil to modern mechanical reproduction in factory work and Taylorism. The introduction of a technology both moderates the scene and suggests the optimization of Mormon practices toward efficiency that might render them dangerously undetectable.

Mormon networking practices were also dangerous in that they reached outward. In film, Mormons were continually staged as vile tricksters who seduced, hypnotized, or otherwise overcame female victims with inexplicable power. Even as Latter-day Saints formally denounced polygamy in 1890 and sought to distance themselves from its image, they focused on missionary work and sending their remade American men out to gain converts. This left their efforts at proselytizing open to distortion. Whatever their gospel messages were, silent films most often turned Latter-day Saints into masters of mesmerist mind control and a whole system of targeting, abducting, and converting victims to become captive Mormons. And this could be accelerated through technological proximity to others, through networks of connection.

Because Latter-day Saints were already connected to the larger world, the trope of contagion and traffic was clearly wrapped up with fears of backward Mormon systems being preached and extended beyond Utah. A telling advertisement for the American film *A Mormon Maid* (1917) promised "big scenes" that "electrify with excitement," and another featured the hypnotic command "buy a Mormon Maid" as an electrified and humming message on the connective communication wires of the nation.[23] Those very wires were also an index of Utah's infrastructural network, which literally linked it to the rest of the nation. In 1897 Lucien Nunn set up the world's largest alternating current transmission system in Utah. In 1899 Utah's streetcar system was electrified and extended, and by 1913 eighteen power companies had merged into Utah Power and Light, putting Utah on course to become one of the most electrified of all western states.[24] Beyond its "first-class electric street railway system" and electric lights, Utah boasted a robust tourist network by the earliest years of the twentieth century.[25] Playing off the threat of sharing electricity with Mormons, *Maid* took up more than the national network its ads promised. The film visualized circulation and traffic on a formal level, by featuring the editing and choreography of bodies that cycle between frames as much as circulate between networks.

At a turning point in the narrative a family of local settlers, the Hogues, are forced to decide between the "the menace of the plains" (Native Americans) or the nearby, but suspect, Mormons. As the Native Americans literally circle the family's home on horseback—creating a visual metaphor of circulation—the Hogues face quite a dilemma. Will they be integrated into what they view as the "savage" network of Indians or into the perceived backward network of Mormons? In which way will they be trafficked? They ultimately decide to go with the Mormons, even though "no tell-bearer escapes" the Mormons' complete control over the flow of information in and out of their community as an intertitle informs the audience. The trope of forced incorporation into the Mormon system allowed the film to project the experience of modernity—as the experience of atomization in masses and being integrated into traffic—onto the past in the most modern of mediums, but couched in historical drag.

Despite being set in the 1840s, *A Mormon Maid* clearly spoke to present national concerns in 1917. Judith Weisenfeld has argued for the film's broader significance and persuasively shown how it "contributed to visions of national belonging that exceeded the concerns of anti-Mormonism" and built on D. W. Griffith's work.[26] Weisenfeld recounts Latter-day Saints' enthusiastic reception of Griffith's *Birth of a Nation* and the uncomfortable but pervasive links "the film's distributors, exhibitors, and critics drew between *Birth of a Nation* and *A Mormon Maid*" two years later, in order to reveal the films' shared reliance on "the construction of white racial innocence and inherent white female virtue."[27] It was the very circulation and violation of this gendered and racial innocence on-screen that helped shape visions of who belonged in America.

Similar tropes guided the success of the 1922 British film *Trapped by the Mormons*. The film opens with a Mormon elder looking directly into the camera with his mesmeric powers, suggesting that we as an audience might just be hypnotized while viewing. The conventional framing of the hypnotic eyes of the antagonist through an uneasy close-up in *Trapped by the Mormons* divulged a most popular subject of silent cinema: crime and the power of suggestion.[28] Combining popular conventions of cinema with the threatening image of Mormons, the film follows the elder as he trains his powers on female victims, who are hypnotized and led into conversion and polygamy as a form of white slavery. The medusa-like threat of Mormon vision was a recurring theme in Mormonsploitation films, but in *Trapped by the Mormons* it catalyzes the entire narrative and is even turned on the audience. As the film suggested, merely looking at Mormons—in movies or in real life—was a thrilling and dangerous act.

Beyond immediate control through hypnotism, a supplementary means of disseminating information and luring victims in *Trapped* comes through pamphlets. They both support and spread the criminal activities of the hypnotic Mormon vampires. The pernicious pamphlets in the diegetic world of the film were even doubled with sly marketing that put scandalous pamphlets into the hands of audience members. One such text reported how modern Mormonism was the same "crude" religion as in the days of Joseph Smith, only their tactics had been updated to "direct the power of their rich Church, to legalizing polygamy in Salt Lake City and instituting it throughout the world."[29] The brochure promised cinematic depictions of "unholy rites," "secrets of the temple," and "the 'sealing' orgy." Unfolding the cover revealed an illustration of a six-armed Mormon man with a woman in each hand, but the verso went further. The other side of the brochure literally folded out to reveal an image of women "trapped" within the folds of the paper and coerced into baptism in a still frame taken from the film. The kneeling woman in white

W. J. MACKAY

who will graphically describe the
thrilling dramatic features in
this wonderful film.

A Pyramid Picture

STAHL PYRAMID FILMS
LTD.
130 WARDOUR ST., W.1

THE HONOUR OF OUR
WOMANHOOD IS AT
STAKE

SHALL ENGLISH GIRLS
BE WHITE SLAVES——
TO MORMONS ?

BROKEN HEARTS AND
BROKEN LIVES

**TRAPPED
BY THE
MORMONS**

THE MORMON
TRAP
FROM WHICH THERE IS
NO ESCAPE

Unholy Rites in Salt Lake City

WOMAN PIERCES THE
SECRETS OF THE
TEMPLE

"SEALING" ORGY

MISSION OF WARNING
TO ENGLISH GIRLS

"I wish to state to the people of this country
that Mormonism as it exists to-day and as I
personally saw it in Salt Lake City is the same
crude, revolting, polytheist, polygamous religion that
it was in the days of the notorious Joseph Smith."

This statement was made to a "Daily Express"
representative recently by Miss Ada Shephard, a
Baptist missionary, who has recently returned to
London after eleven years' sojourn in Salt Lake City.

"Mormonism," continued Miss Shephard,
"has simply taken on a veneer of Christianity
within the last years. The Mormons still worship a
polygamous god, practise polygamy, and, though
they dare not openly advocate a plurality of wives,
glorify it as a divine revelation, and direct the power
of their rich Church to legalising polygamy in Salt
Lake City and instituting it throughout the world."

THE BAPTISM OF A GIRL VICTIM
A Fate Worse than Death.

See—
THE STORY OF THE MORAL
LEPERS OF SALT LAKE CITY

THE SEALING ORGY
THE FAKE MIRACLE
Mormonism
SOUL POISON
Oily Tongues—Vile Intentions

HOME WRECKED BY THE MORMONS

Wife and four girls
lured to White Slavery

Agonised Husband

FATE THAT WAS
WORSE THAN DEATH

"Daily Express' Special Correspondent.

SOUTHAMPTON, Sunday

"Mormonism has wrecked my
happiness and ruined my home."

This tragic declaration was made to me by Mr.
William Jenkins, of Bridges Road, Southampton.

Mr. Jenkins nine years ago was a prosperous
business man with a happy home, a wife and four
daughters. Mormonism robbed him of his wife and
four daughters, broke up his home, and threw him on
the world a grief-stricken and broken-hearted man.

Mr. Jenkins told me how the sinister, snaky
influence of Mormonism personified in the specious
sleek youths from Utah first threw its shadow over
his home.

Pages from *Broken Hearts and Broken Lives: Trapped
by the Mormons*, pamphlet, February 13, 1922.
Church History Library, Salt Lake City, Utah.

surrounded by standing men in all black captured the imagined "baptism of a girl victim," forced into "a fate worse than death." The full experience of *Trapped* included the deft use of both old and new media to render Mormons as vampiric villains adept at abduction and necessitating cinematic instruction on how to avoid their vision and control.

Latter-day Saints appeared as a threatening network of slave traffickers, even after the release of *One Hundred Years* sought to control their image. But the initial blueprint for the feature-length treatment of the Mormon threat first appeared in 1911. The issue of dubious doubles was brought to the fore when Nordisk Film released the motion picture *Mormonens Offer* or *Victim of the Mormons* in 1911, first in Denmark and England. Denmark had been a pioneer in making the international concerns over white slave trade into a cinematic experience with "titillating visualizations of such forbidden spaces as the brothel and the criminal underworld."[30] They were able to couch such sensations in social education and political activism, allowing the sensationally libelous film to feign being born of noble intentions. The programs for *Victim of the Mormons* in England called Mormons "vampires" and stressed the film's social value.[31] The language echoed attacks in print from the British author Winifred Graham, who once expressed just how "thrilling" she had found it "to fight with voice and pen" the Latter-day Saint "kingdom working for self-interest, a vampire in fact, sucking the blood of Europe with its wolf-like emissaries in sheep's clothing hot on the heels of British womanhood."[32] As in the cinematic portrayals, the church was depicted in Graham's work as a system that circumvented laws and was therefore threatening in an illegal and outdated way. The fictitious Mormon doubles were not properly networked into the system of modernity. The film *Victim of the Mormons* might have suggested the "social ambivalence about the competence of women to make responsible, respectable life choices," for Danish audiences, as Julie Allen has suggested. But it certainly also exploited Mormon figures as predatory villains in order to make the promise and threat of modern networks into a cinematic thrill that worked internationally.[33]

The vampiric threat of lawless Mormons was easily translated into the existing cinematic tropes of hypnosis and underground human trafficking. The first ten minutes of *Victim of the Mormons* shows Nina, the white female victim, constantly averting her gaze and avoiding eye contact with the relentless Mormon elder Larson. It is only once she begins looking directly into his eyes in the film's first close-up that he is able to take control of her. This was especially effective, because as Stefan Andriopoulos has shown, theories of hypnotism were closely connected to advertisement strategies and psychology, but also the medium of film itself.[34] Like the feared antics of Mormons, film was understood to trick the mind, as it "forces itself on every spectator," to see motion where there is none, as Hugo Münsterberg stressed in 1916.[35] Mormons were just another one of these manipulative forces that might subtly overtake unsuspecting viewers. Audiences, especially white women, were supposed to learn from the screen how to become discerning enough to recognize the danger and root it out. This meant that Mormons-ploitation films, as colored by the white slave trade genre, contributed to the kind of "contraceptive nationalism" Megan Goodwin has located in later films that demonized minority religions and privileged whiteness, "specifically white sexual innocence or purity allegorized as white womanhood."[36] Of course, Mormon hypnotic vision on film was trained only on white women. The sensational silent films might have targeted Mormons but only as foils to modernity and as a means to eroticize white suffering.

By 1913 the American smash hit *Traffic in Souls* further exploited the cultural fascination with the white slave trade that had been projected onto Mormonism in *Victim*. As Kristen Whissell recounts, around the release of *Traffic in Souls*, human traffickers were reportedly exploiting "a vast network of new technologies increasing in complexity and expansive in reach: the telephone, telegraph, automobile, steamship, railroad, and streetcar." *Victim of the Mormons* shared with *Traffic in Souls* an emphasis on the dangerous traffic of "immigration, transportation, commerce, prostitution, and mechanized communication," which helped to imagine and articulate the *experience* of technological modernity.[37] *Victim* had already embedded Mormon polygamy in the negatively charged figure of traffic. The film also flipped the role of technology. Rather than aiding and abetting the purported Mormon slave trade, technology provided the modern means of combating it.

The same infrastructure that connected Utah Mormons to the nation could thwart their perceived trafficking. In this sense, *Victim* staged the Mormon threat as a fight over the control of data across space and time. Unlike the storage capacity of film, the instantaneous telegraph communication in *Victim* promises the antidote to Mormon seduction and hypnotic control. *Victim* played on audience fears by unleashing scary Mormon abductors and having them narrowly escape several attempts to stymy their efforts through modern media, such as wireless telegraphy signals and automobile chases. This produced suspense through plot and editing and built on the gripping recent capture of wife murderer Hawley Crippen, who was caught by virtue of the telegraph that was quicker than his transatlantic escape in 1910.[38] An excerpt from an English newspaper published in the *Utah Independent* already made the connection to the international scandal explicit. It boasted that London's finest would hunt down any ill-behaving Mormon, and "if you don't believe what I say, send [a telegraph] message to Dr. Crippen and he will tell you all about it."[39] *Victim* simply repackaged the thrill of capturing a Mormon wife abductor through the instantaneous wireless, only to have him slip through the hands of the fallible human operator. A handbill for *Victim* titled the sensational scene "cutting the wires," wherein the Mormon missionary Elder Larson stops telegraph communication from blowing his cover by using the machine's wires to bind the operator to his chair.

The film foregrounded the role of infrastructure and technology in the human trafficking scare by linking them with the Mormon menace, which became a core trope in English and American writing against the Latter-day Saint church in the early twentieth century. Mormonism even became enmeshed in parliamentary debates on how to best deal with the issue in England.[40] In response, Latter-day Saints denounced the film and hoped to mitigate its influence. Leaders of the Church of Jesus Christ of Latter-day Saints were emphatic about their innocence: the church was never involved in any prostitution rings or human trafficking. In the face of denigrating charges catalyzed during the Reed Smoot hearings, church leaders published an open letter in which they, among other things, invited "enlightened investigation" and refuted charges of duping converts or trafficking in souls.[41] But popular representations of Mormons were spreading across the globe, presenting their image otherwise.

DEFAMATORY DOUBLES

In the age of mechanical reproduction, pictures, sounds, and representations of people could spiral out of their control. The ability to create "phantasms of the living" multiplied the presence of disembodied doppelgängers.[42] The discourse network of 1900—with its phonographs and cameras—only increased the means and realistic quality of this effect and more closely connected it with raising the dead. Technologically resurrected and made present, these doubles, replicas, and stand-ins posed new threats to the management of identity and image control. It was soon clear that in the twentieth century, your image—whether your own creation or that of others—could be acted on and consumed by an anonymous mass of others. A similar sense of haunting had suffused the experience of the nineteenth century through industrialization, urbanization, and technologies of reproduction but took on new urgency with portable cameras and an expanding film industry.[43] The most direct reactions to the threat were the creation of new copyright and privacy laws during the early twentieth century and an increased attention to self-fashioning.[44] Struggles in print over image control and defamation only gave verbal expression to the material effect of photographic media.

The cinematograph bound time, but its products also had eerie effects on space. The doppelgänger images or representations of oneself could inhabit multiple spaces at the same time. In this very modern sense, simultaneity was at issue with media that were so readily reproducible. Because of the proliferation of iconic representations on-screen, new debates flared up concerning identity and legality. The right to privacy became increasingly important for film actors, who needed to control the management and monetization of their image. But the Church of Jesus Christ of Latter-day Saints faced a similar threat as it underwent multiple popular and degrading representations during the first decades of cinema.

The inherent ability of the cinematic medium to faithfully render someone's moving likeness as well as multiply that image was itself a prevalent theme in early films. The trick of doubling and threatening images of the self were enjoyable shocks for audiences and generated an impressive spike in gothic figures on-screen. In 1912 *Dr. Jekyll and Mr. Hyde, My Double and How He Undid Me, The Breakdown,* and *His Other Self* all featured doppelgänger characters, and just a year later a remake of *Dr. Jekyll and Mr. Hyde* appeared. Several titles from Europe equally toyed with cinema's ability to double during the same period in film history, including *The Somnambulist's crime* (1909, U.K.), *Dobbeltgaengeren* (1910, Denmark), and a whole slew in Germany, including *Der Doppelgänger* (1909 and 1914) and *Der Student von Prag* (1913). In 1914, the German psychoanalyst Otto Rank wrote an entire monograph on the figure of the double in film and literature with extensive examples to draw from. The time was ripe for the cultural resonance and shocking cinematic effect of doubles, as well as for dealing with anxieties around discerning between originals and copies.

Although suspect of gothic or neoromantic aesthetics, Mormons fit nicely into the psychological issues broached with the figure of the doppelgänger. Doubling Mormons was an interesting prospect, especially because, as Rank wrote, doubles long "for a more exalted existence" and are often "unsure of their identity, are sometimes inhabitants of this earth and sometimes belong to some unearthly region."[45] Mormons too seemed to be ever present, yet not quite fit the modern world. The representations of Mormons dovetailed doubles and popular representations of underground traffic into conspiracy theories of Mormon networks of control and coercion. The Mormons on-screen were seen as dangerous doubles of Americans to national audiences and defamatory doubles of themselves to Latter-day Saint viewers.

Most cinematic representations of Mormonism were damaging the church's image. They were also a stain on the image of Utah, which could be bad for the economy. The Utah business community complained that *Victim of the Mormons* was "a libel on the state of Utah" and sought to have it banned.[46] In 1912, Governor William Spry "threatened to bar Mormon films in Utah" altogether.[47] Apostle Rudger Clawson lamented to the church's first presidency in 1911, "I presume it would be about as easy to inaugurate some method that would prevent the newspapers lying about us, as it would be to prevent these picture shows doing the same thing."[48] But images lied in a different way, and their effect was much more popular and experiential than pamphlet exposés and incendiary newspaper articles.

The popularization and accessibility of photography had increased in the 1880s with the products of Kodak, and they stoked issues around photorealistic representations and privacy. This multiplied possibilities for capturing the likeness of others and inspired countless would-be photographers and journalists. Running rampant and surfacing anywhere, cameras and photographic reproduction carried clear threats to personal space and the control one had over one's own image.[49] New anxieties echoed the tensions around the anatomy laws of the early nineteenth century, which were created to abate the prevalent fear that one's unclaimed body could be legally disinterred and used.[50] Public knowledge of scientific advancement and gothic stories seemed to proliferate new threats to private bodies, raising the question: does one have a right of ownership over one's own body, or the photographic likeness of oneself, once it is out of one's own control?

Conceptions of the right to privacy in the late nineteenth century revolved around legal protection of "private life," essentially determining that no one could intrude on "private property, confidential communications, and personal information."[51] Yet, the burgeoning legal measures taken to protect individuals still did not properly deal with new technologies of infringement on privacy and public image. On the heels of such technological concerns Samuel Warren and Louis Brandeis published their groundbreaking article "The Right to Privacy" in the *Harvard Law Review* in 1890.[52] Although previous legislation had "focused on an external relation between the individual and a community," Warren and Brandeis's article was cutting-edge in its insistence that, as Stephen Kern put it, "the law must recognize the legal status of the relation of an individual with himself."[53] Recording and reproducing devices of the late nineteenth century had fostered and required the updated mindset. New inventions like "photography and newspaper enterprise [had] invaded the 'sacred precincts' of private and domestic life."[54] Warren and Brandeis acknowledged that as "advances in the photographic art have rendered it possible to take pictures surreptitiously, the doctrines of contract and of trust are inadequate to support the required protection."[55] By the first decade of the twentieth century it was widely recognized that anyone who goes out in public "must also anticipate being photographed."[56]

In New York in 1902 the prospect was debated in the court of appeals. Without clear precedent the court recognized the arguments of Warren and Brandeis. They acknowledged that, as Lewis and McConnell put it, a "man has the right to pass through this world, if he wills, without having his picture published, his business enterprises discussed, his successful experiments written up for the benefit of others, or his eccentricities commented upon either in handbills, circulars, catalogues, periodicals or newspapers." Legislators were still feeling out the requisite amount of control. Certainly they could "interfere and arbitrarily provide that no one should be permitted for his own selfish purpose to use the picture or the name of another" without consent, but the move still seemed excessive to some.[57] In 1903 New York was the first state to pass legislation "making it a misdemeanor to use someone's photograph or picture for commercial purposes without first obtaining written consent."[58] Utah followed New York by instituting its own statute on privacy and image use in 1909.[59]

The legal right to control one's image and its circulation was connected to a broader focus on public image, and especially the visual duplication of such. The media landscape of the early twentieth century made visual representation more powerful, present, and contested. The intensification of film, photography, "and the modern 'image industries'—fashion, cosmetics, and advertising, among them—also compelled people to strive to manipulate and perfect their public images." According to Samantha Barbas, "Americans of all backgrounds became not only highly concerned about their images and social appearances, but possessive and protective of them."[60] Latter-day Saint concern with a new image revolved around old perceptions and new developments provoked by polygamy, the Reed Smoot hearings, and sensational films. During this period the church made several efforts to publish statements and defenses in the face of mounting criticism.[61]

The popularity and sensational depictions of *Victim of the Mormons* convinced the church to counteract the damage to their image and reputation by publishing a pamphlet in England and distributing it at screenings.[62] In the pamphlet, the apostle Rudger Clawson, who presided over the church's proselytizing efforts in Europe, expressed his frustration, stating, "We would like the public to know something concerning the weapons used against us in an unequal contest. But when the press is closed to us, we are in a sense most helpless," because, although the images were meant to be Mormons, the productions used fictitious names to protect them from "libel suits." He accused other reporters of attempting to "secure a renewed interest in a vile misrepresentation of a much maligned people, which would put pounds and pence into somebody's pocket." Clawson condemned *Victim of the Mormons* as a "base and cruel libel on the character and lives of the Latter-day Saints" with international influence.[63] In fact, it was at times the international image of Mormonism that was haunting and harming the religion's work to improve its national image.

By 1920 church president Heber J. Grant fully acknowledged the false image by quoting statements made in the U.S. Senate and from one of Winifred Graham's libelous articles in general conference. Grant recounted how Reed Smoot had denounced Graham's incendiary attacks before the Senate. Smoot had scoffed at the declaration that the Mormon Church had at that very moment "twelve hundred girls ready for shipment to Utah" and that it works "secretly" in England and America and "snaps its fingers at law in both countries."[64] Mormon men were, at this very time, cultivating an image of "ideal American citizens."[65] They were charged to obey the laws of the land and learning how to use them to their benefit. If the popular image of Mormonism was one of vampires subverting law, their shift toward legal protection over their image, as well as cultivating one of model Americans, marked a significant turning point in Mormon media practices.

SELF-PROJECTION

As it updated and sanitized their image, *One Hundred Years of Mormonism* adopted American techniques of filmmaking geared toward assimilation. Perhaps inevitably, in Mormonism's attempt to use film to enter modernity by warding off slanderous doubles and controlling their image, they projected themselves as wholly American, white, and victims who emerge victorious. For film was forming a new alternative public sphere where style was often wrapped up with social hierarchy. Even as silent film fostered a diverse audience and brought in immigrant, women, and working-class audiences, it generally instructed them how to act and appear as model Americans. Because movie stars and filmmakers where overwhelmingly white, films taught audiences what kinds of behaviors deserved attention, but also what kinds of bodies ran the industry itself. In its visual filtering between heroes and villains and creators and consumers, silent film offered new possibilities for integrating Mormons and ironing out their race and religion.

From cinema's earliest years, "social Darwinian and eugenics paradigms dominated the meaning of race" and endorsed "the notion of a natural hierarchy of human cultures and histories" as something visual.[66] Coupling aspirations for whiteness with eugenicist thought, Latter-day Saint rhetoric in general conference in 1913 addressed the "melting pot" of America with a hope of perfecting the covenant races of northern Europe now mixed within. Apostle Charles Penrose cautioned listeners not to take it too far, but he praised "the science of eugenics" and its promise to increase life expectancy by bringing forth a superior generation, both spiritually and physically.[67] At the same conference, mission president Melvin J. Ballard proclaimed how "the Lord intends to make this people not only a people intellectual, but a people the physical superiors of any men who have lived upon the earth." Part of the key to this racial superiority was understood to be achieved through pioneer persecutions and sacrifice, like those staged in *One Hundred Years*, which was screening in theaters at the time of Ballard's statement. As Ballard clarified, "In making the sacrifices that our parents did, they were laying the foundation for physical health of manhood and womanhood that shall ultimately produce a perfect race."[68] In flawed logic inflected by eugenicist thought, pioneer suffering on-screen could suggest racial refinement and frontier American identity.

The visual and hierarchical understanding of race is inseparable from American cinema, which was always the display and coconstruction of identities and values of whiteness, or "the garment center of white fabrication," in Gwendolyn Foster's phrasing.[69] In the early twentieth century, misguided racist classifications were welded with subtle cinematic techniques. Against racialized others, white Americans on-screen were often pure feminized victims and virile masculine protectors and victors. It was a vicious reality that the more Latter-day Saints appeased the nation and found belonging by refashioning themselves, the more they took on largely Protestant whiteness that signaled such privilege. This conundrum haunted later Mormon filmmaking as well but is central to their first official foray into film.

Although the medium could be generally inclusive for paying audiences, the effect of many films of the transitional era of 1908–17 was still quite exclusionary. These films forcefully justified the social exclusion of certain groups of people by visually establishing their danger and inferiority. Just as often silent film shored up and constructed whiteness as the default ideal of film stocks, lighting technologies, and American discourse visualized on-screen.

If race is, in Sylvester Johnson's formulation, "a state practice of ruling people within a political order that . . . privileges whites and whiteness, while governing non-white people as in American society, but not of it," then film was an archive of such a practice made visual and structural.[70] D. W. Griffith's early work for Biograph, for instance, often told "the story of the inability of non-whites to fully assimilate into white culture and society."[71] And these kinds of techniques exceeded racist depictions. As Alice Maurice has stressed, race's formative role should be understood "as a broader construct, a structuring principle and rhetorical tool in the development of early cinema" that went beyond stereotypical representations and influenced the very relationship between motion and stillness, as well as between narrative and spectacle.[72] Around the time of *One Hundred Years of Mormonism*, films often wanted to show off what the camera could do by showing off the threat and thrill of performing racialized difference.

Mormons did not want to be on the wrong side of film history and thus sought to combat the libelous representations of themselves. But with their first film, Latter-day Saints also had a clear agenda in establishing a vision of themselves as part of the larger narrative of the country, one that promoted their cinematic whiteness and American belonging. They put John Taylor's 1902 declaration, "to correct misrepresentation we adopt self-representation," into practice.[73] Joining in and embracing cinema allowed the church to better control its public image through conscious self-fashioning.[74] A San Francisco reporter astutely perceived the intention, writing, "It is the plan of the leaders of the church by showing films to offset other motion pictures which portray Mormonism and its leaders . . . in an unfavorable light."[75] Latter-day Saints could enter and even contribute to the newly emerging narrative, feature-length, and logic-driven cinema during the "most profound transformation in American film history."[76] In short, the film industry too was changing its public image.

It was an opportune time for Mormons to share their story as a moving picture. The expanding length of films and their increased emphasis on explication resulted "in a cinema of narrative integration and a gradual displacement of showing by telling."[77] This assimilation of scenes into a longer narrative structured a different film experience and lent itself to the performance of cultural ideals. It also shaped "the formation of a particular narrative system around 1908/1909" that "became closely intertwined with the idealization of domesticity" and the valuation of gender and race.[78]

Film was then increasingly about sequence and visual storytelling, and Latter-day Saints wanted to tell a new story about themselves, especially since their disavowal of polygamy. They fashioned themselves as increasingly in step with mainstream American ideals, and this transformation also made them eager to take full advantage of cinema's new focus on logic, story, and domesticity to produce their own images of Mormonism to shape public perception. Minutes from a June 30, 1910, meeting of the first presidency and quorum of the twelve apostles record President Joseph F. Smith informing the others present that "a man named Hutchison" had proposed to him the "idea of illustrating the chief points in the history of the Church by means of moving pictures." The council decided that it should "co-operate with Mr. Hutchison and that a committee if necessary be appointed to work with him to the end mentioned."[79]

Despite its clear agenda, the film's production history was bumpy. As Randy Astle has detailed, in June 1912 Latter-day Saint leaders "struck a deal with the local Ellaye Motion Picture Company," which had been formed specifically for this project, "to make a huge film telling the church's full history."[80] But within four months Ellaye had broken its contract, and the Latter-day Saint church turned to another production company, Utah Moving Picture Company. Similar adjustments affected the writing. Although it was originally planned that "five men" who had "made a thorough study of Mormon history" would script the film, the young female filmmaker and actor Nell Shipman was eventually hired to write the scenario, and Norval MacGregor directed.[81] The two had worked together in the same capacities with what was possibly Shipman's first film, *The Ball of Yarn*, earlier that same year.[82] Following their work in collaboration with church leaders, *One Hundred Years of Mormonism* premiered at about ninety minutes in length to a select audience in Salt Lake City on February 3, 1913. The production received a "commendation" from President Joseph F. Smith, who was in attendance.[83] Audiences broke into spontaneous applause at the sight of the angel Moroni's appearances, and screenings were scheduled for the next several months.[84] Marketed as "exclusively sanctioned by the Mormon church" and as "the greatest 6,000 feet of reel ever produced depicting an historical sacred and secular story," *One Hundred Years* marked the birth of Mormon cinema and a rebirth of the Mormon image.[85]

Along with its spectacular thrills, *One Hundred Years* plugged Mormons into the network of film traffic and told a new story of an American religion. It was one of the earliest feature-length films in America, but *One Hundred Years* was also the first theatrical film of its length released by a church altogether.[86] That same year the Presbyterian Board of Publications entered a contract with Edison Company to produce a series of religious films.[87] The very next year the Catholic Church allowed the release of a short documentary, *Pope Pius and the Vatican*, and the Federal Council of Churches of Christ published the book *Motion Pictures in Religious Education Work* in 1916.[88] Although religious leaders slowly began acknowledging the potential of actualities to educate their congregants, it was still uncommon for a religion to adopt film as a product sent into the world or to do so with such aspirations for record-setting grandeur.

In order to reach audiences and portray an authentic image of Mormonism, *One Hundred Years* "penetrated farther into the actual life and history of the 'Mormon' people than ha[d] any creed or government."[89] This fresh capacity to animate the church's history from books, paintings, and panoramas into film coincided with "the organization of human sense perception and its transformation in the industrial-capitalist modernity."[90] Cinema was the telos of technological developments that had spread the gospel message. It was Levi Young's optimistic estimation that *One Hundred Years* revealed how "modern invention" and the "gospel" were working together to spread truth and sympathy.[91] In light of the film's premiere, the *Deseret News* celebrated the inventions that had helped network the church, praising how "the railroad, the telegraph, and now the wireless means of communication, all have made it possible for the people of the world" to learn of Mormonism. And now *One Hundred Years* could take full advantage of the infrastructural connectivity, because a motion picture was the great democratizer that spread images, knowledge, and experience in many places simultaneously, reaching those "where the word, both spoken and written would fail."[92]

The film put images of the church's past into motion again, but in a novel way. Much like the panorama work of Philo Dibble and C. C. A. Christensen, *One Hundred Years of Mormonism* shared a pedagogical vision of church history. It used Smith's spectacular vision and a particular view of Mormon history to direct and discipline understandings of Mormonism. This time rather than approximating a moving view—where the experience is closer to that of a traveler witnessing scenes, as if on a train speeding by—the figures in the frame actually moved, through persistence of vision, while audiences sat in darkened nickelodeon theaters. Despite the controversy around persistence of vision as an explanation for motion in films, it provides an apt metaphor for the work of *One Hundred Years*, which updated past images of Mormonism and combined them into a seemingly whole and wholesome vision of the Latter-day Saints. This means the cinematic experience of motion in *One Hundred Years* came from shots of bodies moving within and across a still frame that showed something of the "rise" and movement of Mormons into American enfranchisement.

Although panorama could effectively consolidate vision, movement in film signaled Mormon ascendancy and vitality in ways the panorama could not. In order to achieve this the film eschewed any reference to polygamy and focused on the persecution and frontier struggle of Mormons migrating west and becoming industrious and resilient. By taking full advantage of their infrastructural connection to modernity Latter-day Saints hoped to—in good faith—establish a noble alternative to their portrayal in *Victim* and *Trapped*. They wanted to extend their vision onto the world and train others how to see them properly. It just so happened the vision they peddled was wholly white and American. For urban audiences, Mormonism could finally look modern and fit on-screen as an American story of piety and resilience instead of predation and deviance. Because film "articulated, multiplied, and globalized a particular historical experience" Mormon efforts to show their history could fit their once "backward" ways into praiseworthy modern views.[93]

In John Henry Evans's book *One Hundred Years of Mormonism* (1905), on which the film was based, some of the scenes, including Smith's visions of angels, were said to be simply "beyond description."[94] Yet, on film Smith's visions could finally be rendered photo-realistically and stored for worldwide projection. Double exposure provided the most modern and perhaps the most fitting solution, as it allowed Mormon vision to materialize before the audience's very eyes. Rather than further illustrate David Walker's insight into cinematic satire as the most appropriate to winkingly portray Latter-day Saint history, the technique of double exposure in a history film presented an alternative strategy.[95] Double exposure grounded the affect and effect of (dis)belief in a material technological practice. It made the strangest elements of Mormonism—aside from the ignored element of polygamy—simply appear within American history.

As if they belonged or had always just been there, Smith's visions were now integrated and recorded as scenes from the nation's past. This was still a novel technique for a history film. As early as 1898, the short film *Corsican Brothers* used double exposure to represent ghosts and visions, and the effect spread through early trick films, but not as the staged materialization of what were understood by some to be *actual* historical specters. As the previous chapter outlined, photography still retained certain "links to the occult through spirit photography"; cinema, however, "was a definitively anti-spiritualist medium that was never understood in ontological connection to the paranormal, despite occasional efforts to involve cinema in psychical research."[96] Cinematic ghosts were not hyped as actualities like photographs were. Moroni's spectral appearance then was a powerful blend of the supernatural and the staged. The optical trick literally portrayed a "fissured space" that allowed staged "visitors from another dimension" to share the screen with natural bodies, like Smith's.[97] Where the angel's opacity fluctuates this only underscores the full presence of Smith's solid body and his legible face covered in white makeup. Obviously, viewers knew this was meant to be a fictionalized portrayal of what was believed by Latter-day Saints to be an "actual event." The integration of Mormonism into modern media through *One Hundred Years*, as a history film, allowed viewers "to be fooled and at the same time nobody's fools, to oscillate, swing from knowledge to belief, from distance to adhesion, from criticism to fascination."[98]

Trick photography was only part of the record-breaking production of *One Hundred Years*. The film's epic production participated in, while helping to shape, the burgeoning fashion of feature-length historical films. This effect helped universalize the film's appeal as a huge American production meant for the whole world. Precisely the superlative language that framed the historic production of *One Hundred Years* (six reels) accompanied the descriptions of other contemporary international historical hits. The genre had its origins in the acclaimed Italian spectacles, such as *Dante's Inferno* (1909, five reels), *Fall of Troy* (1910, two reels), and *The Crusaders* (1911, four reels), which whetted American appetites for spectacle incorporated into extended narratives.[99] The blockbuster *Quo Vadis* was released in Italy in the fall of 1912 but played in the spring of 1913 throughout America, and at nine reels long and with 5,000 extras it thoroughly impressed audiences and critics. *Last Days of Pompei* (1913) was released the same year, and then *Cabiria* (1914) outshined them all. The longer films not only displaced one-reelers as the standard product of the film industry, but they had aspirations of respectability.[100] Their attention to set design, cinematography, and marketing helped such films leverage highbrow theatrical trappings and gain social capital. These developments invited the superlative language that helped shepherd the medium's ascendancy in both European and American contexts.[101]

The rise of history films was due in part to their relationship to research and nineteenth-century historicism. This implied that *One Hundred Years of Mormonism*'s vision of the past was authentic. The film's purported material accuracy and marketing claims flaunted its commitment to historical fidelity. In detailing the production process of *One Hundred Years*, it was accordingly noted that "it took months of time and labor to get the true historical value, data and detail." These efforts included "hundreds of horses, oxen, Indians, 'prairie schooners,' mobs and militia" and "fifty thousand dollars" to realize the most accurate and affective portrayal of the Mormon past to date.[102]

Authenticity also came with the control over production. By enlisting surviving members of the original pioneer trek across the plains, the film effectively archived the bodies of those who had actually traversed the terrain. And these individuals were able to see themselves as the stars of an epic feature film.[103] Brigham Young's grandson Frank Young even played the role of his grandfather in the film. Onlookers who caught the filming of a scene of the 1838 "Haun's Mill massacre" of Mormons in Missouri, which ended in enormous flames, were baffled by the spectacle. Thousands clamored together in automobiles and filled a nearby ranch to witness an entire constructed street of buildings burn to the ground. The witnesses "seemed to lose the fact of its being simply a 'picture act' and stood in awed silence until the last house had fallen in."[104] Precisely these kinds of commitments to spectacle were meant to make the film an authentic experience.

The film screened in the New York Theater, "devoted exclusively" to the new development of "feature films," alongside *Last Days of Pompeii, Sapho, Tess of the D'Urbervilles*, and *Monte Cristo*.[105] Typical superlatives colored the report that the companies had paid the "highest price ever agreed upon" to secure the film for screening. At six reels long, *One Hundred Years* was "acknowledged to be the largest in the world" and one of the first feature-length films made in America, as well as a bold first step for Latter-day Saints.[106]

Most importantly the film's narrative and special effects divulged Mormonism's newest means of entering sacred time, since dropping the practice of polygamy, which had connected them to celestial practices. In Jan Shipps's reading, postmanifesto Latter-day Saints could recover some sense of "sacred time" by visiting certain spaces, such as temples, or engaging in rituals.[107] But Peter Coviello's development of Shipps's argument sharpens our appreciation of *One Hundred Years*. For, as Coviello maintains, retelling history itself—from "Smith's revelations" and "years of dire persecution" to the "colonization of the West" and survival after multiple threats—is how Mormons reenter sacred time. In fact, *One Hundred Years* might be best understood as showcasing the newly adopted conviction that "the destiny of sacred time is American belonging."[108] Turning to the past and staging it as a special effect of becoming American was in some measure the compensatory conflation of sacred history with patriotism.

CINEMATIC SENSATIONS

The cinematic rendering of Mormon history was momentous and meant to be overwhelming. Early advertisements with large publicity photographs from the set ran in the *Deseret Evening News* and primed audiences.[109] A description promised "the most thrilling and sensational picture film ever produced."[110] As an exceptional film that would be historical in its unprecedented grandeur, the film was meant to touch audiences beyond the members of the church. By taking on the burgeoning trappings of epic historical filmmaking, the film could appeal to an international and modern audience. The film would depict "the beginning, early struggles, romance, industry and growth of the 'Mormon' people, from New York State to Salt Lake City."[111] And this historical representation would not only bring Mormon producers into business deals but also integrate "authentic" Mormon images into the traffic of film reels. Through sensations, film could share a Mormon vision of their past that viewers, the world over, could experience and accept.[112]

In Connecticut, the local paper reported how the film sought to turn from the "mysticism" around Mormonism to focus on the "struggles, loves, tortures and assassination of Mormon people" with "realism" instead.[113] In the author's estimation, only the modern medium of motion pictures could properly capture the "persecution" of being "driven from place to place across the American continent," all of which was said to be "confirmed by American history."[114] For, if nothing else *One Hundred Years* was the emotional story of America itself—a people moving from religious persecution to a promised land, where they find prosperity. In this regard, *One Hundred Years* was clearly productive, as it implied the role of Latter-day Saints in expanding the frontier and transforming the West from "Indian savagery to white civilization," as they displaced Native populations.[115]

Along with shaping the geography, the story of performing American belonging entailed navigating racial constructions. By treating the imbrication of Progressive Era reform, scientific theories, and Mormon racial prescriptions, Cassandra Clark has turned a useful lens to this time period to tease out the "construction of race in America," as Latter-day Saints sought to deracialize themselves and construct their whiteness.[116] This was particularly charged, because, as Paul Reeve has shown, Mormons in Utah were for a long period imagined as not white but instead as hailing from some ambiguous but "backward racial descent."[117] Rhetoric during the Reed Smoot hearings had compared the Mormon threat with that of African Americans. "Negro domination in the south" would be like "the political control of Mormon hierarchy" over non-Mormons, insisted Idaho senator Frederick T. Dubois.[118] Thus realizing their racial metamorphosis and finding belonging was an uneven and multifaceted process. Mormonism distanced itself from racialized bodies by joining in the performance of American patriotism and by shedding any ethnic markers. Film was one wholly modern mechanism for enacting these very shifts through historical reenactment as new Mormon optics.

To help facilitate and discipline the proper reception of the film, lecturers accompanied the screenings. Norval McGregor performed the role in Los Angeles, William Colvin in San Francisco, and Levi Young in Salt Lake City.[119] Although onstage film lecturers had generally decreased in popularity around 1908, their renewed presence helped signal for *One Hundred Years* "claims asserting the educational value of the medium, in keeping with a middle-class discourse of uplift."[120] It was in the church's best interest to frame the film as uplifting and religious. Large cities, like New York, had recently given more freedom to uplifting films even allowing them to be screened on Sundays, if they were "illustrating lectures of an instructional or educational character."[121] The debates around Sunday entertainment and social reform helped establish certain motion pictures, with moral lessons and happy endings, as "harmless amusement" and "sacred or educational."[122] While a burden for many filmmakers, the reform initiatives proved more inviting for Latter-day Saint purposes and congruent with their conceptions of the medium to educate the public and share a particular vision of Mormonism. Producing an accurate and dramatic history film as social reform and uplift—even for the "poorest and most lowly people," as Levi Young wrote—also positioned Mormons in the role of white, middle-class reformers.[123] In the public sphere Latter-day Saints might now uplift and educate, but on-screen they were first victims.

Most of the sensations of *One Hundred Years* clearly came from witnessing the persecution and struggles of the Latter-day Saints. Now it was their opportunity to cast themselves as the white bodies tortured and persecuted by strange others, a move that would imply their Americanness within cinema. Although only a few scenes are extant, still frames and descriptions of the lost film published in newspapers, along with the book on which it was based, make the film's focus clear. Beyond the custom of literally covering their faces in white makeup, actors in *One Hundred Years* conformed to the widespread practice of "whiteface," or the "performing of whiteness in a way that traces of ethnicity are erased" in American films.[124] Figured as white and heroic, the Mormon screen figures were also subject to victimization at the hands of unscrupulous others. The binary conformed to American film logic, and *One Hundred Years* is, accordingly, structured around the historical events of persecution.

Smith's family being attacked by outsiders serves as the beginning point for the film's cycle of suffering. With sensational detail the film depicts when

Smith was tarred and feathered while his wife and children dressed in white nightgowns huddle together safely inside the sanctuary of their home. At this point in the film audiences had already shared Smith's miraculous vision and seen him sympathetically portrayed as a paragon of white American masculinity. The book too had described Smith as handsome, strong, and a gentleman. Even his "complexion was one of transparency so rare as to be remarkable; the exquisite clearness of his skin was never clouded. . . . His carriage was erect and graceful."[125] His portrayal is an early example of what Brenda Weber refers to as the "Mormon glow," signifying clean living and righteousness.[126] But the idealized Smith is eventually murdered by a mob with blackened "painted faces" as they storm his jail cell in Carthage, Illinois.[127] Then the unjust persecution extends from Smith's body to the larger body of Latter-day Saints.

The film shows how the migrating Latter-day Saints are later attacked by a mob "made up as Indians."[128] As the book had claimed, "Companies of Saints suffered from the depredations of the Indians," when "large bands of these wild people would" create stampedes or otherwise pester the Mormons.[129] The focus and cinematic portrayal seems to have served to make Latter-day Saints victims of strange others, rather than indict the white, especially American, audience members they hoped would view the film. Cinematic histories could now perpetuate racist hierarchies in visual conventions of victimization and triumph. Of course, only two years later Griffith's *Birth of a Nation* radicalized the template with a directly racist instrumentalization of cinema. As legend has it, even President Woodrow Wilson reportedly conceded that now (white supremacist) history could be written with lightning.[130]

While it was apparent in 1910 that "the moving picture show [was] becoming the country's greatest educator in literature and history," it generally taught one view of history.[131] In some ways it did this more persuasively than previous media had. The *Deseret News* noted how "the days of the Prophet Joseph Smith and his devoted followers were known only to our parents, fathers and grandparents. We have the story from their lips, and we have felt the sorrows only in tender sympathy of those who so faithfully laid the foundations of the great work." But reading or hearing retellings of the church's history only aroused interest and "a desire to see those days ourselves," which could now be realized through the opportunity "of having these days return through the medium of the moving picture which either has or will, depict every phase of the west."[132] The commentary revealed the promise of the medium as well as its ability, in America, to make the Mormon story just one of "every phase of the west"—to integrate their story into the larger history of the nation. This was precisely what Latter-day Saints hoped motion pictures could do: visually capture and enact their transformation into good Americans.

Whereas the motion of bodies in Mormonsploitation films thematized threatening networks and traffic, *One Hundred Years* recreated the literal movement of Mormons across the country as the metaphorical movement of Mormons into the nation. Where the former were circular systems of abduction and trafficking, the latter showed a linear movement of Mormons into prosperity and national belonging. The pioneer trek originally enacted to leave the United States in 1847 and to isolate was now reenacted on film to enter the nation and integrate Mormonism into the modern network of mainstream American life. As the film's production sought to mirror the history being depicted, it was reported that "ten states [were] traversed" and "over 1000 people enacted the roles played by their ancestors." Perhaps most importantly, "that acme of modern science—the moving picture camera, faithfully recorded every step of the pilgrimage."[133] This was real history being performed to refashion modern Mormons.

Movement horizontally across the country was meant as movement vertically, as social climbing and acceptance. By "following" them across the plains, through multiple shots and edits, the film—as was representative of early narrative filmmaking—creates continuity and narrative logic. Motion is captured within and between shots, and the general idea of motion, as Mormons on the rise, is central to the film's logic, structure, and purpose. Rather than scenes slapped together, this was a deliberate "history" of overcoming victimization, as the linearization of cinema and Latter-day Saint belonging.

Pioneer citizens who overcame persecution narratively extend from Joseph Smith's prophetic vision into frontier industry and prosperity. By framing Smith's vision and the westward migration within an educational history film for public display, Latter-day Saints bolstered their own cultural enfranchisement. The film's motion is, like the double exposures, the gradual appearance and movement of Mormonism into modernity and mainstream America. As Latter-day Saints translated their vision of history into an American film, they also structured themselves as modern white Americans.

CONCLUSION

Orders for *One Hundred Years of Mormonism* were reportedly received from "London, Berlin, Paris, Rome, St. Petersburg, Montreal, Buenos Ayres, Pekin, Calcutta, and Sydney, Australia, besides all the principal cities of the United

States."[134] The film corporation Pan-American obtained "world rights" and advertised the film for rent as an "exciting historical revelation of Joseph Smith, Brigham Young and their people during one hundred years of American history."[135] The spectacular display, including trick appearances of specters as "historical revelation," was all billed as another part of "American history." The tagline captured the film's effect of incorporating the Mormon past into an American historical narrative. As the motion picture was sold, shipped, and screened, new images of Mormons were cohabitating space and time with their threatening doubles. But the addition of the film *One Hundred Years of Mormonism* into American history marked the church's entry into the shared system of modernity and (inter)national commerce of ideas, images, and influence. Much like the medium of film itself, which synthetically gathers together "discontinuous times" and "discontiguous spaces" into a coherent cinematic body, the Mormon visionary past was gathered in and screened as part of the international cinematic traffic.[136]

Not only had Mormonism forced its place at the table, but perhaps most telling, its first film was explicitly billed as "impossible to duplicate." It was not merely the workforce and spectacle that was unreproducible; it was a legal restriction, due to "exclusive contracts."[137] Although antagonistic and salacious doubles of the church would continue to spawn and spread on celluloid for the next decade, *One Hundred Years of Mormonism*'s self-made representations could be trafficked but not duplicated. By doing their legal homework the producers of the film ensured the images would remain above the common and base practices of slander and demeaning duplication. As an advertisement for the film stated, "Attempts will no doubt be made to imitate this great feature film and spuriously exhibit it by unauthorized producers. . . . We desire to warn all concerned that we are the only authorized producers of this subject, under contract with the Mormon Church, having access to Church archives, and backed by the assistance of Church officials. Any attempt to infringe will be vigorously prosecuted."[138] Although the film was networked and shared, no direct doppelgängers were possible.

One Hundred Years was meant to travel and disseminate a particular and authoritative vision of Mormonism. As Latter-day Saints sought to technologize this vision, they adopted the American style of filmmaking while helping shape its narrative hallmarks. Their entry into modernity as good American citizens implied a standard of whiteness and helped perform their belonging within modernity. By warding off the defamatory doubles of Mormonsploitation films and casting themselves as the wholesome victims of unruly others, Mormons had become cinematically American to audiences everywhere.

Cinematic Traffic

MICROMANAGING DEATH

The direct reproduction of the thing itself can be summoned to any
properly prepared spot. A microfilm, coloured where necessary,
occupying an inch or so of space and weighing little more than a
letter, can be duplicated from the records and sent anywhere.

H. G. Wells, 1938

With a world trembling on the brink of wholesale war and devastation,
there is every possibility that unless we act swiftly and decisively
the records of millions upon millions of our ancestors will be
destroyed beyond all recovery. Apparently the Lord has granted
us a lull to seize this opportunity to rescue the records before
it is too late. At the same time he has inspired the
development of microphotography.

Archibald F. Bennett, 1938

How could Mormons possibly manage all the data of the dead? Already in 1912 the church's Genealogical Society of Utah had lofty ambitions to accomplish the task.[1] The society's clerk, Nephi Anderson, envisioned "the records of the dead and their histories gathered from every nation under heaven to one great central library in Zion." He hoped to eventually enjoy "some elaborate, but perfect system of exact registration and checking, so that the work in the temples may be conducted without confusion or duplication."[2]

This was a far cry from Brigham Young's earlier more rustic understanding of genealogy work, where duplication was welcomed and merely offered the deceased individuals options, while establishing hierarchical claims of the multiple proxy performers of ordinances.[3] In the face of redundancy, surely the dead beneficiaries would choose the performance of ritual on their behalf from the most righteous proxy, or so went the logic. Duplication took on a different resonance once techniques of precision were required to meet the massive volume of records and rituals. With the promise of microphotography, an affordable medium finally seemed up to the task of preserving the world's records and making them accessible. In fact, duplication was now the key. By collapsing space and mechanically duplicating the world's records, microfilm massively expanded the work for the dead. Although some overlap inevitably persisted, microfilming would greatly aid and infuse the experience and understanding of the Latter-day Saint effort to manage and rescue the spirit world—to offer saving ordinances to deceased and disembodied children of God.

In the early 1930s Mormon apostle John A. Widtsoe sent a copy of *Popular Mechanics* with an article on microphotography to the Genealogical Society's new secretary, Archibald Bennett, and included a note stating, "I would watch this. Something may come of it."[4] The magazine piqued the apostle's interest, but the society's eventual adoption of microfilm came through the efforts of German immigrant Ernst Koehler. Although Koehler had first attempted microphotographing genealogical records in Germany, it wasn't until 1938, after his immigration, that he "presented microphotography as a means to obtain records" to the society in Utah and initiated a monumental shift in genealogical work.[5]

Incidentally, 1938 was a milestone for microfilm. That same year major microfilming projects, including Harvard University's Foreign Newspapers Project and Eugene Power's University Microfilms Inc. were founded.[6] From microfilming genealogy and newspapers to rare books and dissertations, these initiatives were understood to contribute to the creation of a shared "world brain" of knowledge for the betterment of humankind and the establishment of peace and order. Microfilming was a benevolent and timely undertaking. Initially, the act of photographing rare originals was "the strangest task any librarian ever performed," but it was also a necessary form of rescue.[7]

For Latter-day Saints, the records, much like the deceased children of God whose spirits inhabited the earth, were in grave danger. The threat of loss—through casualties to fallible bureaucracy or the destruction of war—could impede spiritual progress. In doctrinal terms this portended damnation, or becoming lost and unable to progress. Temples and vicarious work therein became the face of the rescue mission, but the tedious infrastructure to support and make that work sustainable was an expanding process of locating, duplicating, storing, and scanning for the extraction of names. By the late 1930s the fear that precious records of the dead might be destroyed and forgotten became a reality, as world war loomed once more.[8]

Microfilm developments could potentially attenuate entropy and death, and they provided an exciting update to Joseph Smith's vision of techniques, such as "recording practices that could bind earth and heaven and the living and the dead into a single archive" with "salvific action at a distance."[9] As Latter-day Saint apostle Orson Pratt put it in 1859, the work for the dead "is recorded in the sacred records kept on earth; and the recording angel who takes cognizance of the ordinances on the earth makes a record of the same in heaven." In other words, "sacred books kept in the archives of eternity" would be correlated with the books kept on earth.[10]

Rather than a single celestial book, I argue that microfilm offered a *system* of containing the vast universe of deteriorating records and daunting amount of data through visual techniques. It was also understood to fulfill the most expansive visions of redeeming the dead, from Joseph Smith (1840) to Joseph F. Smith (1918). Microfilm turned these prophetic visions into a utopian and cybernetic system through material media practices of members looking at machines. To close the information loop, revelatory moments of visions, guidance, and seeming serendipity attended the tedious labor. Projections on the screen of microfilm readers enabled natural vision to activate spiritual vision. In fact, in the mid-twentieth century, Latter-day Saints reported some of their most miraculous experiences while engaged in genealogy. These feedback loops of communing and connecting with spirits punctuated the practices of photographing, sorting, and saving the dead through microfilmed records. Visions of redeeming the dead were systematized as techniques of pious members.

MICRO MACHINES

A microfilm duplicate was merely a copy, but a photographically *exact* copy. This was precisely its advantage in making surrogate records available anywhere and rendering originals unnecessary. The miracle of microfilm was enabled by the loss of what Walter Benjamin in 1936 would term the "aura" of the original, its specific and perhaps ineffable quality of being created in a unique time and space.[11] Rather than understood in purely negative terms, mechanically reproduced objects stripped of aura enjoyed the freedom of new potential signification and simultaneous existence. As a proxy itself, the microfilmed version required only proper technologies of magnification to be utilized virtually anywhere in the world. This process of microphotographing and viewing old parish records, registers, and family histories was a new application of an already decades-old technology.

In 1870, during the Franco-Prussian War, microphotography was used to reduce documents to a size that could be rolled up and attached to carrier pigeons. The birds brought the miniaturized messages across borders, where the microfilm was enlarged through projection with a magic lantern. Clerks then transcribed the content and relayed it with the telegraph, noting "pigeon" at the end of the telegram.[12] From its inception the technology was clearly able to traverse otherwise impenetrable borders and translations. By the 1930s it was also becoming clear that microfilm could duplicate and store the rapidly expanding "library" or "world brain" of information. It could thereby contain the growing data. When it came to storing massive amounts of research and human intelligence, micro seemed the way to go.[13]

As a storage medium, microfilm was relatively durable and saved space. It did, however, require proper upkeep and regular inspection, and microfilm was also susceptible to chemical and physical damage, which would only be intensified with frequent use.[14] Microfilm also required a reading machine and magnification for the general public to efficiently utilize its magic without squinting into a loop. It required a device to render its shrunken images visible. Mechanical readers—functioning like large microscopes— were affordable means that predated desktop computer techniques and that ergonomically built on other workstation devices, such as sewing machines, typewriters, and counting machines.

As an early desktop screen, readers illuminated static but differing images in sequence by remediating book formats to roll in vertical or horizontal succession. The early years offered several trajectories of development, ranging "from handheld magnifiers to wall projectors to self-contained screen readers."[15] Eyeglasses on which pages of tiny text could be magnified and scrolled through, titled the Fiskoscope, offered promise but soon fizzled.[16] The larger reading machines were generally accepted as the best tool for the task. The Argus machine, purchased by the Genealogical Society of Utah, was one of the most affordable, durable, and dependable. Already by April 1939 two Argus microfilm readers were available at the society's library in Salt Lake City and were reportedly "constantly in use."[17] As Bennett noted, it was

Micromanaging Death

"predicted by some that the reading of microfilms with the reading machine will soon be as common as typewriting with the writing machine."[18] Especially for genealogy work Bennet was right, as generations learned to peer into the clunky devices to seek out and see their ancestors.

Media could extend, professionalize, and develop genealogy in powerful ways. While reading machines made the miniature copies accessible to millions, instructional films could help educate potential users. Radio was even employed to help facilitate genealogy work. Every Tuesday evening a genealogy program broadcast "inquiries from citizens who are seeking definite information or the solution of a problem" across the nation and "free of charge to all who can help."[19] The airwaves connected dedicated genealogists to enhance their scattered work. These supportive media helped spread the perceived value and efficiency of microfilm, ensuring its ascension in genealogy work. In the wake of the new media affordances, libraries began discarding their print assets.[20] Paper products were banished to make room for countless reels of microfilm. For microfilm was foremost a means of reversing the entropy and inefficiency associated with paperwork.[21]

Technologies could systematize and hopefully improve the work for concerned Latter-day Saints, who perhaps more than any other group cared about rescuing records of the dead and making them accessible. In fact, as Christine Kenneally has noted, "the phenomenon [Latter-day Saints have] built out of granite, microfilm, machines, and software is as mind-bogglingly ambitious for our century as the flying buttresses and gargoyles of Notre Dame were in the twelfth century."[22] This pious passion infused articles published in the *Genealogical Helper* that dealt with the excitement and frustrations of microform research. Page 2 of the periodical's first issue included the article "The New Microfilm Records," which excerpted an article from the local newspaper and a response from a reader. The article managed expectations by clarifying that although a large number of records were pouring into Salt Lake City as "tiny photographs," it would still require some time to index, catalog, and make the images accessible. They were not sure "how long it will take to complete this job," just who would be experienced enough "to read the old films, nor how many reading machines and readers it [would] take to carry on the work." The editors anticipated the magnitude of the tasks of sorting, storing, cataloging, and archiving, because as they put it, "if we do not use care in using the records, we will get records so mixed up it will take two millenniums to untangle things." But their ultimate and recurring hope was that God would somehow direct the living "in finding their lost records" in order to complete the work.[23] Even with technological systems, the turn to divine intervention was the linchpin that should make the micromanagement come alive to accurately and efficiently save the dead.

It was a curious arrangement. On the one hand, microfilm duplicated without human error. As Koehler explained, with "the magic of microfilm ... there is no chance for error.... The photo copy is a true copy."[24] Whereas researchers previously had to copy by hand, "the advent of the miniature camera has, however, taken the toil out of the work and substituted a mechanical method," which should preclude mindless mistakes.[25] On the other hand, Latter-day Saints fully expected help from God and spirits from the other side to guide the work, even through the microfilm reading machines. Ghosts in the machine were welcome, even expected.

Microfilm was simply a machine tool of management, but at the hands of Mormon users, microfilm became a means of spiritual rescue. It offered embodied Latter-day Saints the chance to mechanically manage space and time by getting ahold on the vast records of the dead requiring inspired salvation. This impulse harked back to Joseph Smith's innovative revelations concerning proxy baptisms for deceased individuals. As John Durham Peters has argued, Smith's early letters on baptism for the dead evince the "cosmic ambitions of a new world religion and the media-technical project of inscribing the entire human family into a single book."[26] Peters has astutely teased out the techniques involved in managing space, time, and mundane records to enable salvation for the dead in the 1840s. But the concept of the book as storage device for decisive data was itself undergoing revision. By the early twentieth century, microfilm provided a timely solution—not only to getting a handle on the overwhelming amount of records, but to their convenient utilization. Accordingly, early twentieth-century Latter-day Saints prophesied, "through the magic of microfilm and other modern inventions you will see records gathered from these nations to a great central library in Zion, by the hundreds of millions of pages."[27] Here they would be systematically brought within the vision of Saints to turn tiny photos into the salvation of the dead.

Bringing diverse and massive amounts of data into their vision meant technical means and bodily techniques of containment. Microfilm could help contain the ever-expanding problem of data loss, which corresponded with lost spirits. The containment metaphor of microfilm, which would become so telling in the Cold War era as a means to contain and thwart communist threats through data management, also had a suggestive valence for Mormonism.[28] The technical capacity of microfilm to encompass records suggested a theological capacity of the church and its diligent members to encompass the records of the dead to ensure their salvation. Microfilm, which shrunk the records, simultaneously expanded the work available as well as the ability to get a handle on the overwhelming state of affairs.

DAUNTING DATA

In the Latter-day Saint worldview, records had always been bureaucratically and theologically significant. Joseph Smith signaled the central importance of housing and preserving records, reportedly instructing the members to follow "the records of the Church" to avoid apostasy and promising them that the Lord "would never allow the records of this Church to fall into the hands of the enemy."[29] But the connection between vast stores of lost or hidden records and necessary temple work expanded over time.

Proxy work was extended beyond baptism into additional rituals, including endowments and sealings, once the St. George temple was completed in southern Utah in 1877.[30] Then in 1894, just a year after the completion of the Salt Lake City temple, the directive to do genealogy work and seal families together broadened. Genealogy was traditionally rooted in individuals seeking out their ancestors and performing rituals for them.[31] Consequently, the dead were first approached only as family members and were conceptually fewer in number. Wilford Woodruff's desire "to get a record of the genealogy of [his] fathers, that [he] might do something for them before [he goes] hence into the spirit world" was to be expected and represented a widespread Latter-day Saint aspiration.[32] But eventually the whole of the earth's dead required attention, and Woodruff's performance of proxy work for the founding fathers captured this awareness.[33] By using his body to offer baptism to the revolutionary founders of the nation, Woodruff embodied the expanding vision of redeeming the dead and the connections between both worlds.

Appropriately, genealogy was described as "chains" or links between the living and the dead that extended in a linear fashion.[34] But broken links sometimes required inspiration to acquire the names of dead and lost individuals awaiting redemption. In order to reconnect these chains, the living would first need to cultivate the desire to seek out their dead. As Brigham Young taught, "We are now baptizing for the dead, and we are sealing for the dead, and if we had a temple prepared we should be giving endowments for the dead—for our fathers, mothers, grandfathers, grandmothers, uncles, aunts, relatives, friends and old associates, the history of whom we are now getting from our friends in the east. The Lord is stirring up the hearts of many there, and there is a perfect mania with some to trace their genealogies and to get up printed records of their ancestors."[35] The fervor spread as "thousands" of

Americans were actively "laboring to trace the genealogical descent of their Puritan fathers."[36] The spirit of connecting, linking oneself with one's family line, was electrifying a growing number of Americans.

Emphasizing genealogy even allowed some Latter-day Saints to intertwine identity, sacred duty, and national belonging as they had done with their first film, *One Hundred Years of Mormonism* (1913). As Miranda Wilcox wrote, Latter-day Saints "recognized genealogy and hereditary organizations as offering opportunities to leverage their lineage as American social capital."[37] With a new patriotic spin on the Latter-day Saint teaching that the living are "made perfect by [the dead] and they us," work for the dead could also help perfect and position the living genealogists as racially or spiritually superior.[38] When names and places of descent did not make racial lineages clear, at times markers were added. While working on the *Century of Black Mormons* database, Paul Reeve noticed how, despite the absence of a column for indicating race directly in microfilm church records, there are occasions where the word "colored" was inserted next to a black convert's name. For Reeve, the scribal technique "illustrates the way in which white was deemed normal and a variation from white was considered noteworthy."[39] The family histories gathered by the vast majority of Latter-day Saint genealogists were lines of white, European descent. In its destructive application, microfilm could be used to fuel sentiments around racial hierarchy and be connected to eugenicist thought.

Whether sorting racial descent or preparing names for proxy work, genealogy was tedious work full of lacunae. Although genealogical societies in the eastern states could be beneficial, increasingly the work would require research or divine direction to get names and records of unknown individuals. The apostle Orson Pratt assured the Latter-day Saints it would be accomplished by divine inspiration, stating, "We shall learn by the spirit of revelation whom to be baptized for, and whom to officiate for in the holy ordinances of the Gospel. Herein is the necessity of revelation."[40] Fellow apostle George Albert Smith taught that "when we have exhausted all the powers within our natural reason and reach to obtain a knowledge of our dead, and the Lord is satisfied with us, revelations will be opened to our understandings by which we will be able to trace back our genealogy."[41] This kind of revelation from on high was not disconnected from media but often flowed through them.

By the early 1870s Pratt further explained how this revelation might come. Although the records and names of so many were lost, God could reveal them to his prophets. As Pratt put it, God had promised to "reveal unto you hidden things, things that have been kept hid from the foundation of the world." It only stood to reason that the temple work for forgotten dead with no extant records would somehow be enabled through divine intervention, and Pratt suggested it could be accomplished by the technology of a seer stone, or "Urim and Thummim." He went on to explain that once the temple is complete and the "sacred instrument" is "restored to the house of God," then the Lord would, by degrees, reveal through angels and the Urim and Thummim the names of all the ancestors of the Latter-day Saints to enable the proxy performance of their ordinances.[42] In fact Wilford Woodruff's journal entry for May 18, 1888, records how he brought the seer stone used by Joseph Smith to the temple and consecrated it for just such a purpose.[43] Proper labor and devices on earth would invite the inspiration and heavenly communication to fill in the gaps and complete records for vicarious rituals. Fellow apostle Franklin D. Richards concurred. In 1894, as genealogical fervor and the awareness of record quantities were expanding, Richards noted how the "Lord has . . . awakened our souls to trace back that lineage as far as it can be discovered by records, dreams, or vision, or revelation, or by the Urim and Thummim."[44]

Mormons were open to both mundane techniques and divine tools to accomplish the work for the dead. New England and New York had both founded their own genealogical societies in 1844 and 1869, respectively, but it was still relatively forward thinking when the Latter-day Saints organized the Genealogical Society of Utah in 1894.[45] The organization was a concrete response to the call to redeem the dead. Initially relying on indexes and postal networks to accomplish the work, the society was open to innovations. Although revelation through angels, the spirit, or even seer stones could be expected, new modern technologies provided the technological infrastructure to enable data management and rescue, and the anticipated inspiration. The adoption of microphotography proved to be the turning point.

The expectation of a sacred instrument—like the Urim and Thummim—that would reveal and scroll through information at the viewer's pace was partially fulfilled.[46] It was accomplished, first, in the meticulous work of microphotographers, who prepared record duplications, then second, when Latter-day Saints seated at the throne of the microfilm reader could experience the miracles and revelations of the magnified microrecords. This process structured the overall guiding vision of redeeming the dead but also focused it into literal visions in, through, and at microfilm reader machines. While viewing pages of information projected on a screen, Latter-day Saints could fulfill their duty and actualize visions of the dead, both as data and sometimes even as appearances of spirits of the deceased.

Today microfilm is a dead—or at least dying—medium, associated with tedium and headaches, but the initial vitality of microfilm was astounding. Mormon expectations of divine intervention in their efforts to recover lost records in order to meet the ever-expanding obligation to the numberless dead were channeled in more technical innovations and painstaking practices.

Joseph Smith's angelic messengers and stone screens were updated with microfilm and reading machines. Although both could offer answers to lacunae in the historical record and opportunities for divine intervention, microfilm fit the modern mindset of efficiency and containment, while democratizing the efforts to rescue the dead.

The "spirit of Elijah"—as Latter-day Saints often referred to the sense of responsibility to do genealogy and save their dead ancestors—coursed through the potential of microphotographic technologies and capabilities. At the October 1936 general conference, the president of the quorum of the twelve apostles, Rudger Clawson, noted how "the spirit of gathering genealogy is abroad among the nations. Many people are influenced by it."[47] This contagion of genealogical fervor was helpful since the sheer volume of work necessary to save all God's children was becoming clearer. Wilford Woodruff had quantified the issue as early as 1873, stating that there are "about a thousand millions of people on the earth, but in the spirit world they have fifty thousand millions."[48] By 1936, when Clawson spoke, 23,349,280 ordinances had been performed for the dead, yet, as he readily acknowledged, "when you think about the great multitude of spirits that depend on their earthly children for help, it is evident we have hardly touched the problem."[49] The colossal number seemed to dwarf any effort at comprehensive coverage. The apostle Joseph Fielding Smith reiterated in 1948, "Our duty is to search out our dead, and I am very grateful that the Church is helping us in these matters by securing the records of the dead" so that the work in the temples could progress.[50] Based on the numbers alone, Latter-day Saints felt redemption of the dead would be impossible without church organization and divine intervention.

Coincidentally, that same year, Norbert Wiener published his influential book on information systems titled *Cybernetics, or Control and Communication in the Animal and the Machine*. Wiener's ideas about systems for managing data processing and communication would increase in computational engineering, but the instinct to close the loop on systems to ensure efficiency also directly informed corporate practice.[51] For corporate efficiency, all components in a system had to be "oriented toward an objective, . . . orderly and hierarchical," with orderly "communication between them."[52] While not engaged in employing machines that learn and automate all aspects of genealogy work, the process for Latter-day Saints slowly took on more of the influence of systems theory and machine duplication. Machines—counting, duplicating, and sorting—could perhaps provide keys to containing data beyond human capabilities. Although data processing increasingly shaped the Mormon approach to work for the dead, it could never fully equalize individuals and machines in their minds. Embodied work was always paramount, but human, machine, and spirit still had discrete roles to play within a hierarchy.

Even with microphotography mechanizing duplication there remained a massive amount of labor in sorting. Church members soon realized the potential result of their work would be the creation of more work. With an expanded vision of comprehensive redemption, it soon became clear that "a microfilm library may be a hundred times larger than is the library of printed books in the Church Library." The genealogists confessed that the space and labor in sorting made them "dizzy just to think about it."[53] Like priesthood, church governance, education, and Mormonism itself, which were conceived as grand "systems," genealogy eventually needed to be approached and maintained on principles of systems management.[54] Because, as apostle Bruce R. McConkie put it in 1949, "it is one thing to set up a system that will be recognized by men; it is quite another thing to have a system which God will recognize."[55] This was the ultimate goal: mix microfilm and revelation to meet God halfway in an impossible task of managing the dead. The sacred work was increasingly structured and animated by microphotographic technology but still required cultural adjustments at the nexus of new technologies and old habits. It had to become a system.

The number of spirits awaiting the execution of genealogy and temple rituals was staggering and only increased every moment. But to appropriately follow protocol and act on behalf of the dead the church needed to "have their genealogy that a proper record can be made of it and laid up in the archives of the Temple."[56] Genealogical libraries of microfilmed records were the new apex of technological advancement. Further developments of improved systems, apparatuses, and architecture paralleled and prompted the expanding work for the dead.

At the opening of the new genealogical society building on January 17, 1934, the apostle Anthony Ivins remarked how previously "people only did work for their own dead. They did not do it for other people or for other families."[57] This shift to saving the entire human family required advanced infrastructure. Latter-day Saints understood it as divine intervention that during the last hundred years of genealogical development there had "been more development and actual progress in the world . . . than in all of its history before, as far as physical, scientific, and material development is concerned."[58] As concrete evidence of this progress Ivins pointed to their media environment, including "these electric lights, these automobiles with which many of you came here, the radio, which if it were here would carry my voice to the ends of the earth, without limit of time."[59] A long century of work for the dead had included building temples, extending endowments to the dead, and the establishment of genealogical libraries. Now "as a fitting climax" came "the great task of making microfilm copies of millions of pages of hand written genealogical records in Europe and America." Latter-day genealogists touted how the speed and efficiency of "making microfilm records compares with the old process just about as the airplane compares with the oxen."[60] Mormon pioneers with oxen migrating across the plains were now pioneers scanning duplicate records at reader machines. However, the system itself had to be controlled and maintained, which required policy changes and an expanded vision of the work.

THE WORLD BRAIN

This expanded vision then dovetailed with early twentieth-century visions of world networks of records, knowledge, and access. The global promise of networking the world's "brain" was the spread of information to prevent world wars and foster the establishment of peace in this life. The Mormon inflection of the sentiment added peace in the life to come, because work on earth by embodied Latter-day Saints meant spirits could finally rest. Similarly, data integration and improved accessibility meant greater hopes of pacifism across the globe.

In 1912 German scientist Wilhelm Ostwald proposed the assembly of a "world brain" as an antidote to war. As Maxim Gorky described it in 1916, Ostwald had conceived of "a union of the great minds of the world." These flesh-and-blood humans would constitute the "nervous system of humanity, the brain of the world."[61] Ostwald envisioned shared index cards and encyclopedic summaries of knowledge collated, but also housed in embodied beings, regulating scientific knowledge "through organizational, not dictatorial means."[62] These representative figures would need access to the entire library of human knowledge, which would require innumerable sources and space. It was not long after Ostwald's initial vision that microphotography offered the material realization and expansion of such dreams. Microfilm could make the "resources of the great libraries of the world" available anywhere, by making the duplication and dissemination of information much more practical.[63] Microfilm's miniaturization through duplication offered utopian promises of a networked world and liberated information storage from geographic limitations.

In fact, the promise of microfilm caused such a stir that H. G. Wells called it the "beginning of the world brain . . . a sort of cerebrum for humanity."[64] Wells could extend Ostwald's ideas into the material potential of microform. He both stoked and was inspired by the early twentieth-century discourses surrounding microfilm's promise, which foreshadowed the hype around the computer, in the 1980s especially.[65] H. G. Wells was head over heels for the new technology. He gushed: "The whole human memory can be, and probably in a short time will be, made accessible to every individual." In an "uncertain world where destruction becomes continually more frequent and unpredictable," microphotography "affords now every facility for multiplying duplicates of this—which we may call?—this new all-human cerebrum."[66] Wells was convinced microfilm would create the world brain that could unite, unify, and extend all human knowledge, by enabling unprecedented access to records. Microfilm could finally enact "the abolition of distance on the intellectual plane."[67] He even shared Latter-day Saints' urgency, declaring, "I have become a shouting philosopher and I clamour, I clamour with an increasing shrillness for a gigantic effort to pull together the mind of the race before it is altogether too late." Wells was convinced "that an educational revolution, a new Encyclopedism," was required to save the human race from perishing.[68] After the impassioned pleas of Wells and others it is no surprise that when the World Congress of Universal Documentation met in 1937, they resolved to unify systems of "recorded information" by "urging the establishment of microfilm copying services."[69]

Predating the technology's use in salvaging the world brain, microphotography enabled V-mail during World War II, where letters were photographed and a microsurrogate was sent home and then blown up and printed for the addressee to read. Messages and contact across barriers no longer required the same physical space across channels of freight. By the years immediately following the Second World War an information revolution was underway. In order to spark and manage the massive bibliographic impulse, "a heterogenous group of librarians, scientists, engineers, government officials, industrial researchers of various kinds, and commercial entrepreneurs"—we might add genealogists—began "introducing innovative systems, technologies, and new organizational arrangements for the management of information."[70] By midcentury, microfilm had proven itself as a medium of information storage and democratization. An English professor at Columbia, Walter Ginsburg, in the *Educational Screen*, lauded the form, stating, "It makes the library walls disappear! The magic microfilm camera has penetrated the great repositories of recorded culture. Materials we could not even dream of having—the rare, the inaccessible, the cumbersome—now we can have them."[71]

The awareness of records became intimidating. Accordingly, the conception of the spirit world enlarged to an alarming size. The correlation was a unique realization of Friedrich Kittler's assertion that "the realm of the dead is as extensive as the storage and transmission capabilities of a given culture."[72] Microfilm not only contained a vast universe of records but even reduced the space needed for their storage by "more than 85 percent."[73] The efficient use of space coincided with an expanding world of deceased spirits, which took up more space in the Mormon imagination. Driven by this vision and the capability of tiny photographic technologies, the church and its members revolutionized genealogy work and created the most impressive collection of genealogical data in one place by the mid-twentieth century.[74] At that time the genealogical library in Salt Lake City had eighty reading machines with plans to have 400 in the new building. The monumental efforts of the Church of Jesus Christ of Latter-day Saints and its genealogical society were described with echoes of the work performed for their first film, *One Hundred Years of Mormonism*. The money, labor, and technology dedicated to the task were said to approximate the filming of "the biggest epic" ever. Although "no excitement, no glamour, and little publicity" attended the project, the microphotographing of so many historical documents had "implications and ultimate benefits" that would "one day reach all the way around the world."[75]

VISIONARY MEDIA

Doing genealogical work was often described as being animated and inspired by the spirit, sometimes the very spirit of the biblical prophet Elijah, who was understood to preside over ancestral connections. Already at the end of the Great War, apostle James Talmage remarked, "It is a notable fact that the last seven or eight decades have witnessed a development of interest in genealogical matters theretofore unknown in modern times. . . . There is . . . an influence operative in the world, a spirit moving upon the people, in response to which the living are yearningly reaching backward to learn of their dead."[76] One might even unknowingly channel the spirit of Elijah to advance work for the dead and have visionary experiences of communing with them. Supernatural intervention into Mormon work for the dead was often framed by its entanglement with the medium being employed for the work. Before there were "Family Connections from eBay" or "A Google Miracle," there were tedious and rewarding experiences with the deceased through paper and pen, by telephone, and at microfilm reader machines.[77]

Media were always essential to record and make things happen. Efforts to get spirits from one side of the Latter-day Saint understanding of a spirit world to the other—from prison to paradise—required tedious techniques. One Latter-day Saint, Warrin Child, realized this through an inspired dream, in which he saw stranded and starving sheep on a barren farm. After first spreading hay for them, he noticed the adjacent hill was covered with green grass. He only had to move the sheep to that spot, where they would be saved.[78] This, he understood, was echoed in his embodied proxy work with records for, and in behalf of, the dead. He only had to follow the given protocol, and spirits would be saved, by being *moved* across space and time.

A Samoan member of the church in Cardston, Canada, reported how she was inspired by the spirit to get in touch with the temple president before her husband passed away. She was convinced her husband needed to be dressed in his temple clothes before he entered the spirit world, "where he would be directed where to find his dead relatives whose record had been lost," in order to redeem the record and thereby the deceased individuals. The wife tried to call but did not have the temple president's telephone number. Although the wife could not locate the temple president, the telephone operator reported that the switchboard miraculously "illumined with a very pleasant light and the town [where the president was] appeared in letters before her."[79] This is how the spiritual communication was manifested in telephonic connection. Others reported similar miracles while seeking out the dead and their records with microfilm.

Even though it was likely one of the most banal and straightforward devices, the microfilm reader and its ability to expand a lofty vision of redeeming the dead could invite spiritual experiences that infused the tedium with flashes of excitement. Rank-and-file church member Bernice Lorraine Dreier recalled her guided attempts at locating ancestors. After praying, Dreier headed to the library and "sifted through many rolls of microfilm," before the marriage record of her ancestors "suddenly appeared" right before her scanning eyes. "It seemed so real, as though I were there with them in that little Ohio town on February 13, 1845," reported Dreier. She was convinced it was only "with the help of the Holy Spirit [that she] had found these precious records."[80] In 1956, Mormon genealogist Muriel Malphurs of Florida described her experience: "I find that when I am searching in the Library, my whole being is quickened, my vision is better, causing me to scan a page in almost a single glance. (the names of my kindred seem to leap from the page to meet my eye) my thought processes are speeded up, and my spirit is so stirred that I feel I can reach out and touch my dear ancestors."[81] Interestingly, the grand system that contained and managed the records of the dead conceptualized by male church leaders often trickled into personal revelations of female members engaged with the technology. Once again, the big visions of male leadership were animated, refined, or otherwise actualized with small movements by often uncredited women at machines.

In fact, the visions were very much intertwined with the functionality and frustrations of microfilm technology. Sometimes dreams of finding children would recur until the member located the child's name in a record on the microfilm reader. At other times the reader machine would not scan to the next page—the spirit wouldn't allow it—until the name of another individual that had been overlooked was located and copied. Only then would "the pages [roll] easily."[82] The device determined and enabled the pace and progress of the work. Another member of the church, named Carole Wright, was guided in her scanning of microfilmed census records. "I'll try just once more before I quit completely" she thought, a bit frustrated. Just then her eye caught a name on the microfilm reader revealing a long-lost ancestor.[83] Bela Petsco similarly realized the significance of quickened spiritual vision while searching at the microfilm reader. Her mother had gone blind and could no longer scan the microfilm records herself. Instead she would sit next to Bela and stare off at a blank wall. Bela explained how one day she "continued rolling through the reel of film, searching for familiar surnames," when a few minutes later her "mother said, 'Stop.'" The whole time the mother was facing away from the reader, while directing its use. Somehow her lack of sight seemed to result in a heightened level of spiritual vision that was linked to and structured by the reader machine. "Go back." "More." "Stop." Right there, where the blind woman had placed her finger on the screen, was the marriage entry of the deceased parents.[84]

Even as late as the early 1990s an apostle related during his general conference address a miracle of vision at the microfilm reader. He told how a missionary at a reader machine could not discern the names he had retrieved, in order to help a woman accomplish her genealogy work. It was completely illegible. Only after praying three times was his vision enhanced, and the microfilm became perfectly clear.[85] In a technological echo of the story of Jesus healing a blind man through a couple of repetitions of applying hands and spittle, after which he could see everything clearly, genealogical work might invite more miracles and enable more Christlike applications.[86]

More than a new bodily technique of scanning and rolling, the microfilm mission of the Mormon Church represented a huge modern vision of duplicating and preserving records bolstered by personal visions of members doing their own family work, dreaming dreams, and having visions. These experiences not only kept genealogists going; by validating their efforts, they also provided an important sense of closure for both mortal and spiritual realms. This reciprocal relationship between the living and the dead paralleled techniques in Catholicism, where favors are done for deceased loved ones until it is "certified that the prize of heaven has been given."[87] In Mormonism the dead were thought to be cheering the genealogists on. It was, after all, in the deceased's interest that living proxies find them through records and accomplish their work.

Latter-day Saint Archie Graham had seen this in visions as early as 1918. Graham saw how spirits in the spirit world would meet and pray: "Bless all the saints everywhere, both here and on the earth in gathering their genealogies, that the records which are incomplete may be found and accepted in the temples on earth, that our families may come together as one."[88] In Mormonism, the answers to these prayers—divine intervention or spiritual feedback loops—entered the genealogical system through visionary experience. Through supernatural vision one could know that those figurative sheep had been accounted for and moved to the prosperous side. They had been saved.

Methods of accounting for the miraculous work varied by context, but all pointed to the meticulous records kept in temples. In 1932 it was reported that a member previously uninterested in temple work finally agreed to go to Brigham City and copy the names of individuals for whom temple work needed to be done. Although he arrived begrudgingly, as he copied the names individual spirits would enter the room and wait until he was done copying their "name and historical data," at which point they would each disappear.[89] A similar transfer of data storage that echoed the effect of proxy work occurred in a vision reported by Romania Hyde Woolley in 1931. The very individuals for whom Woolley had been baptized the day before rose from their graves at the cemetery, dressed in medieval clothing. At this point Woolley noted, "The tombstones were no longer necessary for records, the graves were opened, and these souls were set free."[90] Each name was an entry of data that required recording, proxy work, and redemption. Woolley knew her work was complete once the stone records were obsolete and spirits arose from their own graves as confirmation.

In a dramatic depiction of the efficacy and importance of temple work as a spiritual feedback loop, Octave Ursenbach, an active Latter-day Saint in Utah, penned a stage drama titled "The Awakening," around 1930. In Ursenbach's play, the principal character enjoys a visit to the spirit world, where spirits (even amid disbelief) await their liberation and their linking together through the proxy work done by embodied spirits in the mortal realm. The physical acts on earth directly affect the lives of the spirits from beyond. "Messages" flash between the realms to indicate the successful performance of ordinances. "Here flashes another message for us," say the spirits on stage while listening "attentively as though receiving a message flashed through space," as the stage direction puts it.[91] The signals between the mortal and spirit worlds were possible only because of a shared teleology; or as Norbert Wiener phrased it, "Within any world with which we can communicate, the direction of time is uniform."[92] Both temporalities pointed toward connection and salvation that was a linear path of progress and work. Even within the jumpy temporality of saving and communing with the dead, the future effect of genealogy was supposed to be sealed in salvation.

Ursenbach's drama only thematized a commonly reported visionary experience. The genealogical worker receives verification that the spirits have themselves received confirmation, in the form of notification or liberation. The relationship between body, machine, and spirit becomes an efficient system. Although genealogy was slowly becoming increasingly systematic, that is, accomplished on the backs of cameras, microfilm, readers, spreadsheets, and temple ledgers, its spiritual feedback loop allowed for the intervention of supernatural elements. Computational thought and mechanical movement could not fully displace the embodied and mindful engagement in the work that made earthly exertion spiritually salvific; and not just for oneself but, more importantly, for dead others.

SYSTEMS OF REDEMPTION

The technological promise of rescuing records bolstered the Mormon doctrine of caring for deceased ancestors through ritual acts. The rites of proxy baptism and then proxy endowments were prepared and realized by fastidious research and recording. Joseph Smith had introduced the concept of the living using their own physical body to perform rituals in behalf of the dead in the early 1840s. Smith taught Latter-day Saints to embrace the opportunity "for the salvation of the dead," by "being baptised by proxy" in order to have the names of the deceased "recorded in heaven."[93] It was clear to his followers that they required the "united energies of living and dead saints" to do this work and that it was mutually salvific. Smith stressed this point, stating, "We [are] made perfect by them and they us."[94] By the mid-twentieth century, the sentiment had developed into a detailed and technological process, which paralleled the mushrooming amount of prospective dead recipients of the work.

With the innovations of cybernetics and computers, the archive of records could be sorted and filtered in more automated ways. This could save time but also represented a computational relationship to records and dead humans. In 1978 these shifts were addressed in general conference. Church leader J. Thomas Fyans described how records are, like telephone numbers, recorded in sequence. He announced the promise of computers to now alphabetically sort and order microfilm cards for genealogy. Fyans explained, "As I sit at a microfilm reading machine and take every name—one by one—from these past records, I do this for everyone whose ancestors are on these records. Hereafter, they will not have to hunt them like a needle in a haystack, but once and for all these names will be rearranged and prepared telephone-book style."[95] The new computer capabilities promised to reshape work with large data sets, as well as connections across space. Just as University of Utah researchers were making innovative developments in digitally simulating objects on-screen through computers and sending their now-famous "Utah teapot" image through the burgeoning ARPANET (Advanced Research Projects Agency Network) to other schools, computers were shaping genealogy work and making some human efforts obsolete.[96] Quantifying individuals made them manageable as data but also represented a potential disenchantment of the work. Sorting and searching were made more efficient—not by spiritual guidance at a reader machine, but by a new computational order.

"Telephone-book style" family history work was a concrete step toward realizing the dreams of previous genealogists. As early as 1947—the same year he was sent to Europe to represent the Genealogical Society of Utah—Archibald Bennett was optimistic about the ability of technology to enhance work for the dead on the level of data transmission and storage. In his imaginative description of a future world, Bennett wrote, "A universal system of intelligent cooperation will bring together on one record sheet every fact in existence regarding a particular family. . . . No sooner will a new fact be uncovered in any part of the world by a researcher than it will be communicated to the Archives center and be assigned to its proper place, on some family record." This new world brain would be made possible by the "process of 'facsimile transmission,'" which was itself "an application of the principle of television."[97] Constant updates across the globe would further enable a networked genealogical effort.

Bennett's description of a fantasy mediascape came two years after Vannevar Bush's famous article in the *Atlantic* on his own imagined "memex" device, which would make information more accessible and allow for a variety of storing and processing functions in one desktop location. Bush considered the "highly suggestive" potential of microfilm to be a cost-effective means of storing and accessing knowledge, if the highest quality technology is utilized to create microfilm. The medium would even be the foundation of the memex machine.[98] Bennett took this a step further, suggesting real-time updates through a centralized network of records, synced across the globe. Receiving sets in each home would gather broadcasts of information from the archive and the church. Bennett's imagined system would technologize Joseph Smith's efforts to inscribe the whole human family into a single book, now with automatic updates across space and time, in order to redeem them all.

CONCLUSION

The desire to rescue and manage the dead by attending to their records was fulfilled through small means and big dreams. The highly specialized and inchoate tenets of cybernetics and goal-driven systems did not so much galvanize Mormon genealogical work, as provide the logical extension of shared mindsets. Microfilm fulfilled Mormon desires to adequately manage the redemption of the dead. Like systems theory, Mormons too sought to achieve an improved genealogical process by limiting error and setting up systems that could self-correct. This development was surprisingly modern and forward thinking. Spiritual feedback loops and menial manipulations were necessary to meet the technical needs of the expanding work for the dead. Once the proper control and instruction were in place the system should function seamlessly. It was the informational materialization of a tenet attributed to Joseph Smith, who reportedly stated, "I teach them correct principles and they govern themselves."[99] But it was never a perfect machine. All manner of noise and parasites invaded while enabling the process.

In order to avoid duplication, policy initially limited people to family connections. But eventually machines allowed for the expansion of this to the wider human family, and temples were fed names of individuals for whom temple attendees could perform ordinances. In September 1941 it was even determined that the opening of the Arizona temple should be postponed to allow for the new system to be properly prepared and installed. This meant changing out sheets for the new cards, which would prevent 12 percent duplication by relying on the new rectigraph and dexigraph machines.[100] The new system could correct and help prevent the "rather shocking" realization in 1942 that "about 50% of the persons now proposed for their vicarious endowments have already had their endowments bestowed upon them."[101] Instead of genealogy work's failure, duplication would become its key.

In the early church, Joseph Smith's concern was that the records in heaven would be neither complete nor efficacious, unless participants properly recorded here on earth. But by the mid-twentieth century, Latter-day Saints worried that the world might completely lose the records to war. In response, in the mid-1950s the church began planning the construction of a vault in the stone mountains of little cottonwood canyon to hold all the microfilm records. Construction began in 1960. Around this same time the church began the actual shift to computers, experts, and an electronic filing system. With a system of seeking out the dead, it was clearly the responsibility of the Genealogical Society to now keep temples busy by providing a steady stream of names.[102]

Microfilm remained integral until the twenty-first century, but the writing was on wall. In 2017 the Family History Center and familysearch.org announced that they had ceased creating and distributing microfilm.[103] The medium was officially dead. Yet, throughout the latter half of the twentieth century Latter-day Saints combined film, photography, miniaturization, and magnification with cultural techniques of managing the dead, to make the most of mundane and sacred practices. They turned visions of the spirit world into concentrated vision at machines to search, record, and save the dead. As they utilized the inspired material of microfilm and were confirmed and sustained in their efforts by spirits offering congratulations from the other side, they were convinced the system was functioning. They turned whatever they could into tools of transcending time and entropy through embodied practices. After all, as Mormon genealogists were acutely aware, "[their] dead are interested in results—not excuses."[104]

BROADCASTING
STANDARDS

Today my television set
Brought greater faith to me—
Not only do I hear the sounds
But now—I even see.

Mirla Greenwood Thayne, 1951

Sessions of this conference are being televised in color over more
than 200 stations in the United States and Canada and will reach
a potential of 40 million homes. "That they may all be one."

David O. McKay, 1967

roadcasting grew out of farming. It had earthy and manual origins
of sowing seeds widely, but in the twentieth century, *broadcasting*
took on a new meaning.[1] It became electronic and expansive, as
mass media with massive reach. For the Latter-day Saint church, television
especially held the potential of scattering a particular postwar vision of Mormon standards, under which to gather its members.

Broadcasting, as both a form of agriculture—shaping the earth through
techniques of cultivation—and also a means of propagating a religious
worldview, dovetailed in the figure of Ezra Taft Benson. Through his overlapping roles as U.S. secretary of agriculture and apostle in the Latter-day
Saint church between 1953 to 1961, Benson spread a public image of conservative religious values. Benson was a model American family man, and his

involvement in both senses of broadcasting worked in tandem under church president David O. McKay's equally telegenic and sanitary American image and McKay's willingness to update the church's infrastructure with broadcast technology.

During these two men's tenure, broadcasting became an organizing force. Television spread the image of church leaders and the "American way" they championed, but it also provided a structural fulfillment of ecclesiastical fantasies of correlation and gathering. Begun in the 1960s, Latter-day Saint Correlation was a major institutional reorganization aimed at clarifying lines of authority, standardizing curriculum, and consolidating power within the Quorum of the Twelve Apostles, as Matthew Bowman has outlined.[2] Indeed, I agree with Bowman's assessment of Correlation as an expression of faith in institutional cooperation to cultivate character, but I extend this analysis by connecting it to broadcast technology and especially the ways television—including the material media of cables, antennae, satellites, and TV sets—made standards into unifying visions shared by scattered members in their homes.

In a broader sense, Lynn Spigel has persuasively demonstrated how American postwar television standardized ideals by addressing possibilities and concerns around public and private space.[3] For television allowed viewers to enjoy distant visions but equally brought the outside world into the home. Maintaining any clear distinction between ideological notions of a masculine public sphere and a feminine private sphere was a function of broadcasting standards "based on [white,] middle-class, Judeo-Christian, heterosexual, two-parent, consumer lifestyles."[4] As Latter-day Saints embraced these postwar American ideals, the process of standardizing Mormonism proceeded with similar assumptions. In fact, Correlation was often couched as a patriarchal bulwark to defend just such a familial arrangement and the cultivation of the home. Combined with television, the authority and vision of church leaders could be consumed and emulated by audiences scattered abroad. Broadcasting standards entailed correlating Mormon vision and gathering Saints as viewers, who were once again taught how to look.

Although the sentiment of a dispersed gathering had been voiced in the early twentieth century, its execution required networks, both architectural and infrastructural. Manuals, curricula, practices, and appearances all had to be in tune. Previously, the gospel was "sown broadcast among thousands, and millions of the human family arose and believed it," leading to the physical gatherings of Latter-day Saints in Ohio, Missouri, Illinois, and then Utah.[5]

Broadcasting Standards

But the church's growth and the accompanying technologies changed the dynamic of this sowing, as well as the gathering of Latter-day Saints. With the church no longer encouraging members to come to "Zion" in Utah, chapels and modern living rooms across the globe became the new sacred domestic spaces where members could be correlated and gathered.

The Correlation Committee standardized doctrine, policy, and practice toward a singular vision of modern Mormonism. But visual broadcasts of general conference, tabernacle choir performances, and wholesome programming also helped solidify the Mormon image and bring members up to the overlapping standards of the church, the nation, and broadcast technology itself. Standards were a filtering process, and Latter-day Saints wielded them to distinguish themselves against a backdrop of others, especially communists and countercultural Americans. Television's ability to decry outside threats and kindle domestic bliss made it complicit in developing Mormonism's postwar American image. The medium brought to life the threat of pernicious content invading the home as communist, progressive, or otherwise menacing televisual influences on the membership. In other words, TV itself made daily threats of invasion real. However, the medium also promised an infrastructural connection to leaders for members scattered abroad. It brought the leading brethren and their message, image, and standards into the home, which itself became a site of correlation and doctrinal emphasis.[6]

Although I am interested in milestones of institutional broadcast history and the ephemeral content of early Mormon television, in this chapter I explore the effect of the medium for the religious culture, by focusing on the essence of simultaneity and standardization.[7] I argue that the form of television—the ubiquitous, electronic simultaneity itself—connected and enabled Mormonism in novel ways. While scholars have recognized some cultural forces at play, including social upheavals of the 1960s and "progressive ideals" that sparked efforts to standardize Mormonism, the galvanizing relationship between television and Mormon correlation has been neglected.[8] For, more than anything else, it synced the Latter-day Saint gaze into a shared vision of what postwar Mormonism looks, sounds, and behaves like.

Television spread the vision of cameras *as visions of white male American church leaders* to be taken on and performed by members everywhere. It provided the visual standard used to gather and correlate Latter-day Saints in the second half of the twentieth century. Whereas microfilm fulfilled visions of managing the dead, television—despite its suggestive connections to spirits—provided a system of managing and correlating the living in the image of patriotic citizen consumers.

Television extended vision horizontally across space but seemed to have come from above. Vertically dispensed in revelatory surges, TV for Mormons was a divine fulfillment with inspiring possibilities. It was somehow fitting that a young, initially uneducated, Latter-day Saint farm boy from Utah was said to have surpassed the most learned priests of physics in inventing television. Philo Farnsworth worked out the mechanics of television while still in high school. By college he set out to improve the process. Once in San Francisco, Farnsworth invented the "image dissector," which he successfully demonstrated for the press in 1927.

Reenacting an echo of Joseph Smith's childhood visionary experience, Farnsworth's revelatory breakthrough in TV technology was understood as an inspired result of effort and prayer, as well as the requisite national circumstances. In fact, Farnsworth's extraordinary inventiveness was explicitly attributed to "the American way of life, in which ingenuity and progress are encouraged by our system of free enterprise," just as much as "to the courage, vision and faith of modern pioneers of American industry."[9] Television might have required and inspired visions, but it was also understood in connection with American exceptionalism and capitalist industry, which were often neatly linked with the rise of modern Mormonism.

David O. McKay, who served as the church president from 1951 to 1970, wrote how Farnsworth visited him and "testified to me that he knows that he was directed by a higher source" in his study and invention of television. McKay continued, "Thank heaven there are hundreds of thousands of people who believe that testimony and repudiate the claims of the communists."[10] Farnsworth's work with television bolstered McKay's belief that technology, capitalist patriotism, and revelation were indeed interconnected. Recognizing and acting on these connections might even mold modern Mormon vision.

Although they may retain the nationalist pride, histories of television have traditionally cut such reports of supernatural inspiration from their accounts. Yet, like Farnsworth's heavenly insights, the earliest conceptions of television or "distant vision" during the late nineteenth and early twentieth centuries emanated from spiritualist, theosophist, and psychic thinkers.[11] Because psychical research and spiritualist optimism were coconstitutive with the technological development and invention of television, the early antecedents to Mormon distant vision were more than antennae placement and TV sets. But these devices made the dream of broadcasting and receiving visual messages across space a reality.

The "optimistic modernism" of the developing concept of broadcasting helped realize spiritualist hopes and technologize agricultural techniques whence the term came.[12] Broadcasting soon shed its earthy roots and blossomed into a ghostly modern technology. It is no wonder that shortly after Farnsworth's death, "Coon Peak," where the church's TV transmitter was located, was renamed "Farnsworth Peak." The mountain's titular change of guard reflected the shift in the semantics of broadcasting. The peak traded its Mormon namesake from a pioneer farmer for that of a modern tele-visionary. For the Mormon faith, however, the medium would retain implications of scattering and gathering, both of images and end users.

The modern technological promise of connecting distant realms was summoned at the event of the initial Mormon devotional use. At the first general conference broadcast by television (to an adjacent building) in 1948, the assistant to the Twelve Apostles, Clifford E. Young, acknowledged the marvelous age, stating, "I thought of these things and thought of this achievement of television [and] I wondered in my own heart if perhaps the time will not come when we can see our loved ones on the other side. That is not beyond the pale of possibility. To us now, of course, it seems impossible. Television was impossible for us not so long ago."[13] This seemingly impromptu sincerity at such an official event lent the confession a near prophetic gravity as it miraculously traveled from one building to the other as audio images. It also underscored a belief in the productive imbrication of innovation and spiritual development.

Young was not alone in linking electronic media to communicating with the dead. Electronic hearing and seeing could potentially be extended across space and time to include the spirit world. Its inhabitants were, after all, material and present in Latter-day Saint understanding. Distant vision was a heavenly promise that television might now fulfill, by extending physical abilities into spiritual capacities for the masses. The intellectually ambitious apostle Orson Pratt had speculated in 1873, "We are limited in our vision here, we can see only a few things round about us. . . . We can not see away off to England," but perfected bodies would eventually experience "an enlargement of vision in the resurrection."[14] In compensatory ways, technology could try to achieve what spiritual metamorphosis promised. In this recognition, the Mormon prophet Joseph F. Smith's (distant) vision of the spirit world in 1918 was closer to early imaginative hopes and conceptions of "tele-vision" than has been acknowledged.[15] Smith reported that his eyes were opened and that he saw other times and places, including the activities of spirits, from the comfort of his own room.[16]

Appropriately, the first Latter-day Saint broadcast was a radio message on May 6, 1922, wherein church president Heber J. Grant read Joseph Smith's account of a heavenly vision, found in section 76 of the Doctrine and Covenants, into the airwaves. Known as "the vision" in the early church when Smith's "first vision" was less familiar, section 76 detailed a personal eyewitness of Jesus Christ, the heavens, and angelic beings. It was itself powerful evidence of enhanced and distant vision. By 1962 the apostle and future president of the church Spencer W. Kimball made the parallel explicit, remarking how "dreams and open vision, like perfected television programs, have come repeatedly" for leaders of the church.[17] At times Latter-day Saints were urged to learn the skills to emulate this kind of spiritual television, but more often they needed to find their place by honing their skills in receiving and accepting the vision of leaders.

Tuning into visions of leaders became a literal media practice with the proliferation of TV sets. Viewers had to learn calibration to receive the desired visions of some, while rejecting others, because it soon became clear that the spirits in TV sets were just as often those to be tuned out. Rather than enabling personalized spiritual communications, electronic media could suffer from "ghosts" within.[18] In fact, TV owners often complained of ghosting, when an image had a fuzzy double, which was particularly common in "fringe areas," away from the hub and antenna.[19] The work of exorcism soon became a practical measure negotiated with the hardware of the television set. Manuals detailed how to reject phantom signals, remove "fluttering" images, and properly calibrate equipment.[20] Through proper tuning, powerful connections could be made and pernicious specters dissolved even while living far from the hub.

Using a TV properly had figurative resonance for scattered Mormon viewers receiving church visions as official broadcasts. But for the nation at large, it was equally important to tune out another kind of looming threat. Karl Marx's provocative line about Europe in 1848 required updates and a new sense of alarmism.[21] For the specter of communism now haunted America, but possibly even in and through the ether of television.

TELEVISUAL MORMONISM

Television shaped viewers through conflict. It consolidated audiences by making shared visions of outside threats visible in the home. According to Lynn Spigel, TV enacted a paradoxical welcoming of public danger into the private domicile, while highlighting its promise to shore up good old American family life.[22] Combined with the spatial arrangement of suburban planning, Americans seemed more standardized and ideologically bundled than ever, after the TV set became a widespread fixture in the home. As a material practice of viewing the same images in TVs, Anna McCarthy has also highlighted how the alignment of "individuals with each other and with broader forms of political authority" was intensified by television's ability "to disperse ideas and automate perception and cognition," which she sees as "enabling, on a massive scale and at a suitably removed distance, the shaping of conduct and attitudes."[23] The ways American ideals were packaged and sold through television against threatening forces often nicely aligned with Mormon culture, even as Latter-day Saints began to double down on conservative family values and cast themselves as defenders of tradition in the face of social upheaval throughout the 1960s.

Television itself engaged these paradoxes by reveling in the threatening news of immanent communist attack or internal division through protests, riots, and demonstrations. Television might have taught how to be a certain model American, but it did so by piping sensational images that might threaten that very model right into the family room. Television was clearly, like all moving-image media, "informed not only by its materiality but also by its political, economic, and social context," which also expressed widespread cultural values.[24] And these were often values of postwar domesticity and a constructed way of life that was equated with the American dream, all of which now seemed to require defending against destructive threats.

With visions of threats to the nation and family and in the face of exponential church growth, the 1950s—the first decade of Mormon television—represented a conditioning period, when Latter-day Saints felt aligned with American ideals and began to recognize the potential of the medium. By the 1970s Mormons were winning awards and gaining public favor with savvy "Homefront" TV spots that branded the church as fundamentally family centered. They had a clear message about family values, honesty, and good citizenship to broadcast to outsiders. As Jan Shipps describes, this was when Mormons began to represent a slice of middle America. It was through television especially that "the dramatic discrepancy between clean-cut Mormons and scruffy hippies" served to finalize "the transformation of the Mormon image from the quasi-foreign" to the "more than 100 percent super-American portrait." By the early seventies, Shipps recalls, Mormons were touted as "more American than the Americans."[25] But in the second decade—the 1960s—television supported and coincided with wide-reaching Correlation efforts to consolidate what it meant to be Mormon, especially in America.

Broadcast technologies shaped the church's efforts to gather and minister to its members. By broadcasting "standards" of living and morality, radio and television provided the technological apparatus and metaphorical counterpart to reaching and gathering worldwide Latter-day Saints under a domestic, patriotic, and divine standard.

Although they soon mastered the medium, Mormon leaders sounded much like their fellow Americans in decrying the potential harm the broadcast media could inflict on the family. The images on the TV set were then contested, precisely because of their formative quality and ability to enter the home. As Gavin Feller has shown, church leaders were even questioned for airing alcohol and cigarette advertisements for their predominantly Mormon audience.[26] Thinking about TV in terms of potential threats to the family by blurring public and private space was already done "by the 1950s, [in] highly conventionalized ways of speaking about household media and emerging technologies."[27] Talk of threatening images carried over from the discourses surrounding earlier media, and while Latter-day Saints certainly gave sufficient attention to the content of TV—often mentioned together with film, magazines, and radio programming—the medium itself offered important logistical affordances.

After all, content was only a secondary consideration for television, as Raymond Williams stressed.[28] The cumulative effect and unifying force of television was also the medium itself, as a presence in the home. In Leo Bogart's 1956 assessment, TV was standardizing "tastes and interests" in general. As he suggested, "The ubiquitous TV antenna" was also "a symbol of people seeking—and getting—the identical message."[29] A print ad for the church's KSL-TV the same year as Bogart's statement promised a utopian image of harmonized families with the caption, "Families see eye-to-eye with KSL-TV."[30] The literal standardization of vision could be used to interpellate and gather Latter-day Saint viewers as it activated their participation in the construction and maintenance of modern Mormonism. The Church of Jesus Christ of Latter-day Saints wholeheartedly adopted the medium when they became one of the only churches to own a television broadcasting company. This move implied the propriety of church members purchasing and properly using TV sets in their own homes, according to certain standards.

STANDARD CONSUMPTION

TV was standardized before it hit the commercial market in an effort to avoid the chaotic and "bitter experience" of early railroads, electric lighting, and radio.[31] As Friedrich Kittler recognized, "Standards determine how media reach our senses," and with television these medium-regulating principles reveal important aspects of the televisual age, as well as Latter-day Saint Correlation.[32] For Mormons using electronic screens, standards were often talked about and performed right before their very eyes. Technical standards dictated how their television worked, but they also implied patriotism, prosperity, and superior content delivery.

After considering various potential implementations, the Federal Communications Committee (FCC) created the National Television System Committee (NTSC) in 1940 to establish the national standard. After "some 12 years" of debate and several technical revolutions the NTSC was able to unanimously prescribe 525 horizontal scan lines as the standard for all American televisions in March 1941. The solution was "another example of the best that is in our democratic system, with the best in the industry" since it was reportedly unheard of that a committee faced with such a permanent decision was able to act in six months.[33] This all replayed in living color when the NTSC announced the color standard and countries around the world were forced to determine their own standardization of color television, which shook out across ideological lines.

While many allies of the U.S. military also adopted the NTSC standard, for "other countries, choosing an alternative standard was a show of political defiance."[34] Some nations could not stomach the imposition of an American standard, especially if they detected weaknesses in its performance. In response France soon developed SECAM (Système Électronique Couleur avec Mémoire, or Sequential Color with Memory), which was also adopted in its colonies, as well parts of the Middle East.[35] West Germany's development of PAL (Phase Alternating Line) became the standard for most of Europe, Asia, and Africa, but the Soviet Union's adoption of SECAM signaled their contested chumminess with France as much as their antagonism toward America.[36] Since the French had already tried to discredit the NTSC standard, "the accord was greeted in the French press as a great victory for the technical genius of the country and as an American defeat."[37] Even decisions about technical standards were framed with militaristic language seemingly raising the stakes of television's future as inextricably linked to the nation's prosperity.

In America a sense of "technological nationalism" was a guiding force in early television development that wove together capitalist prosperity and national pride. The sentiment took on embodied performance in July 1959, in the now famous "kitchen debate" in Moscow, when U.S. vice president

Richard Nixon verbally sparred with Soviet premier Nikita Khrushchev on television. The two men discussed politics as they walked around a model home outfitted with modern appliances. Nixon explained to Khrushchev, "There are some instances where you may be ahead of us. For example, in the development of the thrust of your rockets for the investigation of outer space. There may be some instances, for example color television, where we're ahead of you."[38] The light debate, in the throes of ideological and linguistic barriers, highlighted the spirit of antagonism that shaped early television developments. After all, the need for radar and missile guidance systems had advanced the technology in the first place. In fact, the very equipment leftover from World War II was used by the Church of Jesus Christ of Latter-day Saints to facilitate the first broadcast of general conference.[39]

Because the war had originally hoarded television technology and halted its public use, the arrival and prompt domestication of the TV set signaled the nation's triumph. "Victory has been won. Peace is here. Television is ready to go," NBC's president Niles Trammell assured the FCC.[40] From that moment America was decidedly an NTSC nation. Beyond the content geared toward inculcating anticommunist sentiment in American audiences, the very form and its standards taught American superiority, exceptionalism, and the democratic ideals of capitalism. Simply put, if you were in the Soviet Union you watched television with a 625 line standard; in America you watched with a 525 line standard, solidifying an ideological and technological gap that only increased with color TV.[41] But the amount of lines on your TV set meant more than just quality or resolution. It reflected a shared national resolve and trajectory.

Efforts to correlate, control, and homogenize Mormonism during the mid-twentieth century employed a similar sense of standard, as a cultural or religious benchmark. Although both Latter-day Saint Correlation and the NTSC format were top-down decisions to regulate, both standards were often welcomed as opportunities for patriotism or devotion or both—to perform conformity. Their implementation was understood as an act of obedience and harmonization. And both implicitly signaled the acceptance and enjoyment of a higher standard of living, which was often connected to American exceptionalism. As Ezra Taft Benson remarked at general conference in 1960, the Soviets' "success in the field of rocketry is in sharp contrast to their backwardness in general standards of living."[42] Television helped make the spirit of capitalism and industrial life into media practice. It electrified—shaped, while spreading—both American ideals and Mormon standards, which were seen as intertwined.

In the decades following the war, consumerism "was a civic responsibility designed to improve the living standards of all Americans," as "a critical part of a prosperity-producing cycle."[43] Owning a television set soon "became a technological ruler by which to measure the American Dream."[44] TV culture and American ideals broadcast the notion that "private consumption and public benefit . . . went hand in hand."[45] The made-for-TV conception that an ideal nation would consist of consumers continued to flourish into the 1960s, even when marketing shifted from targeting monolithic audiences to segmented ones. The capitalist mode traded the medium's genealogy of spiritual vision for market foresight. Although TV promised "immediacy and immensity, where all possible subjects and objects are co-present to each other," the implementation replaced "visual extension" with "visible distinction."[46] TV was a form of conspicuous consumption. Rather than a meaningless activity, viewing was conflated with selecting and consuming, as ideas and products were sold to the country through their TV sets.

The effect was dramatic. Already by the end of the 1950s more than half of all revenues at most big advertising firms came from television spots.[47] The advance in consumerism was supposed to connote a unified and connected society. Television provided the "material embodiment and simultaneously gave audio-visual form to the systematic integration that the individual in the domestic sphere had with this material advancing society."[48] If audiences were watching television in the home and acting in accordance with its invitation to buy, behave, and believe in certain ways, they were meant to feel connected to the greater cause of the nation. In short, they were up-to-date and contributing.

The connection to consumer culture and gendered domesticity that was shaping the nation also structured Mormon television from the very first commercial broadcast. The Church of Jesus Christ of Latter-day Saints acquired a permit for their television station KSL-TV in 1948. May that year the church's department store ZCMI (Zion's Co-operative Mercantile Institution) invited customers to "SEE TELEVISION broadcast tonight in our South Temple window. . . . COME IN and see the newest, finest developments in television instruments."[49] The broadcast was presided over by several well-known men, including Governor Herbert B. Maw, Mayor Earl J. Glade, ZCMI manager Harold Bennett, and the first counselor in the Latter-day Saint first presidency, J. Reuben Clark. After these prominent figures addressed the audience of shoppers through TV sets placed throughout the store, the summer fashions were shown. And with an electrical surge, window-shopping became the first activity to be electronically extended by Mormon television.

If the televisual display was not enough to link consumerism and broadcasting, the next segment took the show onto the floor among the shoppers in action. An interviewer with a microphone got "real people" to answer questions, allowing them to see themselves on TV as they shopped. The broadcast in ZCMI had a strongly gendered configuration, as men of prominence and technical acumen delivered content to receiving women. The dynamic was even caught in close-up. A photograph from the event shows how "pretty model, Shirley O'Connor, looks distractingly 'untechnical' as she learns from Dave Sear, television technician." The show of technology, to every "woman in the store," catered to the conflation of women, housewives, and shoppers.[50] The televised spectacle could even be viewed at several different locations simultaneously.[51] Each store would be in sync.

Eventually, television would extend this sentiment by bringing the store into the home. Both viewers and shoppers were free to consume standardized images and goods with their eyes at the same time. The emerging television culture fashioned a nationwide consumer economy that endorsed "conceptions of gender and domesticity that both eased patriarchal tensions about messages coming into the home and broke the audience into markets."[52] Along with children, a key target was decidedly the housewife and mother, who was assumed to be home during the day to watch more television. TV programming and advertisements targeted women by dishing up in-home delivery of the latest trends, tastes, and standards that were paramount in constructing and directing consumerism and domestic behavior. Women viewers were invited not only to buy products but, more importantly, to buy into a configuration of standardization and gendered uses of television that brought postwar national ideals into everyday life.

By May 1949, there were reportedly 4,200 TV sets throughout Salt Lake City, and programming was geared toward peak hours after work and dinner, when families would be available to discipline their bodies into new daily routines. A newspaper article in Utah recognized the subtle shift, stating "television is developing a new race of sitters—a vast, immovable population of living-room squatters, as it were."[53] There could also be an attendant decrease in social interaction: "The decline in conversation at house parties in television belts had become alarming. Guests hardly speak to one another or to the hostess," described the reporter.[54] With adjustments to new domestic screen culture, visions and communications were coming from outside the home, while directly affecting the behavior and practices within.

Although Latter-day Saints consistently voiced warnings against the moral pitfalls of potentially lewd content entering and corrupting the home, their technological practices demonstrated a deep commitment to utilizing the medium. Instead of producing peculiarly Mormon content, what KSL-TV provided was primarily family oriented and American in flavor. Shows like *Junior Council* and the "audience favorite" variety show *Uncle Roscoe's Playtime Party* were clear extensions of radio and knockoffs of other popular American genres.[55] The programs utilized a nonnarrative variety format that broke up the entertainment, allowing distracted housewives to continue working between segments and rooms. The shows also employed an interactive element that allowed nonactor participants to perform or talk about their hobbies and pets. The programs were filled with square dances, answering questions that had been sent in by audience members, and playing clue games taken from the church's magazine the *Children's Friend*.[56] These strategies helped to vicariously involve home viewers, but they also presented what a "normal" American child or audience was like. As one might expect, the ideal child viewer was clearly white and middle class.

The focus on children in programming appealed to housewives as the gateway to the home and suggested the register and tone of wholesome Mormon content. Television's ability to invade the home made it a thief in the night, and discourse around managing this threat often turned to mothers. It was her responsibility to safeguard the home and protect the children from other programs not within the Latter-day Saint standard. In 1955, local Salt Lake City church leader S. Dilworth Young broached the dilemma in general conference by asking the audience, "How would you like to have a man walk into your home and" try to show your daughter some "pictures of half-dressed people performing antics, doing lewd things or questionable things or uncultured things?" Supplying the answer, Young continued, "You would do anything in your power to keep him from entering your house, and yet at the touch of a button that is what you have if you do not take care."[57] The women's *Relief Society Magazine* recommended mothers encourage their children to read novels instead of watching television, as a safer alternative and superior mode of promoting imagination.[58] After all, the evils of the world and conspiring men could be "brought to the very heart of the home by radio and television."[59]

Additionally, mothers were taught to familiarize themselves with television programming in order to best guide their children. Again, women in the private sphere could gain patriarchal knowledge and guidance from the proper sources. A 1955 article stressed how "an intelligent appraisal of programs by the mother of the home will enable her to plan the child's time so he receives benefit and not harm." But then the author considered that "still a child cannot be and, perhaps, should not be shielded from all awareness of practices not in conformity with Latter-day Saint standards. But the mother should point out those destructive practices and teach to her children the truth."[60] This balanced gesture toward media literacy was rare, however. For the most part Mormon anxiety around content would only increase, which coincided with a shift in American television from the 1950s' "golden age" directed at domesticity and bringing the family together to the 1960s' more subversive and adventurous views of family life.[61] Where Latter-day Saints nicely fit and endorsed the wholesome fare of the 1950s, the increasingly subversive programming of the following decade helped solidify their urgency to correlate and defend postwar ideals.

MODEL AMERICANS

Early Mormon programming was generally for children, musical, or wholesale preaching. But *Let Freedom Ring* was the breakthrough 1962 special that helped catapult KSL-TV into national broadcasting and justify investing in quality color equipment.[62] The show utilized talent from outside the church and focused on American history through music and spoken word, the same format utilized around general conference.[63] The special was musical family entertainment with a strong patriotic message. As *Let Freedom Ring* garnered awards and praise it was clear that good TV was not distinctly Mormon but rather American.

A similar brand of faintly Mormon patriotism had been illustrated in the 1950s when Ezra Taft Benson, secretary of agriculture and Mormon apostle, appeared with his family on Edward R. Murrow's popular television show *Person to Person*. Producers hoped the 1954 episode would showcase the Benson family, as an exemplary American family, engaged in family home evening. Although the Bensons initially hesitated, they were eventually convinced it would be advantageous to put a Latter-day Saint family on national display.[64] In the segment, the daughters take turns performing song and dance, and the mother, Flora explains how she is living up to their religion's belief that women's greatest career was "to be a real homemaker and a mother" as well as a "support to [her] husband." Mr. Benson doesn't say much. He lets his family perform their patriotism and unity, until finally he sings in harmony with the entire family the hymn "Love at Home." At the time Benson was already cultivating an image of a model American. Intensely anticommunist and a dedicated Christian family man, Benson was a paragon of American masculinity. He was even "doing [his] duty" by "serving the government," as he described it in the show. Once broadcast through television, Benson was able to perform and portray the visual equivalent of proper patriotism to the nation. Of course, the televised image of Benson was literally broadcast in 525 NTSC scan lines and therefore discernable, but much more importantly it was an acceptable standard of living and appearance to be emulated.

Benson projected a model of character, honesty, and intelligence that was "almost too good to be true."[65] In 1953 and again in 1956 Benson's picture also adorned the cover of *Time* magazine.[66] His appearance on *Person to Person* and *Time* connected the dots of wholesome American family values, capitalist work ethic, masculinity, and technology. His appearances in Latter-day Saint general conferences equally portrayed this image for insiders. Although television was "a great blessing to the people," Benson wrote in his journal of the first televised general conference, "to me it adds to my worry and anxiety to realize that I am not only on the air during my remarks but being photographed also."[67] Becoming a face of modern Mormonism in the age of television brought increased awareness of visibility and public image that was seen by thousands, even millions simultaneously. Because Latter-day Saints had become good modern capitalists and (nuclear) family oriented, the 1950s saw the heyday of the Mormon media image.[68] Engaged in politics, running their own TV station, and standing by American values and traditional gender roles, Mormons like Benson were surprisingly well accepted, and Mormonism and Americanism converged as never before. Focused on family and the fate of the nation, Mormons were up-to-date consumers and patriots.

A certain brand of patriotism also united the apostle Benson and the prophet David O. McKay. Although Benson would clash with McKay on issues concerning Benson's endorsement of the ultraconservative John Birch Society, they both agreed on the general threat of communism.[69] McKay clarified in general conference in 1966, "The position of the church on the subject of communism has never changed. We consider it the greatest satanical threat to peace, prosperity, and the spread of God's work among men that exists on the face of the earth."[70] Benson was more radical in his anticommunism and actively gave the "impression that Mormonism and conservatism were irrevocably aligned," even reportedly suggesting the difficulty in being a "good Mormon" and a "liberal democrat."[71] For the threat was among Americans themselves, and liberal democracy was too close to communism for Benson. As Benson's 1969 book *An Enemy Hath Done This* suggested, communism and the destruction of the nation could come from misled and unscrupulous Americans, masquerading as patriots.[72] The possibility of fellow Americans not living up to patriotic standards and even undermining them made technology and television politically charged. Publications, such as *Counterattack*'s "Red Channels," sought to expose communist-leaning dissidents who were corrupting the broadcast technologies of radio and television, as Benson feared. Although his passionate tirades did not go unchecked, Benson's warning of the communist infiltration of American minds and technology was louder than many of his critics.[73]

Putting Benson's and many viewers' paranoia into televised imagery, the popular science fiction / fantasy series *The Twilight Zone* satirized Cold War mentalities around technology and outside threats. The show's 1960 episode "The Monsters Are Due on Maple Street" pitted neighbors against one another. When the power goes out and all automobiles and electronics cease to function, the frustrated suburbanites become suspicious of each other and some entertain the possibility of an alien invasion. Playing with an ending that confirmed the reality of such an invasion, the episode showed that although "the external threat was real (as depicted by the two men in spacesuits), the true threat lay in the neighbors quickly and ruthlessly turning on each other," as Heather Lunney has written.[74] Focusing on internal division is certainly a sound reading of the episode. However, the political valence of media at the time also suggests that the episode's real horror was a reversal of America's ideological relationship to power and technology.

The episode flipped the patriotic use of infrastructure, electricity, automobiles, phones, radios, TVs, and so on into a sign of foreign invasion and influence. After the disorienting outage, if someone's car inexplicably starts or someone's radio actually works, it is taken as a sign those people are aliens in disguise. Reliable infrastructure and advanced technology—hallmarks of the American standard of living—are uncomfortably coupled with dissent. They become incriminating evidence of treason. Whether the interloper was alien or communist, this exposed a deep-seated anxiety in suburban middle-class families who lived and thrived through such infrastructures.

Devices utilizing power were a hallmark of the warm, happy American home. An ad for the Utah Power and Light Company in 1951 even cartoonized electricity, which was "more popular than ever," by showing him as a cute masculine figure entering the home from the wall outlet with a smile and a ready hand.[75] Because of their connective powers, media enhanced and troubled inside and outside distinctions, especially when connections could switch between welcome appearances and threatening invasions. Clearly both the internal finger-pointing and the external threat of invasion sent up in *The Twilight Zone* spoke to Cold War anxieties, but the thematization of electricity and technology as inverted in connotation was precisely the kind of psychological terror behind Benson's warnings and often captured in television.

Evil threats had to be countered with the reception of the right messages through proper channels. While piping sports, sitcoms, and "up-to-the-minute" "Tele News" to TV sets, the new network of broadcast could also bring church messages into homes. Like friendly electricity itself, church leaders' figures and voices could be televised into the home offering instruction, but also the sights and sounds of proper Mormonism. Following by sight—actually seeing all the apostles and prophets in close-up—was a thrilling prospect that had been impossible since the earliest days of the faith. Beginning in May 1949, Thursday nights at 9 P.M. viewers could witness President J. Reuben Clark give an address beyond the semiannual general conference broadcasts of church leaders.[76] And this was just the beginning. Throughout the next decade more and more members were able to use TV sets outside Utah, then the nation, to attend general conference in local church buildings or eventually their own homes. Viewers only had to invite the leaders in by powering the television set on and tuning in to the appropriate channel.

TUNED IN

Standards had to be kept for proper communication from beyond or above. Once the enemy was tuned out, users had to be properly "in tune." Much like experiments with telekinesis, broadcast technology worked only when "sender and receiver were precisely tuned to each other."[77] Because of the remarkable process of channeling invisible information, both radio and television revitalized the conceptualization of revelatory experiences. Joseph Smith was now understood to have been "in tune, like unto the delicate instrument of the radio, and thus under that influence," when as a young boy he "went out into the woods to pray, and communed with God."[78] In like manner, Mormons were admonished to get "themselves in tune with the Spirit, just like a large radio transmitting station."[79] By 1971, the apostle Bruce R. McConkie taught,

The minute, however, in which we tune a radio to the proper wave band and tune a television receiving set on the proper channel, we begin to hear and see and experience what otherwise remains completely unknown to us. And so it is with the revelations and visions of eternity. They are around us all the time. This Tabernacle is full of the same things which are recorded in the scriptures and much more. The vision of the degrees of glory is being broadcast before us, but we do not hear or see or experience because we have not tuned our souls to the wave band on which the Holy Ghost is broadcasting.[80]

The technology had helped offer models and metaphors for understanding the transmission of spiritual data. Even the cultural techniques of tuning and channel selection could inspire devotional understanding. With similar hopes of reaching unity, the Latter-day Saint church initiated several midcentury projects that epitomized the process of tuning the membership through a focus on standards.

In the face of outside threats even the faith's holy scriptures, or "standard works" as they were termed, required renewed emphasis. As Philip Barlow has traced, accusations of communist influences in the 1952 academic Revised Standard Version of the bible influenced Mormon responses to double down on their adherence to the King James Version (KJV) as the Latter-day Saint standard. Church leaders Mark E. Peterson and J. Reuben Clark sought to consolidate the KJV's centrality by voicing arguments for its privileged status throughout the 1950s. For any Latter-day Saint with access to media, KJV was clearly *the* bible that all should simultaneously use together. As an October 1952 editorial in *Church News* declared, "For the Latter-day Saints there can be but one version of the bible," which was unequivocally the King James Version.[81] Clark, who was also the first church leader to appear on local television, published his defense of the decision as the book *Why the King James Version* in 1956.

A parallel effort to standardize the image of Mormons was increasingly enforced at the visible site of maturation: the church-owned Brigham Young University in Provo, Utah. College students represented the church itself as well as its future. A new BYU honor code was initiated in 1948, the same year of the first TV broadcast in Utah. This mostly expanded earlier efforts to monitor and enforce adherence to the church's health code, the Word of Wisdom, and academic honesty. It emphasized "honesty, integrity, and moral cleanliness."[82] From the 1950s into the early 1960s, however, the focus on the interior of the body and integrity would shift to an increased focus on codes of conduct and appearance, including dress and grooming standards.

The apostle Spencer W. Kimball addressed the students at BYU on "modesty in dress and its relationship to the Church" as early as 1951.[83] Although modesty and virtue had been topics of discussion in the church previously, his talk "defined standards of modesty" as specific ways of clothing the body.[84] The emphasis on the Mormon appearance coincided with the spread of television ownership in the 1950s, which shot from .02 percent of homes with TVs in 1946 to 65 percent by 1955. The following decade showcased the cultural influence of the new media infrastructure, as TV presented images of hippies against clean-cut TV personalities reporting the news of demonstrations. Incidentally, David O. McKay was also the first clean-shaven prophet of the church since Joseph Smith. Grooming standards discussed and performed in conference and on campus were then packaged for the youth of the church. The first *For the Strength of Youth* pamphlet, detailing how to dress and act as a Mormon youth, was published in 1965.

That same year BYU president Ernest Wilkinson continued to clarify and enforce grooming standards at the university. Wilkinson's push to determine student behavior and appearance was entangled with his consumption of national media, which broadcast confirmation of a lost American youth upsetting the status quo. Wilkinson hoped these rough-looking youth fighting for civil rights and against the Vietnam War would not influence the youth of the church. The unrest on the University of California–Berkeley's campus during the free speech movement suggested wayward American young adults might radicalize at any university. The sensational TV footage made the threat palpable. In 1966 the assistant to the twelve apostles Henry D. Taylor pointed out to the Latter-day Saints how TV and radio offered a barrage of the "unrest that exists in the world today." As he described it, "Wars, bloodshed, riots, and acts of lawlessness are characteristic of the times."[85] In the wake of these developments, public image as dress and grooming coalesced in the 1960s as a demarcating cultural technique against new fashions associated with hippies, "beatniks," "go-go girls," and "surfers," as BYU's President Wilkinson grouped them.[86] The university administration offered their students a narrowed and increasingly defined parameter of dress standards with the hope they might differentiate themselves from some of the popular trends they saw as morally degenerate.

Along with dress codes aimed to consolidate a standard look, Mormon life became increasingly bundled through the standardization of architecture and curricula.[87] The construction of cookie-cutter chapels across the world during the 1950s and 1960s reflected growth in membership and attempts to homogenize the worldwide experience of Mormonism. The year 1952 saw the first suggested set of lessons for proselytizing missionaries to share with those they taught. By 1961 even this was redone and titled *A Uniform System for Teaching Investigators*.[88] In learning, performing, or teaching the culture of Mormonism, it was imperative to live up to the proper standards.

During these same decades teaching the importance of living up to gospel "standards" in general conference skyrocketed in frequency. If broadcast technology allowed church leaders to enter the home and chapel of members scattered abroad, then standards did the work of fostering and cultivating a specific vision of patriotic and family-centered Latter-day Saints. As David O. McKay put in in 1961, "A home keeping the standards of the Church, is a happy home; an unbroken home."[89] Members were taught to "refrain from things which lower our standards of joy, lower our standards of life," and to "live up to the standards of the church"; "this was not a day for compromising standards."[90] They needed to "conform their lives to [the gospel's] standards" and to "set [their] standards high."[91] Although these few examples come from the first couple of years of instituting Correlation, similar rhetoric peppered the entire decade. Through discourse and example in televised general conferences, members were encouraged to live up to standards in their own homes throughout the global regions of an interconnected Zion. In 1971 the church's magazine for adults was even retitled with a synonym for a standard: *Ensign*.

The Correlation Committee implemented the clearest effort to harmonize under the banner of a common standard with their goal of uniting auxiliaries under the priesthood authority. Certainly, one model for correlation was the American corporation and its centralized power.[92] In fact, as part of their efforts to correlate the church, leaders hired two consulting firms and deliberately worked toward functioning as an efficient corporation, with committees, clear lines of authority, and quantitative measures.[93] Yet the efforts toward harmony and simultaneity were also animated with the appeal of electronic media. The discourse of Correlation efforts mirrored the technical standards of commercial television in form, while also disseminating normative standards of conduct.

In microcosm and limited to auditory regulation, similar standardization had already been a concern with radio broadcasting. In the 1930s Mormon mission president Roscoe Grover led and created radio programs for the eastern states mission. In an effort to standardize the broadcasts, Grover wrote up and disseminated a list of commonly mispronounced words. Before the homogenizing effect of radio, church members—even leaders—were apparently pronouncing "ah-poss-tull" for apostle and "ee-pis-tull" for epistle. Heber J. Grant, for instance had to unlearn his pronunciation of California as "Californy."[94] Grover feared a wider audience "could spot them as hicks from the west if they mispronounced these words."[95] Since the group performing on the national air would have the "responsibility of presenting a picture of the entire 'Mormon Church' to the nation," they utilized "every opportunity for perfecting themselves in radio technic."[96] During an early practice run in New Jersey, participants realized that this would be "one of the finest efforts yet made for reaching a million people at a time."[97] The way Grover molded Latter-day Saints to work on air offers a concrete example of American music scholar Jake Johnson's contention that Correlation is fundamentally a policy of disciplining the Mormon voice. As Johnson puts it, "Through correlation, the voice has, over the last several decades, become just as disciplined and codified as the Mormon body and its accompanying demeanor."[98]

The concerted effort to homogenize Mormonism was meant to cultivate unity. After listening to the broadcast of music and the spoken word in 1936, McKay stated in general conference, "Your unison in song in the national broadcast this morning deeply impressed me. . . . I would that the same oneness, unity and harmony manifested in that congregation singing might characterize every righteous endeavor of the Church."[99] Voice and harmony across the airwaves already suggested the unifying effect of broadcast, but two decades later conference was televised. As President McKay quoted in conference, a telegram from California received that very day reported how members "gathered in homes enjoyed the TV broadcast of conference this morning." And from Tijuana came the report "The Saints gathered here in Mexico enjoying good conference reception." After reading the messages of successful televisual connection, McKay concluded, "As you see . . . we are just one great, united Church—united in love."[100]

Beyond shaping pronunciation, cadence, and appearance, Mormon Correlation functioned as a response to perceived threats to family and manhood. Church leaders warned that "the failure of patriarchal leadership in the home" was a leading threat to what they saw as divinely ordained and rigid gender roles.[101] Correlation was an act to intervene and shape patriarchy and doctrines with a clear gender hierarchy.[102] It also simplified things and streamlined activity. The apostle appointed by President McKay to head up Correlation, Harold B. Lee, explained their mandate as threefold: to simplify programs, stress the priesthood as the guiding authority and stress the home as the center of Mormonism.[103]

In October 1962 the members of the newly appointed Correlation Committee reported on their objectives and progress. Lee began by first emphasizing how Correlation would only enhance domestic life. Lee clarified, "The home is the basis of a righteous life and no other instrumentality can take its place nor fulfil its essential functions. The utmost the auxiliaries can do is to aid the home in its problems."[104] In the face of nuclear and civil threats, including communism, both national survival and personal progress were rooted in the home, which was divinely ordained in Mormon thought.[105] In fact, by the 1970s the Latter-day Saint standard works of holy scripture included the statement that "only the home can compare with the temple in sacredness."[106] The home had been elevated but needed to be cultivated, protected, and instructed against the evils of the modern world. And a correlated vision of the church provided the answer through manuals and magazines, as well as radio and television broadcasts.

During the October 1962 general conference, apostle Gordon B. Hinckley suggested that the Correlation Committee could be compared to the central "nervous system whose responsibility is to keep the various aspects of the great teaching program of the Church operating harmoniously together."[107] Fellow member of the quorum of the twelve Spencer W. Kimball even referenced the parallel potential of broadcast technology to extend the instruction out to the world. Kimball reflected how "in these days of radio and television, we may preach to all the world. Yesterday, the human voice could be heard only hundreds of yards. Today, the Lord having opened the way, modern inventions permit our bearing witness to all the people of the earth. From yards to miles to Telstars to planets."[108] As Kimball referenced, the Telstar satellite was a cutting-edge recent development in broadcast technology. As it was launched in the context of the space race and in response to Russia's Sputnik satellite of 1957, Telstar was also a symbol of American advancement.

The Telstar satellite was sent into orbit in July 1962, and that same month the Mormon Tabernacle Choir participated in the first formal worldwide television program. The previous televised work of the choir had already "sealed the association between Mormonism, religious 'wholesomeness,' and Cold War patriotism," as Joanna Brooks wrote.[109] And they would go on to sing at the presidential inaugurations of Johnson and Nixon.[110] But now they were invited to perform their talents as assimilated quintessential Americans to eighteen different countries at once. Positioned at the base of Mount Rushmore, the Latter-day Saint singers belted out what one participant called "the message of America to the world."[111] In the broadcast, the choir appears following a patriotic montage, including footage of baseball, President Kennedy, Seattle's Space Needle, buffalo, and "real life cowboys."

The choir is framed in a long shot and sings "A Mighty Fortress Is Our God," which provides the magisterial soundtrack to the camera's work of moving from human singers to close-ups of the founding fathers' faces carved in the mountain's stone facade. The performance of good Mormonism on satellite television was the performance of good patriotism. Even an implicit vision of race and gender was on display. With men and women clearly separated among an all-white ensemble singing in exquisite harmony, the Mormon Tabernacle Choir demonstrated key ideals of one brand of American culture to an international audience.

ELECTRONIC GATHERING

With broadcast technology the need to gather geographically lost some of its necessity. Instead, television brought church standards to audiences, who were gathered and correlated where they live, simultaneously. Latter-day Saint Correlation was, after all, a visionary management of space. Correlation wanted nothing less than to enter the home of members and connect that domestic space with the hub through patriarchal priesthood. This force would endow the home with exalting ties and gather members as so many scriptural declarations had promised.

Although similar notions of a dispersed gathering had been taught as early as 1912, the architectural, standardized, and technological means to support such a policy were not in place until the late 1960s.[112] Originally the Latter-day Saints had gathered through physical migrations and looked forward to a day when all would gather in the prophesied future utopia of New Jerusalem, in Missouri. The directive to live among one another in tight-knit communities, where Zion could be built through individuals becoming increasingly unified and "of one heart and mind" was rooted in scripture.[113] The amazing account of the City of Enoch provided inspiration. For, as the story goes, Enoch was so successful in knitting the citizens' hearts as one that the entire city was taken up to heaven.[114] In fact, in their articulation of Correlation's initiatives, Latter-day Saint leaders connected it to the City of Enoch, crediting that city's success to its implementation of Correlation.

Harold B. Lee described how to attain Zion by adhering to church standards and reminded audiences that "the all-important thing is not where we live but whether or not our hearts are pure."[115] The ability to develop pure hearts, proper character, and unity was to be facilitated by Correlation. As the apostle and future church president Thomas S. Monson stated, "The battle plan whereby we fight to save the souls of men is not our own. It was provided . . . by the inspiration and revelation of the Lord. Yes, I speak of that plan which will bring us victory, even the Correlation Program of the Church."[116] This ecclesiastical overhaul's primary intention was to make priesthood the mediating and "coordinating agency between the home and the church program."[117] Employing standards and standardization not only regulated families but simultaneously shaped the definition and the very performance of that ideal. Soon Correlation was articulated as a divine inspiration finally being restored to bless the face of the earth and gather the faithful where they stand.

Even when, as historian Richard Jensen has noted, "a resurgence of LDS emigration from Europe took place in the years immediately following World War II," the church responded by providing "Europe and other areas with greater access to opportunities found in the United States, including the temples, more substantial local meeting places, and local leadership." This strategy reinforced the church's message "to build Zion wherever Saints were found." [118] As a result emigration from Europe dwindled. Between 1960 and 1975 the church created "approximately 100 non–United States stakes," and similar organizational clusters were "found on every continent of the world."[119] At a conference in Mexico in 1972, Apostle Bruce R. McConkie taught that "every nation is the gathering place for its own people."[120] With the proper infrastructure of instruction in place, gathering could be enacted across the globe. The eventual international reach of televised church-sponsored content solidified the hope print materials had fostered for a century. God's children—living up to standards and properly tuned in—could be electronically gathered *while scattered*.

But even this implementation of priesthood Correlation initially required bodies to meet together in closed-circuit, semiannual "priesthood" broadcasts available only in designated chapels. The Correlation Committee also charged men who held the priesthood to go in groups of two to visit the homes of their fellow congregants in an effort to support spiritual growth and help parents "maintain genuine Latter-day Saint homes."[121] Church leaders hoped to extend the "uniformly deeper" curriculum of "instruction, activities, and all proper wholesome interests" into the home to better supervise its members.[122] Visits from men with the priesthood would also provide regular inspections to determine the physical, financial, and spiritual health of Latter-day Saints.

While television taught priesthood-holding men how to accomplish the work of Correlation in closed-circuit meetings, TV sets in homes also supplemented their instruction. Any member with a TV set was able to tune in to public broadcasts of general conference, which tethered members to the faces, image, and standards of the church being taught and performed in real time. At the first broadcast of general conference, it was noted that now finally "housewives . . . unable to leave young children to attend . . . could watch conference speakers Friday while sitting on their living room sofas—if they owned television sets."[123] The expected audience quickly expanded, but the author's assumptions of gendered roles, spaces, and audiences was telling. As the televised programs bore out, men—because they held the priesthood authority—did the teaching, and women did the listening. In fact, between 1931 and 1984 women did not speak in the general sessions of general conference. That role was reserved for men and meant to be emulated in the home, where it was modeled on the TV.

Mormons scattered abroad looked forward to the broadcasts and reported feeling a new connection to the church's leadership by tuning in.[124] For many it was the first and only time seeing their leaders in medium close-up. Viewers were even invited to raise their hand to sustain "by common consent" the leaders of the church during each conference broadcast. This unifying action at a distance was powerful. It meant viewers interacted with the television in religiously significant ways through embodied performances of devotion. As Latter-day Saint scholar Joanna Brooks has argued, "General Conference was the most important 'rite of assent' . . . in Mormon life," especially because it was "an act understood by many orthodox Mormons as a promise not to dissent and as a fulfilling of sacred covenants they had made in LDS temples to consecrate themselves entirely to the Church."[125] Raising a hand at home collapsed space and gathered the flock through televisual prompts that enabled their pious participation. TV seemed to be restoring some sense of intimacy that had been difficult to maintain as the church grew internationally. Now in a modern mass media form Correlation could gather and unify without every member gathering in one physical location. Broadcast met the globalizing church halfway.

At its very core this was precisely television's magic. TV could electronically gather and reintegrate after diffusion and transmission. With the cathode ray tube, TV could dissolve, disseminate, and reveal images for those tuned in and attentive. The technology did this spreading and gathering on its own, but it also involved the viewer of the TV set in fleshing out its miniature but intimate images. Because television images were a "mosaic mesh" of points on lines, Marshall McLuhan was convinced they were more than meets the eye. He thought TV required the active involvement of the viewer's body and imagination to fully grasp the images as a whole and decipher their meaning. With a signature counterintuitive interpretation, McLuhan argued in his 1969 *Playboy* interview that TV does not just extend the viewer's sight. For McLuhan, television extended the viewers' "central nervous system" as the technology "washes over [their] entire body."[126] This was precisely the kind of active involvement Latter-day Saints sought in their viewers. Looking at lines of low-quality images got viewers to see more than what was on-screen. It invited them into the restoration and fleshing out of television and its deeper message through bodily movements and mental incorporation.

Getting viewers involved and harmonized was indeed the draw of domesticated television and correlated Mormonism. The effort to pull together distanced people—to bind them in unified and intentional ways of seeing the larger picture of domestic and spiritual threats as well as redeeming standards—suffused Mormon Correlation's hopes. These hopes were partially fulfilled in bringing visions of the church leadership and their performance of standards into the home. Viewers needed only to help flesh out the meaning and instructions of the televised images. With careful attention and proper techniques members could aid the priesthood in the work of restoring and gathering. Although member involvement and sight were essential in this gathering process, the animating and authorizing force was always understood to be the Spirit or priesthood power.

At the first television broadcast of general conference, in April 1948, church patriarch Eldred G. Smith described the priesthood as the power to restore seemingly destroyed or scattered elements. Smith explained how Latter-day Saints had always taught the "doctrine of the indestructibility of matter," but he had gained a personal insight while helping to develop the atomic bomb. Smith explained, "We were working, you might say, with an invisible ray, because we took the material, put it through a certain process which made it invisible to the eye. Then it was caught again in a separated condition, separating the $U235$ and $U238$ and other elements of uranium." Smith continued, "As a result of using those materials, elements of the earth were dissipated into the air." But Smith noted how everything that was vaporized could be restored completely. In a description that aligned priesthood, nuclear physics, and television technology, Smith proclaimed that the Lord can "exercise his power to call together elements or put them into action for our benefit. . . . God has those powers, and he has given them to us through the power of the priesthood."[127] Priesthood power—the consolidated authority under Correlation's mandate—was understood to work miracles, including the ability to connect and correlate across space. Like TV, its invisible power was made manifest in pulling back together elements and souls that had been scattered.

CONCLUSION

Speaking at Farnsworth's funeral the apostle Richard L. Evans suggested "that the unseen, the unheard, is as real as that which we can see and touch. Philo helped to demonstrate that. A turn of a switch, the tuning of an instrument—and sight and sound come in from all the earth and from out into the reaches of outerspace."[128] Where Mormon materialism had been the basis for its early visions of material spirits inhabiting the earth among the living, but generally invisible to the naked eye, TV now proved the existence and possible perception of the otherwise invisible through NTSC visions in the home. Now Latter-day Saints could "turn a little gadget and bring the President of the United States" or the president of the church right "into [their] front room" with broadcasts that demonstrated and disciplined a normative vision of how Latter-day Saints look, speak, and believe.[129] Turning dials, raising hands, and attending meetings from afar gathered the flock under the standard of a clean-cut wholesome image of harmony.

Television shaped domestic vision as much as governance and compliance did. It was a medium geared toward unifying segments of viewers and shaping behavior. Afraid of what might enter the home, American Mormonism also adopted television and the standards of a connected, capitalist nation of nuclear families. For just as soon as church leaders articulated postwar Latter-day Saint standards, the standards were said to be under attack. The specters of communism and social upheaval could be both represented and vanquished through cultural techniques of tuning in. The standardizing effect of synchronized broadcast technology together with Correlation allowed for the existence and performance of a particular type of Latter-day Saint. As a gradual creationary process, standards of the broadcast/Correlation era molded a modern Mormonism that, in many ways, persists into the present with lasting tensions for a global church.

Television changed the relationship to consuming and conforming to visions of Mormonism. Rather than learn from leaders' words in print, for the first time since the earliest days of the church Mormons could see their leaders and hear them speak from afar. This new sense perception and sense of being perceived—being seen by numberless audiences—shaped codes of conduct. The Latter-day Saints' shared vision through NTSC screens entailed strict obedience and conformity to the standards and public image of the church, especially as each member was eventually conceived of as an extension of the institution—a medium transmitting the message of the gospel to the rest of the world.[130] Television just helped standardize this work by getting Latter-day Saints to look at and like the same images of Mormonism.

Adhering to a standardized appearance and tuning in allowed the scattered to be brought up to standards and therefore gathered, at a distance. To borrow Vivian Sobchack's formulation on the power of moving-image media, broadcast television "not only historically *symbolized* but also historically *constituted* a radical alteration" of previous cultural forms of Latter-day Saints interacting and gathering.[131] Just as much as leaders or individual initiatives, television itself shaped and disseminated the vision of modern Mormonism as good, harmless patriots. Correlated and seemingly homogenous, Latter-day Saints were taught to look the same way, into screens and for the world.

CONCLUSION

May the Latter-day Saints be haunted, if it need be, by the memory
of those who pioneered the work of gathering in this dispensation,
and be haunted by the memory of the teachings and work of
Adam and Moses; of Joseph Smith and Brigham Young.

Harold B. Lee, 1948

This book has been a séance of sorts. It has conjured up a communion with the dead media of Mormonism's past to recognize the technologies that brought the religion to life in the first place. These technologies don't just neutrally disseminate Mormonism—as I've argued—they equally construct it, hence my emphasis on media interactions as distributed agency throughout the book. As I've contended, Mormonism should be understood as a series of visions, which were always embedded in media practices enacted through users and technologies. Of course, this process of shaping Latter-day Saint vision—disciplining how to look at media in order to see a certain way—continues into the present.

In 2016 an article announcing a new exhibit in the Church History Museum in Salt Lake City invited potential viewers to "experience the First Vision as if you were there."[1] The installation of a 220-degree panoramic screen in the museum updated the concept of shared panoramic vision from chapter 2 into a modern movie theater. Now visitors could see as Smith did through an immersive technology. With viewers sitting on log benches in a darkened room, the panoramic screen stitched footage together from multiple special cameras to present an equally stitched-together rendition of Smith's "first vision," composited from the various extant accounts describing that event.

In fact, this video formally enacted what contemporary Latter-day Saints were challenged to do conceptually. After the internet had proliferated different descriptions of Smith's account—some unknown and troubling to many Latter-day Saints because of apparent discrepancies—Mormons had to look at LED screens and somehow see a still unified and unifying vision of the church and its history. They have to continue doing this in the age of general religious atrophy, when young adults especially, with their own devices full of innumerable views, show little interest in sharing a traditional religious vision.[2] Latter-day Saints have to find ways of stitching together uncorrelated and unruly elements of Smith's vision into a richer but living vision. Once again, however, the panoramic presentation in the museum was a stabilized and standardizing way of seeing the "first vision." Because personal digital screens can be seen as a detriment to a unified vision of the church's past, Smith's visions of embodied beings and his seeing into stones needed to be reincorporated in the digital age. Bringing viewers to a shared screen was inviting, but conceptualizing revelation through the new screen culture also seemed necessary.

The exact same year as the exhibit, in June 2016, Latter-day Saint apostle Dieter F. Uchtdorf drew an analogy between Smith's looking in seer stones and modern-day Latter-day Saints looking at smartphones. "Most of us use a kind of 'seer stone' every day," he suggested. "My mobile phone is like a 'seer stone.'" For Uchtdorf, the handheld technology had finally caught up with and approximated the miraculous media practices of Smith and bolstered his early visionary claims. As Uchtdorf put it, "If it is possible for me to access the knowledge of the world" by looking at a small digital screen, then "who can question that seer stones are impossible for God?"[3] Importantly, Uchtdorf made the statement as a post on Facebook, and the explanation spread quickly through shares, likes, and quotations in articles just as multiple "first vision" accounts beyond the canonized version had rocked some members' sense of the "official" narrative and tone of Smith's vision. This, coupled with a growing awareness of Smith's less familiar use of a seer stone, as detailed in this book's introduction, left the religion's founding vision(s) in crisis for some because the information didn't seem to comport with what church members had learned or what they had been conditioned to see. But according to the apostle's statement, looking in the glowing screen of your phone might be the closest experience you have to seeing as Joseph Smith did.

I mention these recent impulses because they capture the thrust of this book. The museum's technology and the apostle's analogy both seek to update Smith's vision in the twenty-first century, to make Mormon seeing in the digital age, yet again, a process of Latter-day Saints seeing together by virtue of but beyond what is in front of them. As ever, media practices train Latter-day Saints' eyes where to look and discipline how to understand what is seen. And the ecclesiastical purchase as well as spiritual potential of these initiatives are entangled with and inseparable from material media. The panoramic film and the glowing digital display enable these turns to tuning retinae and linking the visions with particular feelings and meanings.

To be sure, many Mormons will make the pilgrimage to visit the museum's sensational exhibit and see the "first vision" in its panoramic and cinematic form. But most members across the globe will see into the "seer stone" of their portable screens every day. And that media practice is fraught for the church and deserves its own book someday. But it also foregrounds what I have shown here, by treating the first 150 years of the religion: Mormonism is in large measure media made and navigated through the management of vision. With the proliferation of screens in the current age there is no reason to believe this heritage will diminish.

In its simplest formulation the preceding chapters have highlighted how *Mormons are fashioned by looking at stuff to see things*. That stuff just happens to be media projects with formative value, and the passive construction of that statement is important. For in this looking they have been enabled to perform and measure what it means to be a member of the Church of Jesus Christ of Latter-day Saints within a given network of technologies. Thus, media, as much as members have determined Mormonism through visionary practices.

Technology and the Mormon body have been entangled in a process of getting members to take on and live within the visions and dreams of others. Standardizing vision and spiritual literacy through print forged and disciplined anxious eyes, craving visions but susceptible to deception. It got them to see spiritual visions by looking at text in intentional ways. Bodily techniques informed the clustering principle of church members standing at the panorama displays that solidified a shared vision of the past and future of the church after Joseph Smith's murder. Women at machines got others to look at patriarchal visions around the turn of the twentieth century with a critical eye to see beyond them. Their channeling and radical alterations of these visions exposed just how much ways of seeing are often dreams for some and nightmares for others.

Energizing connections between vision and embodiment continued to shape religious devotion, as film was employed to appeal to human bodies in getting them caught up and involved in sensational cinematic experiences.

Both anti-Mormon dramas and the Latter-day Saint church's first feature film lent viewers sights that were otherwise impossible and perhaps unbelievable. But these thrilling projections on-screen would shape how audiences viewed the modernization of Mormons beyond the theater and on the national stage. And in the first Latter-day Saint motion picture, screen Mormons were persecuted, white, frontier pioneers who had found their place in American history and culture.

Patriotic Latter-day Saints then enjoyed a welcome sense of freedom to enhance their visionary management of both the living and the dead. By the mid-twentieth century, scrolling through rolls of microfilm at reader machines enabled diligent genealogists to receive revelations and manage the growing volume of spirits to redeem. And broadcast technologies locked viewing audiences into scheduled programming and standardized looks. Vision and personal appearance were tightly bundled in the broadcast era, when tuning in to look at the right things and look the right way made Mormonism and gathered Latter-day Saints scattered abroad under a common standard.

In each media moment treated herein, the Mormon body was not only adapting to these new technologies; it was also being trained and disciplined to see correctly, to look at the right things to see the grander vision of Mormonism. From discerning supernatural sights to conditioning ways of looking into electronic screens, Mormon vision is made in its doing. And while the media they look at in order to see beyond does not dictate that all users must look this exact way, it is nevertheless integral to this process and prescribes certain parameters. Thus, adopting technologies always meant navigating unintended consequences.

Technology is not neutral. We must remember that instead of overcoming or transcending human bias, technology is shaped and used in the image of its creators and thus perpetuates and enhances—even when it conceals—these biases behind a sheen of neutrality.[4] Taking up technology entails negotiating the inherited technicality and techniques associated with that technology, which often help some while hurting or neglecting many others. Media visions of Mormonism's past are then haunted, not just because they can return after being repressed or because they are often populated with spirits, but also because they can carry with them the specter of oppressive tendencies. Performing Mormonism required a sender and receiver of visions and simultaneously assumed an unspoken third—an uninvited and absent outsider against whom Latter-day Saints could be filtered. The absent figures of Mormon visions, often based on race, sexuality, or belief, hover just outside the community's normative peripheral vision and require recognition. Even well-intended cultural techniques can have malevolent consequences for the filtered out, as well as the filtered.

Confronting the unfamiliar figures and facts of dead media conditions should be as inspiring as it is haunting for the present. In the internet age it is precisely this duality that provoked projects like the museum's panoramic film and the apostle's explanation, especially because, as they have for many religions, new media environments created new ecological issues for Latter-day Saints. The beehive of Mormonism, "Deseret" in the religion's own idiom, became digitized, and something similar to the contemporaneous phenomenon of bee colony collapse disorder ensued. Without overstating the trend, new online hives apart from the orthodox community offered appealing habitats of respite for some Mormons questioning their faith. The digital Deseret was confronted with visions unlike what had been used to unify the Latter-day Saints before. Some of this migration away from the singular vision of the church within virtual environments was a result of the accessibility of disturbing information and welcoming alternative communities. But beyond the content, personal computers and other portable screens were enabling catalysts. The possibilities for looking exploded exponentially and were increasingly private as "screen time" monopolized the masses.

Once again, training vision and a properly productive screen culture seems the church's only hope of fortifying the flock after strange specters of Mormonism's past resurfaced that were not part of Correlation in the TV age. They had lingered just outside its unified gaze. Online Mormons have to find ways to deal with the ghosts of history that had been conjured by the internet and seem to haunt the Mormon present. In 2011 Latter-day Saint church historian Marlin K. Jensen described the forces facing Mormonism in the age of Google by stating that since the first decade of the faith, "we've never had a period of—I'll call it apostasy—like we're having right now, largely over these issues."[5] The *New York Times* ran an article on the phenomenon and stated that in the information age the "Mormon Church is grappling with a wave of doubt and disillusionment among members who encountered information on the Internet that sabotaged what they were taught about their faith."[6] Visions in the screen of seer stones were once the original spark of Mormonism for a singular prophet but were now technological quagmires for Latter-day Saints everywhere gazing in their own screens of 1s and 0s.

The founding of the Joseph Smith Papers documentary editing project to publish primary sources connected to Smith, the composition of "Gospel Topics" essays that explain the church's perspective on difficult issues, and an aggressive online presence with superlative SEO tactics formed a sort of Van Helsing or Peter Venkman of Mormonism. The projects were supposed to overpower the threatening undead of the church's past. These unruly elements were not manicured and shimmering like Mormon author Stephenie Meyer's undead.[7] No, the revenant supplements to the traditional church narrative were messy, challenging, and potentially faith diminishing. They were for some Latter-day Saints difficult and dangerous to look at.

As I was employed at the Joseph Smith Papers from 2015 to 2018, the importance of directing eyes toward primary sources and away from misinformation was a constant concern, whether it involved lay members or academic scholars. We hoped to empower any interested parties with the most accurate information and sources. But looking into digital screens was clearly a charged practice for Latter-day Saints, and some felt their belief, perhaps even salvation, was at stake. It was not uncommon to hear Latter-day Saints in worship services state their fear of looking online to learn about their own faith. The church's directive was to pray, read scriptures, turn to the prophets, and seek out divinely inspired sources.[8]

Because sources and sites online are potentially dangerous, digital sight requires direction. Even in the case of the internet maximizing the production and circulation of sexually explicit content, the church has responded with ocular guidance. As Gavin Feller has written, "While online porn threatened to tear nuclear Mormon families apart, alongside it was online genealogy promising to weld together the entire human family."[9] But this was not just drowning out lewd images with a deluge of genealogical tools. It was just as much another iteration of teaching members, essentially, to "look here" (at genealogy) "not there" (at porn). This was more broadly an instruction in "how to look" into screens. And the same schema was taught concerning sites, blogs, videos, memes, and threads that hosted information antagonistic or simply not in line with the church's teachings and vision. Training eyes to look and *look away* in the digital age poses one of the church's biggest challenges. For users increasingly addicted to devices and in the candy store of digital possibilities, it has gradually become clearer that looking away altogether is not sustainable in the age of Web 2.0.

Jensen's successor as church historian, Steven E. Snow, described in 2013 how "the difficulty with some information online is that it is out of context and you don't really see the whole picture."[10] Being able to withstand the shocks and blows of digital screens in order to see the bigger picture for Snow is predicated on spiritual preparation. Looking into scriptures and toward prophetic visions is supposed to provide an antidote to "anti-Mormon" distortions. By pushing social media fasts, source criticism, and a new transparency, the Latter-day Saint church hopes to assemble a shared and sustainable media practice for the new age. One of the most productive ways Mormonism might shape its outlook is to continue to turn to, explore, and learn from its past without the potential blinders of correlated expectations.

Revisiting earlier discourse networks should inspire care, attention, and innovation in current media practices. As a Joseph Smith revelation put Paul's words to the Hebrews, "They without us cannot be made perfect—neither can we without our dead be made perfect."[11] Speaking of proxy baptism for the dead, Smith continued the thought, stating, "The earth will be smitten with a curse unless there is a welding link of some kind or other between the fathers and the children, upon some subject or other."[12] I would suggest that turning the hearts of the living media children to the fathers of dead media conditions should be mutually galvanizing, and that recognizing the assumed logic of who gets to do that turning or be turned to is a first step to working through its exclusionary violence. By taking stock of their past and present media entanglements, Latter-day Saints might generate new horizons of inclusion and sever problematic ties to harmful or dangerously limited visions. Looking back can help those looking to appreciate the role of technology in miraculous innovations or in problematic missteps of the past.

Because each chapter has its own unique context and media interaction, I hope each can maintain individual lessons and insights. Yet taken together, they reveal a tendency toward using media visions in an effort to survive assimilation into American mainstream culture. Media treated herein were always at least geared toward cultivating Latter-day Saints, but they were also techniques of filtering. They offered chances to build and maintain a community by creating the very processes for measuring, feeling, expressing, and conceptualizing what that meant at any given moment. The performance of Mormonism is then inextricably linked to media practices and has historically profited by and suffered from its alignment with American belonging.

On this model, early Mormon print texts sought governance through proliferating visions, but they also spread radical visions of an Amerindian apocalypse and the primary role Native Americans would play in God's plan. After Joseph Smith's death, panorama consolidated a vision of Latter-day Saint persecution and removal from the nation, where transgressive visions such as polygamy could thrive. Even into the turn of the twentieth century there remained some room to think outside the mainstream. The suggestive visionary work with machines of Elfie Huntington and Susa Young Gates were precisely opportunities to inspire alternative ways of envisioning gender against or beyond the American Protestant norm. Visions thereafter—including through film, microfilm, and television—only evince the further internalization of bundled ideas around race, gender, and sexuality.

Even the generative power of the dead in Mormonism gradually shifted to histories and figures that emphasized a European American lineage. The shocking spectral figures of Native American prophets appearing to early church members often morphed into more acceptable visions of family members, founding fathers, and a genealogy that shored up Latter-day Saint racial purity and American belonging. The dead no longer made the performance of Mormonism radical or incompatible with life among fellow citizens of the nation. Mormonism and its media practices might have always remained a little weird, but they were no longer pitted against the nation or provocative enough to hazard provoking its punishing gaze.

In seeking after America's version of "religious liberty," Latter-day Saints have been forced to mute their visionary impulse. They learned to be good citizens and how to perform as the "quintessential American religion." They were then free to strip themselves of any radical visions of sexuality, race, and gender. This shift in media visions is not a secularization narrative in the sense that Latter-day Saints dropped their belief system as they modernized, but rather an example of how American religious politics have always sorted acceptable and deviant religions and how this takes place by and through media. The larger narrative of this book is a survival story of Mormonism and suggests ways to embrace its global media visions and disentangle itself from the pernicious inheritances of oppressive American structures, actions, and attitudes.

I am not suggesting Latter-day Saints or other religious individuals and organizations should liberate themselves from media. They are not doomed by the media that prescribe their use. In fact, what I hope shines through this book's pages is the profound potential inherent in recognizing the interplay between humans, media, and things—even dead ones. If we acknowledge the ways media set the terms and dictate the fields of action that enable Mormonism, then it also means the Latter-day Saints emerging from these operations can be re-created over and again to become a new creature, one that holds onto its peculiarity while extending more understanding and inclusivity beyond the divides facilitated by cultural techniques. For these very divides, gaps, and glitches also enable radical restorations and opportunities for understanding. It should become clear that the webs of actors and actions could be reassembled in new ways, to see things in new ways. This not a damning determinism. It is a promising plasticity.

NOTES

INTRODUCTION

1. "History, circa Summer 1832," 2.

2. See 2 Nephi 25:18; 26:16; 3:18–20 in the Book of Mormon.

3. "'Church History,' 1 March 1842," 707.

4. "Lucy Mack Smith, History, 1845," 95.

5. Bushman, *Joseph Smith*, 49–52.

6. It is difficult to know exactly when Smith used the stones in silver bows (or "interpreters"), and when he used his previously obtained stones. See M. MacKay et al., *Joseph Smith Papers: Documents*, xxix–xxx. Smith also had visions and dictated revelations without stones or the interpreters, but his use of seer stones continued throughout his entire lifetime. Spencer, "Seers and Stones," 44–49.

7. Nolan, "Materialism and the Mormon Faith," 70.

8. Abraham 4:18.

9. See Nolan, "Materialism and the Mormon Faith," 73; Park and Watkins, "Riches of Mormon Materialism," 161–62; Welch, "New Mormon Theology of Matter."

10. "Discourse, 17 May 1843–B," [18].

11. See, for instance, Fessenden, *Culture and Redemption*, 4, 17–19; and Sullivan, *Impossibility of Religious Freedom*, 8.

12. Webb, *Mormon Christianity*, 36.

13. Ogden, *Credulity*, 8–10; and McGarry, *Ghosts of Futures Past*, 8.

14. Lassander and Ingman, "Exploring the Social," 205.

15. Allred, "Mormonism and the Archaeology of Media."

16. Shapiro, *Archaeologies of Vision*, 3.

17. Kittler, *Gramophone, Film, Typewriter*, xxii; Winthrop-Young, *Kittler and the Media*, 2.

18. Kittler, *Discourse Network*, 369.

19. Parikka, *What Is Media Archaeology?*, 7.

20. J. Peters, *Marvelous Clouds*, 11.

21. B. Meyer, "Medium," 61.

22. Siegert, *Cultural Techniques*, 7.

23. See J. Peters, "Recording beyond the Grave"; Siegert, *Cultural Techniques*; Stolow, *Deus in Machina*.

24. Stolow, *Deus in Machina*, 3–5.

25. Latour, *Reassembling the Social*, 65.

26. J. Bennett, "Edible Matter," 134.

27. Latour, *Reassembling the Social*, 91.

28. Törneman, "Queering Media Archaeology," 4.

29. Dolphijn and van der Tuin, *New Materialism*.

30. Keller and Rubenstein, *Entangled Worlds*, 1.

31. Barad, *Meeting the Universe Halfway*, 152.

32. Barad, *Meeting the Universe Halfway*, 66.

33. Barad, "Posthumanist Performativity," 823.

34. Barad, *Meeting the Universe Halfway*, 26; Siegert, *Cultural Techniques*, 1–3; J. Peters, *Marvelous Clouds*, 37; Latour, *Reassembling the Social*, 9–11.

35. Lasswell, "Structure and Function of Communication," 37.

36. Vismann, "Cultural Techniques and Sovereignty," 87.

37. Plate, *Key Terms in Material Religion*, 4.

38. Morgan, "Introduction: The Matter of Belief," xiii.

39. Plate, *Key Terms in Material Religion*, 4.

40. Modern, *Secularism in Antebellum America*, 46.

41. Coviello, *Make Yourself Gods*, 25–27, 43.

42. M. Jones, *Contemporary Mormon Pageantry*, 3; J. Johnson, *Mormons, Musical Theater, and Belonging in America*, 45.

43. Nietzsche, *Gay Science*, 51.

44. Barad, "Posthumanist Performativity," 819.

45. Mitchell and Hansen, *Critical Terms for Media Studies*, 40–41.

46. Barad, "Posthumanist Performativity," 802.

47. Barad, "Posthumanist Performativity," 828.

48. Letterbook 1, 2.

49. Doctrine and Covenants (hereafter D&C), section 90:11.

50. D&C, section 1:24; D&C, section 21:5.

51. Pratt, *Absurdities of Immaterialism*.

52. See Beardsley, "Celestial Mechanics"; and "The Female Absorption Coefficient."

53. J. Johnson, *Mormons, Musical Theater, and Belonging in America*, 20.

54. Harris and McMurray, "Sounding Mormonism," 34.

55. See Schmidt, *Hearing Things*.

56. Chen, "Internet as Battleground," 62–63.

57. See Feller, "Media as Compromise."

58. Feller, "Media as Compromise," 13.

59. B. Peters and Peters, "Introduction: Small Means, Great Things," 17–18.

60. Winthrop-Young, "Cultural Techniques: Preliminary Remarks," 14.

61. For an example of doubling-down on the determinism of material media, see Ernst, *Chronopoetics*.

62. Winthrop-Young, "Cultural Techniques: Preliminary Remarks," 14–15.

63. Wegenstein, "Body," 27.

64. Kraidy, "Body as Medium in the Digital Age," 287.

65. Morgan, *Embodied Eye*, 5.

66. S. Brown and Holbrook, "Embodiment and Sexuality in Mormon Thought," 293–94; Coviello, *Make Yourself Gods*, 8–9.

67. Welch, "New Mormon Theology of Matter," 69.

68. Blanco and Peeren, *Spectralities Studies Reader*, 2.

69. S. Brown, *In Heaven as It Is on Earth*, 35.

70. Asad, *Formations of the Secular*, 13.

71. Modern, *Secularism in Antebellum America*, xxix.

72. J. Peters, *Speaking into the Air*, 193, 142.

73. J. Peters, *Speaking into the Air*, 193, 142.

74. Derrida and Stiegler, "Spectographies," 38.

75. Orsi, *History and Presence*; Seeman, *Speaking with the Dead*; and Laqueur, *Work of the Dead*, esp. 65–74.

76. Modern, *Secularism in Antebellum America*, xxix.

77. Shapiro, *Archaeologies of Vision*, 3.

78. Stoker, *Dracula*, 59.

79. Kittler, *Discourse Network*, 258.

80. Taves, *Fits, Trances, and Visions*, 4.

81. Huhtamo, "Screen Tests," 145.

CHAPTER 1

1. L. Smith, *Biographical Sketches of Joseph Smith*, 92.

2. Bushman, "Joseph Smith and His Visions," 111.

3. By the mid-nineteenth century this account, which was included in the *Pearl of Great Price*, was the most prevalent; however several other accounts were printed by the early 1840s and were in circulation, including Pratt, "Interesting Account" (1840); Hyde, *Ein Ruf aus der Wüste* (1842); and "Church History,' 1 March 1842," 706–7.

4. Walker, *Diary of Charles Lowell Walker*, 2:755–56.

5. D. Jones, *Gothic Machines*, 19, 21.

6. B. Anderson, *Imagined Communities*, 6.

7. "Discourse, 7 April 1844," [135].

8. "Discourse, between circa 26 June and circa 4 August 1839–A," 71.

9. Kittler, *Literature, Media, Information Systems*, 40.

10. Taves, "History and the Claims of Revelation," 186.

11. Dunlap, *Life of Charles Brockden Brown*, 48–49.

12. Schmidt, *Holy Fairs*, 148.

13. Quoted in Barber, "Phantasmagorical Wonders," 81.

14. Barber, "Phantasmagorical Wonders," 80.

15. Castle, "Phantasmagoria," 30.

16. Warner, *Phantasmagoria*, 139.

17. Nicholson, "Narrative and Explanation," 148.

18. Bellion, *Citizen Spectator*, 7.

19. Kant, "Dreams of a Spirit-Seer," 308–9.

20. Kant, "Dreams of a Spirit-Seer," 327–28.

21. Qtd. in Andriopoulos, *Ghostly Apparitions*, 30.

22. Andriopoulos, *Ghostly Apparitions*, 42–43.

23. Castle, "Phantasmagoria."

24. Hawthorne, *House of the Seven Gables*, 167.

25. Carlyle, *French Revolution*, 1:165.

26. Page, "Letter."

27. Thomas, *Romanticism and Visuality*, 2.

28. Kittler, *Gramophone, Film, Typewriter*, 10.

29. Modern, *Secularism in Antebellum America*, xxix.

30. Jarvis, *Accredited Ghost Stories*, 5.

31. Kittler, *Optical Media*, 104.

32. Nord, *Faith in Reading*, 114.

33. C. G. Brown, *Word in the World*, 21.

34. See Pratt, "Interesting Account," 525; Mormon 8:15, 3 Nephi 13:22, D&C 4:5, 27:2, 55:1, 59:1, 82:19, 88:67.

35. Thomas, *Romanticism and Visuality*, 3.

36. Crary, *Techniques of the Observer*, 5, 17.

37. Jütte, *History of the Senses*, 191.

38. "Try the Spirits," 743.

39. Crary, *Techniques of the Observer*, 6.

40. Bellion, *Citizen Spectator*, 20.

41. Qtd. in Jarvis, *Accredited Ghost Stories*, 110.

42. Perry, "Many Bibles of Joseph Smith," 760.

43. D. Walker, "Humbug in American Religion," 36.

44. Taves, "History and the Claims of Revelation," 187.

45. T. Givens and Grow, *By the Hand of Mormon*, 40.

46. "Testimony of the Three Witnesses," in Joseph Smith, *Book of Mormon*, appended unpaginated.

47. Siegel, *Forensic Media*, 39–40.

48. "And Also the Testimony of the Eight Witnesses," in Joseph Smith, *Book of Mormon* appended unpaginated.

49. John Durham Peters, "An Afterword," 45, and Paul Frosh, "Telling Presences," 60, both in Frosh and Pinchevski, *Media Witnessing*.

50. Derrida, "Demeure: Fiction and Testimony," 41.

51. Kittler, *Discourse Network*, 369.

52. Savoy, "Rise of the American Gothic," 174.

53. Fiedler, *Love and Death in the American Novel*, 144.

54. Steinberg, *Lost Book of Mormon*, 178.

55. Savoy, "Rise of the American Gothic," 167.

56. C. B. Brown, *Edgar Huntley*, xiii.

57. Bergland, *National Uncanny*, 1.

58. Cooper, *Last of the Mohicans*.

59. McGarry, *Ghosts of Futures Past*, 66–93.

60. Hickman, "*Book of Mormon*," 429–30.

61. Coleridge, *Biographia Literaria*, 36.

62. Crary, *Techniques of the Observer*, 14.

63. Bellion, *Citizen Spectator*, 27.

64. T. Reid, *Inquiry*, 411.

65. Hazen, *Village Enlightenment*, 11.

66. Darley, *Ghost Stories*.

67. Andriopoulos, *Ghostly Apparitions*, 75.

68. Carpenter and Kolmar, *Ghost Stories by British and American Women*, xv.

69. Pulsipher, "History of Zera Pulsipher," 3.

70. Sedgwick, *Stories for Young Persons*, 41.

71. The first published vampire narrative was John Polidori's *The Vampyre* in 1819.

72. Joseph Smith, Letter to John Taylor; *Saints*, 1:70–71.

73. Hatch, *Visions*, Manifestations, and Miracles, 96.

74. B. Brown, *Testimonies*, 7.

75. B. Brown, *Testimonies*, 8.

76. Loughran, *Republic in Print*, 23.

77. Modern, *Secularism in Antebellum America*, 62.

78. Pulsipher, "History of Zera Pulsipher," 7.

79. Crocheron, *Representative Women of Deseret*, 24.

80. See Hatch, *Visions*, Manifestations, and Miracles.

81. Bushman, Joseph Smith, 41.

82. K. Davidson, Jensen, and Whittaker, Joseph Smith Papers: Histories, 38.

83. P. Pratt, *Autobiography*, 65.

84. Clapp, "Mormonism."

85. K. Davidson, Jensen, and Whittaker, Joseph Smith Papers: Histories, 38.

86. K. Davidson, Jensen, and Whittaker, Joseph Smith Papers: Histories, 2:22.

87. MacKay and Dirkmaat, Joseph Smith Papers: *Documents*, 1:270 (D&C 46:7–8).

88. K. Davidson, Jensen, and Whittaker, Joseph Smith Papers: Histories, 38.

89. "Recollections of the Prophet Joseph Smith."

90. "Letter to Hyrum Smith, 3–4 March 1831," [1].

91. "Revelation, circa 8 March 1831–A [D&C 46]," 78.

92. D&C 28:11.

93. J. Peters, "Mormonism and Media," 409.

94. Fielding, Diary of Joseph Fielding, September 2, 1841, 75–76.

95. Blythe, "Ann Booth's Vision," 122.

96. "Revelation, 9 May 1831 [D&C 50]," 82.

97. Ashurst-McGee, Grua, and Kuehn, *Documents*, 510; see also S. Brown, *In Heaven as It Is on Earth*, 188–91.

98. Defoe, *Secrets of the Invisible World Disclos'd*, 16.

99. "Instruction, 9 February 1843 [D&C 129]," 53, 54.

100. S. Brown, *In Heaven as It Is on Earth*, 171.

101. Ashurst-McGee, Grua, and Kuehn, *Documents*, 547; Martha Jane Knowlton Coray, Notebook.

102. Martha Jane Knowlton Coray, Notebook. Discourse also reproduced in B. Rogers, Allred, Dirkmaat, and Dowdle, *Documents*, 83.

103. See Schmidt, *Hearing Things*.

104. "Discourse, 1 May 1842," 94.

105. Morgan, *Embodied Eye*, xvii.

106. Modern, *Secularism in Antebellum America*, 107–9.

107. "Instruction, 2 April 1843," 69.

CHAPTER 2

1. Dibble, Reminiscences.

2. Copyright Records, State of Illinois, vol. 18.

3. Stout, Journal, April 10, 1845; *Nauvoo Neighbor* 3, no. 13 (July 30, 1845).

4. See Bernhisel, "Letter to Brigham Young, Sep. 10, 1849."

5. Assmann, "Collective Memory and Cultural Identity," 129.

6. Dibble, "Brother Philo Dibble's Sceneries, Museum, &c.," 11.

7. Woodruff, *Wilford Woodruff's Journal*, 2:199.

8. Kittler, *Gramophone, Film, Typewriter*, xxxix.

9. Orsi, *History and Presence*, 108.

10. Sobchack, *Carnal Thoughts*, 150.

11. J. Peters, *Marvelous Clouds*, 2.

12. Quinn, "Mormon Succession Crisis of 1844," 188.

13. Carmack, "'One of the Most Interesting Sceneries'"; and D. Jensen, "Philo Dibble's Dream."

14. Carey, *Communication as Culture*, 15.

15. Pallasmaa, "Hapticity and Time," 83.

16. Griffiths, *Shivers Down Your Spine*, 37.

17. Huhtamo, *Illusions in Motion*, 1–9.

18. Byerly, "Prodigious Map beneath His Feet," 84.

19. Oetterman, *Panorama*, 323.

20. Oetterman, *Panorama*, 313.

21. Morgan, *Lure of Images*, 161.

22. Huhtamo, *Illusions in Motion*, 184.

23. Barringer, "World for a Schilling," 83–84.

24. Otto, "Artificial Environments, Virtual Realities," 167.

25. Carmack, "One of the Most Interesting Sceneries," 25.

26. G. Smith, "History of George Albert Smith." See also Villela, "Beyond Stephens and Catherwood," 156.

27. M. Godfrey, McBride, Smith, and Blythe, *Joseph Smith Papers: Documents*, 242.

28. Schivelbusch, *Railway Journey*, 64.

29. Crary, "Gericault, the Panorama, and Sites of Reality," 9.

30. Dibble, "Brother Philo Dibble's Sceneries," 11.

31. Dibble, "Brother Philo Dibble's Sceneries," 11.

32. Dibble, "Brother Philo Dibble's Sceneries," 11.

33. Stout, Journal, September 2, 1845.

34. Dibble, Reminiscences; and Stout, Journal, September 8, 1845.

35. R. Bennett, Black, and Cannon, *Nauvoo Legion in Illinois*, 234.

36. Stout, Journal, September 18, 1845.

37. Morgan, *Lure of Images*, 162–64.

38. Dibble, "Brother Philo Dibble's Sceneries," 11.

39. Grow et al., *Administrative Records, Council of Fifty*, 408–9.

40. Mahas, "Remembering the Martyrdom," 300–305.

41. Jessee, "Return to Carthage," 18.

42. Daniels, *Correct Account of the Murder*, 8, 19.

43. Oaks and Hill, *Carthage Conspiracy*, 168.

44. Crary, *Techniques of the Observer*, 122.

45. D. Walker, "Railroading Independence," 32.

46. D. Walker, *Railroading Religion*, 202.

47. Halbwachs, *On Collective Memory*, 175.

48. Wind, "Warburg's Concept of *Kulturwissenschaft*," 193.

49. "Murder," 585; Poulsen, "Fate and the Persecutors of Josephs Smith," 63–68.

50. D. Godfrey and Godfrey, *Diaries of Charles Ora Card*, 386.

51. B. Johnson, *My Life's Review*, 117; Dahl and Cannon, *Encyclopedia of Joseph Smith's Teachings*, 644.

52. Blythe, "'Would to God, Brethren,'" 2, 7.

53. Quinn, "Mormon Succession Crisis of 1844," 194.

54. Blythe, "'Would to God, Brethren,'" 11.

55. Speek *"God Has Made Us a Kingdom,"* 25.

56. Barnett, "Canes of the Martyrdom," 206.

57. See Stout, Journal, April 10, June 3, and August 6, 1845.

58. Woodruff, *Wilford Woodruff's Journal*, 2:479; *Journal of Discourses* 5:58–60; L. Snow, "Iowa Journal," 268.

59. M. Kimball, *Journal of Mary Ellen Kimball*, 31–33.

60. Clayton, *Intimate Chronicle*, 174; Lightner, *Life and Testimony of Mary Lightner*, 63–65; O. Huntington, *History of the Life of Oliver B. Huntington*, 7–8.

61. *Journal of Discourses* 4:286. See also Blythe, "'Would to God, Brethren,'" 11.

62. Woodruff, journal entry for August 6, 1844, in Wilford Woodruff's Journals and Papers, 1828–1898, CHL. See R. Walker, "Six Days in August," 161–96.

63. Woodruff, *Wilford Woodruff's Journal*, 2:434.

64. Watson, *Manuscript History of Brigham Young, 1801–1844*, 528–30.

65. Qtd. in Juanita Brooks, *On the Mormon Frontier*, 238.

66. J. Johnson, *Mormons, Musical Theater, and Belonging*, 36.

67. See Jorgenson, "Mantle of the Prophet"; and Van Wagoner, "Making of a Mormon Myth."

68. Woodruff, "Priesthood and the Right of Succession."

69. A. Rogers, *Life Sketches of Orson Spencer*, 331–32.

70. Woodruff, "To the Officers and Members of the Church," 138.

71. J. Cannon, "Image as Text and Context," 340.

72. Major, "Artworks in the Celestial Room," 48.

73. Dibble, Reminiscences, 2.

74. Dibble, "Brother Philo Dibble's Sceneries, Museum, &c.," 11.

75. Stout, Journal, March 7 and April 10, 1845.

76. *Wilford Woodruff's Journal*, 2:539.

77. Huhtamo, *Illusions in Motion*, 8.

78. S. Brown, *In Heaven as It Is on Earth*, 295.

79. Griffiths, *Shivers Down Your Spine*, 42.

80. Dibble, "Brother Philo Dibble's Sceneries, Museum, &c.," 12.

81. Qtd. in Jütte, *History of the Senses*, 194.

82. "Patty Sessions," 135.

83. Woodruff, *Wilford Woodruff's Journal*, 3:340.

84. Landsberg, *Prosthetic Memory*, 21.

85. "Interesting Meeting."

86. Amy Brown Lyman, "In Retrospect," 6.

87. Dibble, "Brother Philo Dibble's Sceneries," 12.

88. Woodruff, *Wilford Woodruff's Journal*, 3:340.

89. Qtd. in T. Givens and Grow, *Parley P. Pratt*, 232.

90. Balázs, "'Visible Man,'" 96.

91. Nicholas of Cusa, *Vision of God*, 3–6.

92. de Certeau, "Gaze: Nicholas of Cusa," 11–12.

93. Kittler, *Optical Media*, 34.

94. W. Reid, *Lectures on the Revelation*, 25.

95. W. Reid, *Lectures on the Revelation*, 273.

96. Morgan, *Lure of Images*, 161–62.

97. Whitney, "Discourse by Bishop Orson F. Whitney," 264.

98. Godfrey et al., *Joseph Smith Papers: Documents*, 2:343.

99. Woodruff, "Church and Kingdom of God," 199.

100. Pratt, "Preparations for the Second Advent," 310.

101. G. Cannon, "Discourse," 677.

102. Durham, *Discourses of Wilford Woodruff*, 285.

103. J. Smith, "Remarks," 449.

104. D. Jensen, "Philo Dibble's Dream," 21.

105. Flake, *Politics of American Religious Identity*, 115.

106. Dibble, Letter to John Taylor.

107. *Deseret News*, June 26, 1878.

108. Dibble, *Philo Dibble's Reminiscences*, 53.

109. Carmack, "One of the Most Interesting Seeneries," 33.

110. Richard L. Jensen, *C. C. A. Christensen, 1831–1912*, 15.

111. Arrington, *Mormon Experience*, 124.

112. Osterhammel, *Transformation of the World*, 901.

113. Dearinger, *Filth of Progress*, 125.

114. Chevalier, *Society, Manners, and Politics*, 307.

115. Carey, *Communication as Culture*, 157.

116. Stevenson, *Child's Garden of Verses*, 41.

117. S. Clark, *Round Trip*, 164.

118. J.M.S., "In Switzerland," 185.

119. Schivelbusch, *Railway Journey*, 62; Sternberger, *Panorama*, 50.

120. *History, 1838–1856*, volume F-1, August 5, 1844, 7: addenda, 10.

121. *Wilford Woodruff's Journal*, 2:434.

122. *Wilford Woodruff's Journal*, 2:439.

123. D. Walker, "Railroading Independence," 30.

124. Qtd. in Richard L. Jensen, *C. C. A. Christensen, 1831–1912*, 18.

125. Harper, *First Vision*, 109.

126. The initial painting of the "first vision" has been lost. See Richard L. Jensen, *C. C. A. Christensen, 1831–1912*, 91.

CHAPTER 3

1. Iverson, *Seventy-Eighth Annual Conference*, 70.

2. Stolow, "Salvation by Electricity," 685.

3. See Price and Thurschwell, *Literary Secretaries / Secretarial Culture*; and Gaboury, *Image Objects*, 118.

4. Rozmarin, "Living Politically," 472.

5. Jantzen, *Becoming Divine*, 102.

6. Jantzen, *Becoming Divine*, 119.

7. Dolphijn and Tuin, *New Materialism*, 62.

8. Wajcman, *TechnoFeminism*, 6–7.

9. Hoyt and Patterson, "Mormon Masculinity," 73, 80.

10. Howe, "Professional and Business Opportunities," 24.

11. Irigaray, *Sex Which Is Not One*, 76.

12. Schor, "This Essentialism," 67.

13. "Springville Notes"; "Springville Celebrates."

14. Hood, *Comic Annual*, 94–98; Steward, *Vision of Aorangi*, 180.

15. Piner, *Werner's Readings and Recitations*, 8.

16. Bertolini, "Fireside Chastity," 719–21.

17. "Proceedings of Societies."

18. Novak, *Realism, Photography*, 3.

19. Novak, *Realism, Photography*, 4.

20. Mulvey, *Visual and Other Pleasures*, 13.

21. Irigaray, *Speculum of the Other Woman*, 133–34.

22. Snyder, *Bachelors, Manhood, and the Novel*, 32–33.

23. Crary, *Techniques of the Observer*, 13.

24. Kent, "Points of the Ideal Woman"; Gates, "Perfect Woman."

25. Gates, "Perfect Woman," 451.

26. D. Davis, "Appreciating a Pretty Shoulder," 132.

27. Campbell, *Charles Ellis Johnson*, 91–114.

28. Crowl, Letter.

29. "Gambling Resumed at Poker Joints."

30. L. Williams, "Motion and E-motion," 111–13.

31. C. Jones, *Women's View*, 5–6.

32. Campbell, "Mormonism, Gender, and Art," 245.

33. See, for instance, the verso of photograph of George A. Smith in Bathsheba Smith Photograph Collection, ca. 1865-1900, CHL.

34. "Springville Notes"; "Springville Celebrates."

35. Owen, *Darkened Room*, 11.

36. Modern, *Secularism in Antebellum America*, 40–42.

37. Bitton, *Ritualization of Mormon History*, 86; R. Walker, *Wayward Saints*, 282–84; Braude, *Radical Spirits*.

38. D. Walker, "Humbug in American Religion," 31, 39.

39. Geoghegan, "Mind the Gap," 903.

40. Sconce, *Haunted Media*, 12; Walkowitz, "Science and the Séance," 9.

41. Braude, *Radical Spirits*, 3, 83.

42. McGarry, *Ghosts of Futures Past*, 126.

43. Stolow, "Salvation by Electricity," 672.

44. Sconce, *Haunted Media*, 18.

45. Holzapfel and Hedges, *Through the Lens*.

46. J. Cannon, "Images as Text and Context," 355–65.

47. Robinson, *Elements of a Pictorial Photograph*, 39.

48. Lindsey, *Communion of Shadows*, 117.

49. Manseau, *Apparitionists*, 7.

50. Harvey, *Photography and Spirit*, 30.

51. Allred, "Developing the Dead."129.

52. "Curious Trial—Spirit Photography."

53. Gunning, "To Scan a Ghost," 226.

54. Tucker, *Nature Exposed*, 3.

55. H. A. Anderson to Susa Young Gates; C. Orlob to Susa Young Gates.

56. Tait, "'Young Woman's Journal': Gender and Generations," 51, 53.

57. James Allen and Embry, "Provoking the Brethren to Good Works," 115.

58. Lynott, "Susa Young Gates 1856–1933," v.

59. Caldwell, "Biographical: Susa Young Gates," 124.

60. Gates, "Relief Society Organized at Nauvoo," 1.

61. Stoker, *Dracula*, 207; Wicke, "Vampiric Typewriting," 470.

62. Kittler, *Gramophone, Film, Typewriter*, 14.

63. E. Wells, "New Civilization."

64. Gates, "Importance of Record Keeping," 17.

65. Gates, "To My Mother's Mothers," *Improvement Era*, 777. See also, Gates, "To My Mother's Mothers," Susa Young Gates Papers.

66. Price and Thurschwell, *Literary Secretaries / Secretarial Culture*, 3.

67. Keep, "Blinded by the Type," 159.

68. Thurschwell, "Typist's Remains," 2.

69. A. Davis, *Present Age and Inner Life*, 285.

70. Kontou and Willburn, *Ashgate Research Companion*, 67.

71. Keep, "Blinded by the Type," 158–59.

72. Owen, *Darkened Room*, 11–12.

73. Schmidt, *Heaven's Bride*, 112.

74. "Scientific News," 519.

75. "New Publications"; Wade, *Posthumous Memoirs*, 1.

76. Qtd. in J. Jones, *Thaumat—Oahspe*, 7, 13.

77. Tate, "'Great World of the Spirits of the Dead.'"

78. Roberts, "Comprehensiveness of the Gospel," 397.

79. Tait, "Susa Young Gates and the Vision," 318.

80. Gates, "Vision of the Redemption of the Dead," 21.

81. Gates, "Lion House Memories," 6.

82. Gates, "Editor's Department," 86.

83. Gates, "Witchcraft," 396, 399, 397.

84. Beardsley, "Celestial Mechanics," 48–54.

85. Typewriter in custody of the Church History Museum, Salt Lake City, Utah.

86. Whitaker, Daily Journal, 30–31.

87. Historical Department Office Journal, January 1, 1909. See also Robin Jensen, "Archives of the Better World."

88. Gates, *History of the Young Ladies'* Mutual Improvement Association, 168.

89. Gates, "Message," 450.

90. Seymour, "Type-Writing," 426.

91. Wershler-Henry, *Iron Whim*, 92.

92. Harline, Polygamous *Wives Writing Club*, 159.

93. Daynes, *More Wives Than One*, 135.

94. L. Foster, *Women, Family, and Utopia*, 207.

95. T. Simpson, *American University*, 18; H. Jensen, "Aesthetic Evangelism," 144.

96. See Tait, "'Young Woman's Journal' and Its Stories."

97. Lizzie Smith, "Equality of the Sexes," 176.

98. Howe, "Professional and Business Opportunities," 24–25.

99. Coviello, *Make Yourself Gods*, 204.

100. Seltzer, *Bodies and Machines*, 10.

101. Shiach, "Modernity, Labour and the Typewriter," 115.

102. Gates, Notes on Life History.

103. Plummer, "Gates, Susa Young," 536.

104. Gates, Autobiographical Sketches.

105. G. Cannon, "Influence and Sphere of Woman," 67.

106. Gates, "Boy versus Girl," 30.

107. Gates, "Women's Place in the Plan of Salvation," 5.

108. Gates, "Women's Place in the Plan of Salvation," 5.

109. Glover [Eddy], *Science and Health*, 303.

110. Shirts, "Role of Susa Young Gates," 105, 139.

111. Tait, "'Young Woman's Journal' and Its Stories," 12.

112. Alexander, *Mormonism in Transition*, 132.

113. Gates, Autobiographical Sketches.

114. Gates, "From a Mother to Her Babe."

115. Lynott, "Susa Young Gates 1856–1933," vi.

116. Gates, Autobiographical Sketches.

117. Burt, "Susa Young Gates," 2.

118. Burt, "Susa Young Gates," 3.

119. Flake, *Politics of American Religious Identity*, 118–21; Harper, *First Vision*, 129.

120. Gates, "Vision Beautiful," 543.

121. Gates, "Vision Beautiful," 542.

122. See Paulsen and Pulido, "'Mother There,'" 9–10; F. Givens, "Feminism and Heavenly Mother," 558.

123. Embry, "Grain Storage," 60.

124. Alexander, *Mormonism in Transition*, 125.

125. Hoyt and Patterson, "Mormon Masculinity," 79–80.

126. C. Madsen, "'New Woman' and the *Women's Exponent*," 72–77.

127. Stapley, "Women and Priesthood," 573.

128. Wershler-Henry, *Iron Whim*, 225; Kittler, *Gramophone, Film, Typewriter*, 200–214.

129. *Deseret Weekly*, April 6, 1889, 451.

130. Blythe, *Terrible Revolution*, 191–93.

CHAPTER 4

1. *Deseret News* 3 (January 25, 1913): 8.

2. Tybjerg, "Seeing through Spirits," 121–22.

3. Natale, "Short History of Superimposition," 140.

4. Bazin, *What Is Cinema?*, 15. See also Elsaesser, "Media Archaeology as Symptom," 201.

5. Coviello, *Make Yourself Gods*, 25–27, 43.

6. See T. Simpson, *American University*, 54–91.

7. See Flake, *Politics of American Religious Identity*.

8. Bunker and Bitton, *Mormon Graphic Image*, 140–43.

9. See M. Jones, *Performing American Identity*; T. Givens and Grow, *Viper on the Hearth*; and Reeve, *Religion of a Different Color*, 140–41.

10. Whissell, *Picturing American Modernity*, 166.

11. Whissell, *Picturing American Modernity*, 163.

12. Edwards, "Infrastructure and Modernity," 186.

13. See T. Simpson, *American University*, 26.

14. Hoyt and Patterson, "Mormon Masculinity," 78, 73.

15. See D'Arc, "Mormon as Vampire."

16. B. Cannon and Olmstead, "'Scandalous Film,'" 63.

17. Arrington, *Mormon Experience*, 243.

18. Hoyt and Patterson, "Mormon Masculinity," 73, 80.

19. R. Nelson, "Commercial Propaganda in the Silent Film," 149.

20. D. Walker, "Mormon Melodrama," 262.

21. B. Cannon and Olmstead, "'Scandalous Film,'" 42.

22. Gunning, "Now You See It, Now You Don't," 76.

23. See *Motion Picture News* 15:1505; and "A Mormon Maid," Internet Movie Database, accessed May 13, 2022, www.imdb.com/title/tt0008319/.

24. May, *Utah: A People's History*, 164.

25. *Tourist's Handbook*, 53.

26. Weisenfeld, "Framing the Nation," 29.

27. Weisenfeld, "Framing the Nation," 32–33.

28. Andriopoulos, *Possessed*, 4.

29. *Broken Hearts and Broken Lives*.

30. Julie Allen, *Danish but Not Lutheran*, 165.

31. B. Cannon and Olmstead, "'Scandalous Film,'" 46.

32. W. Graham, *That Reminds Me*, 59.

33. Julie Allen, *Danish but Not Lutheran*, 183.

34. Andriopoulos, *Possessed*, 91–92.

35. Münsterberg, *Photoplay*, 57.

36. Goodwin, *Abusing Religion*, 7.

37. Whissell, *Picturing American Modernity*, 162–63.

38. E. Larson, *Thunderstruck*.

39. Peet, "Anti-Mormon Crusade in England," 1.

40. *Debates of the House of Commons*.

41. Alexander, *Mormonism in Transition*, 246.

42. J. Peters, *Speaking into the Air*, 141–43.

43. Modern, *Secularism in Antebellum America*, xxix.

44. Andriopoulos, "Terror of Reproduction," 501–20.

45. Rank, *Double*, xiii.

46. B. Cannon and Olmstead, "'Scandalous Film,'" 53.

47. *Motion Picture News* 5:12.

48. Clawson, Letters to the First Presidency, December 15, 1911; see also letter of March 5, 1912.

49. Mensel, "'Kodakers Lying in Wait,'" 28.

50. S. Brown, *In Heaven as It Is on Earth*, 54.

51. Warren and Brandeis, "Right to Privacy," 199.

52. Warren and Brandeis, "Right to Privacy."

53. Kern, *Culture of Time and Space, 1880–1918*, 189.

54. Kern, *Culture of Time and Space, 1880–1918*, 189.

55. Warren and Brandeis "Right to Privacy," 211.

56. "Ethics and Etiquette of Photography," 107–8.

57. Lewis and McConnell, *Equity Jurisdiction, Bills of Peace*, 356–58.

58. Kern, *Culture of Time and Space*, 189.

59. R. Smith, *Law of Privacy Explained*, 12.

60. Barbas, "Gossip Law," 133.

61. Alexander, *Mormonism in Transition*, 248–49.

62. B. Cannon and Olmstead, "'Scandalous Films,'" 49.

63. Clawson, "Anti-'Mormon' Moving Pictures."

64. Grant, *Ninetieth Annual Conference* (1920), 6.

65. Hoyt and Patterson, "Mormon Masculinity," 73.

66. Bernardi, *Birth of Whiteness*, 4.

67. Penrose, *Eighty-Third Annual Conference*, 57.

68. Melvin Ballard, *Eighty-Third Annual Conference*, 19.

69. G. Foster, *Performing Whiteness*, 2.

70. S. Johnson, *African American Religions*, 394.

71. Bernardi, "Voice of Whiteness," 112.

72. Maurice, *Cinema and Its Shadow*, 5.

73. Qtd. in Peery, "Bureau of Information," 215.

74. Alexander, *Mormonism in Transition*, 239.

75. "Motion Pictures to Tell."

76. Keil and Stamp, *American Cinema's Transitional Era*, 1.

77. Keil, *Early American Cinema in Transition*, 10.

78. Grieveson, *Policing Cinema*, 81.

79. Historical Department, Journal History of the Church, June 30, 1910, 8.

80. Astle, *Mormon Cinema*, 195.

81. "Noted American Writer."

82. Armatage, *Girl from God's Country*, 355.

83. "Century of 'Mormonism.'"

84. "Amusements."

85. "100 Years of Mormonism," *Logan Republican*, February 4, 1913, 4; "Mormon Story to Be Told by Film."

86. Astle and Burton, "History of Mormon Cinema," 24.

87. E. Godfrey, *Film and Education*, 15.

88. Moffett, "Doing the Impossible."

89. "History of 'Mormonism' in Picture."

90. Miriam Hansen, *Cinema and Experience*, 4.

91. L. Young, "Mormonism in Picture," 75.

92. "History of Mormonism' in Picture."

93. Miriam Hansen, "Mass Production of the Senses," 68.

94. J. Evans, *One Hundred Years of Mormonism*, 40.

95. D. Walker, "Mormon Melodrama," 259.

96. Solomon, *Disappearing Tricks*, 8.

97. Gunning, "To Scan a Ghost," 213.

98. Commolli, "Historical Fiction: A Body Too Much?," 68.

99. Pearson and Khullar, "Reverse Flow," 110–11.

100. Gunning, *D. W. Griffith*, 257.

101. Allred, *Weimar Cinema, Embodiment, and Historicity*, 45.

102. "History of 'Mormonism' in Picture."

103. *Deseret Evening News*, March 22, 1913.

104. L. Young, "Mormonism in Picture," 78.

105. *Moving Picture World* 18:1015.

106. "History of 'Mormonism' in Picture."

107. Shipps, *Mormonism*, 125–29.

108. Coviello, *Make Yourselves Gods*, 208–9.

109. *Deseret Evening News*, September 7, September 14, 1913, and March 15, March 22, 1913.

110. *Deseret Evening News*, March 15, 1913.

111. *Deseret Evening News*, March 15, 1913.

112. Sobchack, *Carnal Thoughts*, 149.

113. "'100 Years of Mormonism' in Pictures at the Empire," 13.

114. "'100 Years of Mormonism' in Pictures at the Empire," 13.

115. C. Prescott, *Pioneer Mother Monuments*, 25.

116. Cassandra Clark, "No True Religion," 50.

117. Reeve, *Religion of a Different Color*, 8.

118. Qtd. in Reeve, *Religion of a Different Color*, 252.

119. *Moving Picture World* 15:875.

120. Miriam Hansen, *Babel and Babylon*, 96.

121. Musser and Nelson, *High-Class Moving Pictures*, 192.

122. Grieveson, *Policing Cinema*, 84.

123. L. Young, "Mormonism in Picture," 77.

124. G. Foster, *Performing Whiteness*, 47.

125. J. Evans, *One Hundred Years of Mormonism*, 358.

126. Weber, *Latter-day Screens*, 94.

127. J. Evans, *One Hundred Years of Mormonism*, 350.

128. "100 Years of Mormonism," *Logan Republican*, February 4, 1913, 8.

129. J. Evans, *One Hundred Years of Mormonism*, 447.

130. Qtd. in Benbow, "Birth of a Quotation," 528.

131. "What Moving Pictures Teach," 154.

132. "History of 'Mormonism' in Picture."

133. "100 Years of Mormonism: The Days of '47."

134. "History of 'Mormonism' in Picture."

135. *Moving Picture World* 19:1129.

136. Sobchack, *Carnal Thoughts*, 152.

137. *Moving Picture World* 16:1163.

138. *Moving Picture World* 14:1331.

CHAPTER 5

1. The society had been established in 1896. See James Allen, Embry, and Mehr, *Hearts Turned to the Fathers*.

2. N. Anderson, "Genealogy's Place in the Plan of Salvation."

3. Wagoner, *Complete Discourses of Brigham Young*, 64.

4. Qtd. in Mehr, "Microfilm Mission of Archibald F. Bennett," 69.

5. Koehler, Letter to the Board of Directors; Wesemann and Wesemann, *Arthur Clemens Ernst Koehler*, 2, 7.

6. Kuhlman, *Archives and Libraries*, 106.

7. Detzer, "Rescue of the Books."

8. A. Bennett, "Magic of the Microfilm."

9. J. Peters, "Recording beyond the Grave," 843.

10. Pratt, "Elijah's Latter-day Mission," 84.

11. Benjamin, *Illuminations*, 221.

12. Patterson, *Peripheral Vision*, 10.

13. See, for instance, Lemov, *Database of Dreams*.

14. Noll, "Maintenance of Microfilm Files."

15. Cady, "Machine Tool of Management," 154.

16. Lemov, *Database of Dreams*, 84.

17. "Progress in Microfilming."

18. A. Bennett, "Monthly Letter."

19. Lynch, "Germany's Service to Genealogy."

20. Baker, *Double-Fold*, 73.

21. See Lindström, "Drömmar om det minsta."

22. Kenneally, "Mormon Church."

23. "New Microfilm Records."

24. Qtd in J. Hansen, "Juniors Visit the Genealogical Society," 242.

25. Qtd. in Bennett, "Modern Method of Copying Records," 146.

26. J. Peters, "Recording beyond the Grave," 844.

27. A. Bennett, *Saviors on Mount Zion*, 3.

28. Auerbach and Gitelman, "Microfilm, Containment, and the Cold War," 746.

29. W. Nelson, "Joseph Smith, the Prophet," 543; E. Clark, "Testimony of Ezra T. Clark."

30. The Endowment House had been used for some of these but was primarily for the living.

31. Woodruff, "Necessity of a Temple," 190–91.

32. Woodruff, "Necessity of a Temple," 191.

33. Woodruff, *Discourses of Wilford Woodruff*, 160–61; *Wilford Woodruff Journal*, 7: 367–69.

34. O. Pratt, "Temples to Be Built," 261; J. Taylor, "Honesty of Purpose," 298.

35. B. Young, "Increase of Saints," 138.

36. Woodruff, "Necessity of a Temple," 190–91.

37. Wilcox, "Sacralizing the Secular," 41–42.

38. B. Rogers, Allred, Dirkmaat, Dowdle, *Documents*, 10.

39. Qtd. in "Recovering Identities of Black Latter-day Saints."

40. Pratt, "Elijah's Latter-day Mission," 86.

41. G. Smith, "Sacrament—Self Examination," 97.

42. Pratt, "Temples to Be Built," 260–61.

43. Woodruff, *Wilford Woodruff's Journal*, 8:500.

44. F. Richards, "Discourse," 403.

45. Otterstrom, "Genealogy as Religious Ritual," 145.

46. Whitmer, *Address to All Believers in Christ*, 12.

47. Clawson, *One Hundred Seventh Semi-annual Conference*, 117.

48. Woodruff, "Unchangeableness of the Gospel," 269; Durham, *Discourses of Wilford Woodruff*, 151.

49. Clawson, *One Hundred Seventh Semi-annual Conference*, 117.

50. J. F. Smith, *One Hundred Eighteenth Annual Conference*, 135.

51. G. Brown and Campbell, "Control Systems," 57; Lieberman, "Mathematical Model." See also "Information Retrieval," 24; and Timms and Pohlen, *Production Function*, 11, 430.

52. Mockler, "Systems Approach," 53.

53. "Church Microfilm Program."

54. Bennion, *One Hundred Twenty-Seventh Annual General Conference*.

55. McConkie, *One Hundred Nineteenth Annual General Conference*, 91.

56. Clawson, *One Hundred Seventh Semi-annual General Conference*, 117.

57. Qtd. in A. Bennett, "Collection of Faith Promoting Stories," 2.

58. "Hundred Years of Genealogical Progress."

59. Qtd. in A. Bennett, "Collection of Faith Promoting Stories," 2.

60. "Hundred Years of Genealogical Progress."

61. Gorky, "War and Civilization."

62. Ostwald, "Ein Weltreich der Wissenschaft."

63. Metcalf, "Microphotography for Libraries," 60.

64. Qtd. in *Address before World Congress*.

65. M. Buckland, "Emanuel Goldberg," 290.

66. H. G. Wells, *World Brain*, 87.

67. H. G. Wells, *Science and the World Mind*, 35.

68. Qtd. in Fadiman, *I Believe*, 422–23.

69. "World Congress of Universal Documentation," 303.

70. Rayward, "Information Revolutions," 690.

71. Ginsburg, "Electrifying English," 187.

72. Kittler, *Gramophone, Film, Typewriter*, 13.

73. National Archives, *Second Annual Report*, 65.

74. A. Bennett, "Record Copying Program," 228.

75. "One of the Biggest Film Epics."

76. Talmage, "Genealogy and Work for the Dead," 49.

77. Bradshaw, *True Miracles with Genealogy*, 47, 106.

78. A. Bennett, Collection of Faith Promoting Stories.

79. A. Bennett, Collection of Faith Promoting Stories, 2.

80. Qtd. in Rector and Deputy, *Celestial Connection*, 151.

81. Qtd. in A. Bennett, "Joy of Temple Building," 9–10, with punctuation and casing as shown.

82. Rector and Deputy, *Celestial Connection*, 59.

83. Wright, "Clue in an Obituary," 21.

84. Petsco, "My Mother and Genealogy."

85. Haight, "Personal Temple Worship."

86. See Mark 8:22–25.

87. Orsi, *History and Presence*, 171.

88. A. Graham, "Visit beyond the Veil."89. A. Bennett, Collection of Faith Promoting Stories, 2.

90. Qtd. in A. Bennett, Collection of Faith Promoting Stories, 4.

91. Ursenbach, "Awakening," 11.

92. Wiener, *Cybernetics*, 35.

93. B. Rogers, Allred, Dirkmaat, Dowdle, *Documents*, 289.

94. B. Rogers, Allred, Dirkmaat, Dowdle, *Documents*, 10.

95. Fyans, "Ours Is a Shared Ancestry," 39.

96. Gaboury, *Image Objects*, 108–10.

97. A. Bennett, "Great Cause of Tomorrow," 20.

98. Bush, "As We May Think," 113.

99. Qtd. in Erastus Snow, "Discourse," 159.

100. "Minutes of Meeting Sep. 10, 1941."

101. Letter from First Presidency.

102. James Allen, Embry, and Mehr, *Hearts Turned to the Fathers*, 181.

103. "Familysearch Digital Records."

104. "What Young People Have Accomplished," 125.

CHAPTER 6

1. J. Peters, *Speaking into the Air*, 207; *Utah Agricultural College Bulletin*, 6.

2. Bowman, "Zion," 15, 19–21.

3. Spigel, *Welcome to the Dreamhouse*, 192–93.

4. Spigel, *Welcome to the Dreamhouse*, 5.

5. J. Taylor, "Revelation from God," 163.

6. See Rose, "Correlation Program," 48–50.

7. For histories that more closely chart institutional and technological developments, see Feller, "Media as Compromise," ch. 3; and Baker and Mott, "From Radio to the Internet," 339–60.

8. Bowman, "Saturday's Warriors."

9. Everson, *Story of Television*, 11.

10. D. McKay, *One Hundred Thirty-Ninth Semi-annual Conference*, 136.

11. Given, *Turning of the Television*, 30.

12. Gripsrud, "Television, Broadcasting, Flow," 20.

13. C. Young, *One Hundred Eighteenth Annual Conference*, 38.

14. O. Pratt, "Revelation on the Judgments," 336–37.

15. For the context of Smith's vision, see Tate, "'Great World of the Spirits.'"

16. Tait, "Susa Young Gates and the Vision," 318.

17. S. Kimball, *One Hundred Thirty-Second Annual Conference*, 64.

18. Sconce, *Haunted Media*, 125–27.

19. Zante, *Household Equipment Principles*, 469.

20. See, for instance, I. Davidson, *Receiving Aerial Systems*, 39, 42, 69; E. Anderson, *Audels Television Service Manual*, 198; Kiver, *Television Receiver Servicing*, 5; W. Smith and Dawley, *Better Television Reception*, 56–58.

21. Marx and Engels, *Manifest der kommunistischen Partei*, 3.

22. Spigel, *Welcome to the Dreamhouse*, 192.

23. McCarthy, *Citizen Machine*, 3.

24. Sobchack, *Carnal Thoughts*, 136.

25. Shipps, *Sojourner in the Promised Land*, 100.

26. Feller, "Media as Compromise," 125.

27. Spigel, *Welcome to the Dreamhouse*, 2.

28. R. Williams, *Television*, 25.

29. Bogart, *Age of Television*, 5.

30. "Families See Eye-to-Eye on KSL-TV."

31. Fink, *Television Standards and Practice*, 1.

32. Kittler, *Optical Media*, 36–37.

33. Fink, *Television Standards and Practice*, 3.

34. G. Taylor, *Shut Off*, 2, 36.

35. Doleniewski, *Telecommunications Essentials*, 292; see also Chaplin, *Turning on the Mind*, 33.

36. Hollister-Short, *History of Technology*, 1–2.

37. Crane, *Politics of International Standards*, 72.

38. Reed and Reed, *Encyclopedia of Television*, 299.

39. A. Madsen, Yorgason, and Peterson, *Infinite Journey*, 153.

40. Qtd. in Falk, *Upstaging the Cold War*, 120.

41. Murray, "'Never Twice the Same Colour.'"

42. Benson, *One Hundred Thirtieth Annual Conference*, 98.

43. Cohen, "Consumer's Republic," 236.

44. Falk, *Upstaging the Cold War*, 127.

45. Cohen, "Consumer's Republic," 236.

46. Dienst, *Still Life in Real Time*, 12.

47. Cohen, *Consumers' Republic*, 302.

48. Hirsch, "New Technologies and Domestic Consumption," 163.

49. "Department Store Sees Television."

50. "Department Store Sees Television."

51. "Salt Lake City 13th to Have Television."

52. Sewell, *Television in the Age of Radio*, 14.

53. Phillips, "Good or Bad, Television."

54. Phillips, "Good or Bad, Television."

55. "Talented Uncle Roscoe."

56. "18th Ward Primary Presents."

57. S. Young, *One Hundred Twenty-Fifth Annual Conference*, 100.

58. Jacobs, "Literature—the Literature of England," 635.

59. Wirthlin, "Evil Designs."

60. "Take Time to Safeguard Children."

61. Spigel, *Welcome to the Dreamhouse*, 61, 109.

62. A. Madsen, Yorgason, and Peterson, *Infinite Journey*, 155–56.

63. Prince, *David O. McKay*, 129.

64. Dew, *Ezra Taft Benson*, 298.

65. Lythgoe, "Changing Image of Mormonism," 47.

66. *Time* magazine, April 13, 1953, and May 7, 1956.

67. Qtd. in Dew, *Ezra Taft Benson*, 235.

68. Lythgoe, "Changing Image of Mormonism," 53–54.

69. M. Harris, "Breaching the Wall," 7–8.

70. Qtd. in Benson, *Enemy Hath Done This*, 297.

71. Harris, *Watchman on the Tower*, 8, 88.

72. Benson, *Enemy Hath Done This*, 3–13.

73. Quinn, "Ezra Taft Benson," 12–13.

74. Lunney, "Exploring the Cold War," 47.

75. Advertisement, *Improvement Era* 54, no. 2 (February 1951): 127.

76. "New Television Outlet."

77. Andriopoulos, *Ghostly Apparitions*, 148.

78. E. Wesley Smith, *Ninety-Fifth Semi-annual Conference* 114.

79. Eldred Smith, One Hundred Twenty-Seventh Semi-annualConference, 75–76.

80. McConkie, *One Hundred Forty-First Annual Conference*, 98–99.

81. Qtd. in Barlow, "Why the King James Version," 25.

82. Blakesley, "'Style of Our Own,'" 22.

83. S. Kimball, *Style of Our Own.*

84. Blakesley, "'Style of Our Own,'" 20.

85. H. Taylor, "When the Lord Commands, Do It," 529.

86. Waterman, "Ernest Wilkinson," 88.

87. Prince, *David O. McKay*, 208–9.

88. Lund, "Proclaiming the Gospel in the Twentieth Century," 231–32.

89. D. McKay, *One Hundred Thirty-First Annual Conference*, 96.

90. Isaacson, One Hundred Thirtieth Annual Conference, 59–62; Tanner, One Hundred Thirty-First Annual Conference, 106–10; F. Richards, One Hundred Thirty-First Annual Conference.

91. Romney, One Hundred Thirty-Second Annual Conference, 16–20; Hunter, One Hundred Thirty-Third Annual Conference.

92. Bowman, *Mormon People*, 195–96.

93. Bowman, "Zion," 22.

94. Grover, Interview, 33.

95. Grover, Interview, 34.

96. McAllister et al., Letter to Broadcaster.

97. Kirkham, Letter to James Kirkham.

98. J. Johnson, *Mormons, Musical Theater, and American Belonging*, 138.

99. D. McKay, *One Hundred Seventh Semi-annual Conference*, 102–3.

100. D. McKay, *One Hundred Twenty-Sixth Semi-annual Conference*, 128.

101. Petrey, *Tabernacles of Clay*, 35.

102. Hanks, *Women and Authority*, xi–xxx.

103. Qtd. in Bowman, "Zion," 22.

104. Lee, *One Hundred Thirty-second Semi-annual Conference*, 72.

105. Benson, "Our Homes Divinely Ordained."

106. *Bible Dictionary*, s.v. "Temple."

107. Hinckley, *One Hundred Thirty-Second Annual Conference*, 72.

108. S. Kimball, *One Hundred Thirty-Second Annual Conference*, 55, 118.

109. Joanna Brooks, *Mormonism and White Supremacy*, 90.

110. Hicks, *Mormonism and Music*, 164.

111. K. Johnson, "Mormons and a Mission."

112. See Arrington, *Mormon Experience*, 140.

113. Lee, *One Hundred Thirty Eighth Semi-annual Conference*, 61.

114. Moses 7:69.

115. Lee, *One Hundred Thirty Eighth Semi-annual Conference*, 62.

116. Monson, "Correlation Brings Blessings," 247.

117. All Church Coordinating Council Secretary, meeting minutes, May 3, 1962.

118. Richard Jensen and Hartley, "Immigration and Emigration," 676.

119. Hartley, "Coming to Zion," 18.

120. McConkie, *Official Report of the First Mexico*, 45.

121. Lee, "Report from the Correlation Committee," 938–39.

122. R. Evans, *One Hundred Thirty-Second Semi-annual Conference*, 76.

123. "LDS Confab Seen on Video."

124. "Heber G. Wolsey interview," 25–26.

125. Joanna Brooks, *Mormonism and White Supremacy*, 145.

126. McLuhan and Zingrone, *Essential McLuhan*, 246.

127. E. Smith, One Hundred Eighteenth Annual Conference, 98–99.

128. R. Evans, Philo T. Farnsworth funeral remarks.

129. Cowley, "Miracles."

130. D. McKay, *One Hundred Twenty-Ninth Annual Conference*, 122.

131. Sobchack, *Carnal Thoughts*, 138.

CONCLUSION

1. A. Johnson, "Heavens Are Opened," 40.

2. Riess, *Next Mormons*, 224–25.

3. Dieter F. Uchtdorf, post from June 21, 2016, facebook.com/lds.dieter.f.uchtdorf.

4. See, for instance, R. Benjamin, *Race after Technology*; Noble, *Algorithms of Oppression*.

5. Q&A session reproduced in Smoot, "Reports of the Death of the Church." For more on "apostasy" in the late 1830s, see Esplin, "Joseph Smith and the Kirtland Crisis."

6. Goodstein, "Some Mormons Search the Web."

7. S. Meyer, *Twilight*.

8. "Answering Gospel Questions."

9. Feller, "Media as Compromise," 210.

10. S. Snow, "Balancing Church History."

11. D&C, section 128:15; Hebrews 11:40 (KJV).

12. D&C, section 128:18.

BIBLIOGRAPHY

Abbot, Lyman. "The Timid Woman's Touch." *Christian Union* 39, no. 6 (February 7, 1889): 176.

Address before World Congress of Universal Documentation, 1937, Paris. Washington, D.C.: Science Service.

Alexander, Thomas. *Mormonism in Transition*. Champaign: University of Illinois Press, 1986.

All Church Coordinating Council Secretary. Meeting minutes, May 3, 1962. Church History Library, Salt Lake City, Utah.

———. Meeting minutes, 1966. Church History Library, Salt Lake City, Utah.

Allen, James B., and Jesse L. Embrey. "'Provoking the Brethren to Good Works': Susa Young Gates, the Relief Society, and Genealogy." *BYU Studies* 31 (Spring 1991): 115–38.

Allen, James B., Jessie L. Embry, and Kahlile B. Mehr. *Hearts Turned to the Fathers: History of the Genealogical Society of Utah, 1894–1994*. Provo, Utah: BYU Studies, 1995.

Allen, James B., and Glen M. Leonard. *The Story of the Latter-day Saints*. Salt Lake City, Utah: Deseret, 1976.

Allen, Julie K. *Danish but Not Lutheran: The Impact of Mormonism on Danish Cultural Identity, 1850–1920*. Salt Lake City: University of Utah Press, 2017.

Allred, Mason Kamana. "Circulating Specters: Mormon Reading Networks, Vision, and Optical Media." *Journal of the American Academy of Religion* 85 (2017): 527–48.

———. "Developing the Dead: Mormonism, Spirit Photography, and Noise." *Journal of Mormon History* 48 (2022): 106–30.

———. "Mormonism and the Archaeology of Media." *Mormon Studies Review* 5 (2018): 46–52.

———. *Weimar Cinema, Embodiment, and Historicity*. New York: Routledge, 2017.

"Amusements." *Salt Lake Tribune*, February 4, 1913, 9.

Anderson, Benedict. *Imagined Communities: Reflections on the Origin and Spread of Nationalism*. 1983. London: Verso, 2006.

Anderson, Edwin P. *Audels Television Service Manual*. New York: Theo. Audel, 1965.

Anderson, H. A. Letter to Susa Young Gates, April 12, 1890, Provo, Utah. Susa Young Gates Papers, Correspondence Files, Church History Library, Salt Lake City, Utah.

Anderson, Nephi. "Genealogy's Place in the Plan of Salvation." *Utah Genealogical and Historical Magazine* 3 (January 1912): 12–22.

Andriopoulos, Stefan. *Ghostly Apparitions: German Idealism, the Gothic Novel, and Optical Media*. New York: Zone Books, 2013.

———. *Possessed: Hypnotic Crimes, Corporate Fiction, and the Invention of Cinema*. Translated by Peter Jansen and Stefan Andriopoulos. Chicago: University of Chicago Press, 2008.

———. "The Terror of Reproduction: Early Cinema's Ghostly Doubles and the Right to One's Own Image." In "Modernism after Postmodernity," edited by Andreas Huyssen. Special issue, *New German Critique* 99 (Fall 2006): 151–70.

"Answering Gospel Questions." Gospel Topics, The Church of Jesus Christ of Latter-day Saints (website). Accessed May 18, 2022. www.churchofjesuschrist.org/study/manual /gospel-topics/answering-gospel-questions.

Armatage, Kay. *The Girl from God's Country: Nell Shipman and the Silent Cinema*. Carbondale: Southern Illinois University Press, 2003.

Arrington, Leonard. *The Mormon Experience*. Chicago: University of Illinois Press, 1992.

Asad, Talal. *Formations of the Secular: Christianity, Islam, Modernity*. Palo Alto, Calif.: Stanford University Press, 2003.

Ashurst-McGee, Mark, David W. Grua, and Elizabeth A. Kuehn, eds. *Documents*. Vol. 6, *February 1838–August 1839*. Joseph Smith Papers. Salt Lake City, Utah: Church Historian's Press, 2017.

Assmann, Jan. "Collective Memory and Cultural Identity." *New German Critique* 65 (1995): 125–33.

Astle, Randy. *Mormon Cinema: Origins to 1952*. New York: Mormon Arts Center, 2018.

Astle, Randy, and Gideon Burton. "A History of Mormon Cinema." *BYU Studies Quarterly* 46, no. 2 (2007): 12–163.

Auerbach, Jonathan, and Lisa Gitelman. "Microfilm, Containment, and the Cold War." *American Literary History* 19 (Fall 2007): 745–68.

Baker, Nicholson. *Double-Fold: Libraries and the Assault on Paper*. New York: Random House, 2001.

Baker, Sherry Pack, and Elizabeth Mott. "From Radio to Internet: Church Use of Electronic Media in the Twentieth Century." In *A Firm Foundation: Church Organization and Administration*, edited by David J. Whittaker and Arnold K. Garr, 339–60. Provo, Utah: Brigham Young University Religious Studies Center, 2011.

Balázs, Béla. "The Visible Man." Translated by Erica Carter and Rodney Livingstone. *Screen* 48 (2007): 91–108.

Ballard, M. Russell. "Be Anxiously Engaged." Transcript. Library, General Conference, October 2012, Saturday Afternoon Session, The Church of Jesus Christ of Latter-day Saints (website). www.churchofjesuschrist.org/study/general-conference/2012/10 /be-anxiously-engaged.

Ballard, Melvin J. *Eighty-Third Annual Conference of the Church of Jesus Christ of Latter-day Saints, April 1913*, 16-21. Salt Lake City: Church of Jesus Christ of Latter-day Saints, 1913.

Barad, Karen. *Meeting the Universe Halfway: Quantum Physics and the Entanglement of Matter and Meaning*. Durham, N.C.: Duke University Press, 2007.

———. "Posthumanist Performativity: Toward an Understanding of How Matter Comes to Matter." *Signs* 28 (Spring 2003): 801–31.

Barbas, Samantha "Gossip Law." In *When Private Talk Goes Public: Gossip in American History*, edited by Kathleen Feeley and Jennifer Frost, 123–38. New York: Palgrave Macmillan, 2014.

Barber, Theodore. "Phantasmagorical Wonders: The Magic Lantern Ghost Show in Nineteenth-Century America." *Film History* 3, no. 2 (1989): 73–86.

Barlow, Philip. "Why the King James Version: From the Common to the Official Bible of Mormonism." *Dialogue* 22, no. 2 (1989): 19–42.

Barnett, Steven G. "The Canes of the Martyrdom." *BYU Studies Quarterly* 21 (1981): 205–11.

Barringer, Tim. "The World for a Schilling: The Early Panorama as Global Landscape, 1787–1830." In *On the Viewing Platform: The Panorama between Canvas and Screen*, edited by Katie Trumpener and Tim Barringer, 83–106. New Haven, Conn.: Yale University Press, 2020.

Barrionuevo, Alexei. "Honeybees Vanish, Leaving Keepers in Peril." *New York Times*, February 27, 2007. www.nytimes.com/2007/02/27/business/27bees.html.

Bathsheba Smith Photograph Collection, ca. 1865–1900. Church History Library, Salt Lake City, Utah.

"Battlefield of the Mind: A Conversation with Arch L. Madsen." *Meridian Magazine*, May 19, 2000. latterdaysaintmag.com/article-1-4573/.

Bax, Christina E. "Entrepreneur Brownie Wise: Selling Tupperware to America's Women in the 1950s." *Journal of Women's History* 22 (Summer 2010): 171–80.

Bazin, André. *Bazin at Work: Major Essays and Reviews from the Forties and Fifties*. Translated by Alain Piette and Bert Cardullo. Edited by Bert Cardullo. New York: Routledge, 1997.

———. *What Is Cinema?* Vol. 1. Berkeley: University of California Press, 2005.

Beardsley, Amanda. "Celestial Mechanics: Technologies of Salvation in the Church of Jesus Christ of Latter-day Saints and American Culture." Ph.D. diss., Binghamton University, 2019.

———. "The Female Absorption Coefficient: The Miniskirt Study, Gender, and Latter-day Saint Architectural Acoustics." *Technology and Culture* 62 (July 2021): 659–84.

Bell, Susan Groag, and Karen M. Offen, eds. *Women, the Family, and Freedom: The Debate in Documents, 1880–1950*. Vol. 2. Stanford, Calif.: Stanford University Press, 1983.

Bellion, Wendy. *Citizen Spectator: Art, Illusion, and Visual Perception in Early National America*. Chapel Hill: University of North Carolina Press, 2011.

Benbow, Mark E. "Birth of a Quotation: Woodrow Wilson and 'Like Writing History in Lightning.'" *Journal of the Gilded Age and Progressive Era* 9 (October 2010): 509–33.

Benjamin, Ruha. *Race after Technology: Abolitionist Tools for the New Jim Code*. Cambridge, U.K.: Polity Press, 2019.

Benjamin, Walter. *Illuminations*. 1936. Edited by Hannah Arendt. New York: Schocken Books, 2007.

Bennett, Archibald F. Collection of Faith Promoting Stories, Church History Library, Salt Lake City, Utah.

———. "The Great Cause of Tomorrow." Genealogical Society. March 1956. From the Book of Remembrance of Archibald F. Bennett, Church History Library, Salt Lake City, Utah.

———. "The Joy of Temple Building and Temple Service." March 1956. Genealogical Society. From the Book of Remembrance of Archibald F. Bennett, Church History Library, Salt Lake City, Utah.

———. "Magic of the Microfilm." *Improvement Era* 41 (November 1938): 685.

———. "The Modern Method of Copying Records." *Utah Genealogical and Historical Magazine* 29, no. 4 (October 1938): 145–47.

———. "Monthly Letter to Stake Genealogical Representatives." *Utah Genealogical and Historical Magazine* 29, no. 3 (July 1938): 119.

———. "The Record Copying Program of the Utah Genealogical Society." *American Archivist* 16, no. 3 (July 1953): 227–32.

———. *Saviors on Mount Zion*. Salt Lake City, Utah: Deseret Sunday School Union Board, 1950.

———. "An Urgent Appeal." *Utah Genealogical and Historical Magazine* 30 (July 1939): 189–91.

Bennett, Jane. "Edible Matter." *New Left Review* 45 (2007): 133–45.

Bennett, Richard, Susan Easton Black, and Donald Q. Cannon. *The Nauvoo Legion in Illinois*. Norman, Ill.: Arthur H. Clark, 2010.

Bennion, Adam S. *One Hundred Twenty-Seventh Annual Conference of the Church of Jesus Christ of Latter-day Saints, April 1957*, 115–18. Salt Lake City, Utah: Church of Jesus Christ of Latter-day Saints, 1957.

Benson, Ezra Taft. *An Enemy Hath Done This*. Salt Lake City, Utah: Parliament, 1969.

———. *One Hundred Thirtieth Annual Conference of the Church of Jesus Christ of Latter-day Saints, April, 1960*, 96–100. Salt Lake City, Utah: Church of Jesus Christ of Latter-day Saints, 1960.

———. "Our Homes Divinely Ordained." *Improvement Era* 52, no. 5 (May 1949): 278.

Bergland, Renée L. *The National Uncanny: Indian Ghosts and American Subjects*. Hanover, N.H.: University Press of New England, 2000.

Bernardi, Daniel, ed. *The Birth of Whiteness: Race and the Emergence of U.S. Cinema*. New Brunswick, N.J.: Rutgers University Press, 1996.

———. "The Voice of Whiteness: D. W. Biograph Films, 1908–1913." In *The Birth of Whiteness: Race and the Emergence of U.S. Cinema*, edited by Daniel Bernardi, 103–28. New Brunswick, N.J.: Rutgers University Press, 1996.

Bernhisel, John M. "Letter to Brigham Young, Sep. 10, 1849." Brigham Young Office Files, Church History Library, Salt Lake City, Utah.

Bertolini, Vincent. "Fireside Chastity: The Erotics of Sentimental Bachelorhood in the 1850s." *American Literature* 68 (December 1996): 707–37.

"Best Advertised Screen Feature in America: 'A Mormon Maid.'" *Motion Picture News* 15, no. 10 (March 10, 1917): 1504–5.

Bible Dictionary. Salt Lake City, Utah: Church of Jesus Christ of Latter-day Saints, 1979.

Bitton, Davis. *The Ritualization of Mormon History, and Other Essays*. Urbana: University of Illinois Press, 1994.

Blakesley, Katie Clark. "'A Style of Our Own': Modesty and Mormon Women, 1951–2008." *Dialogue* 42, no. 2 (Summer 2009): 20–53.

Blanco, Maria del Pilar, and Esther Peeren, eds. *The Spectralities Studies Reader*. London: Bloomsbury, 2013.

Blythe, Christopher James. "Ann Booth's Vision and Early Conceptions of Redeeming the Dead among Latter-day Saints." *BYU Studies* 56, no. 2 (2017): 105–22.

———. *Terrible Revolution: Latter-day Saints and the American Apocalypse*. New York: Oxford University Press, 2020.

———. "'Would to God, Brethren, I Could Tell You Who I Am': Nineteenth Century Mormonisms and the Apotheosis of Joseph Smith." *Nova Religio* 18 (2014): 5–27.

Bogart, Leo. *The Age of Television*. New York: Frederick Unger, 1956.

Bolter, Jay David, and Richard Grusin, eds. *Remediation: Understanding New Media*. Cambridge, Mass.: MIT Press, 2000.

Bowman, Matthew. *The Mormon People*. New York: Random House, 2012.

———. "Saturday's Warriors." *Slate.com*, April 15, 2012. slate.com/human-interest/2012 /04/mormon-correlation-the-bureaucratic-reform-policy-that-redefined-mormon -culture.html.

———. "Zion: The Progressive Roots of Mormon Correlation." In *Directions for Mormon Studies in the Twenty-First Century*, edited by Patrick Q. Mason, 15–34. Salt Lake City: University of Utah Press, 2016.

Bradshaw, Anne. *True Miracles with Genealogy: Help from beyond the Veil*. Lexington, Ky.: Createspace, 2011.

Branch, Olive. "Good Nurses." *Woman's Exponent* 15, no. 8 (September 15, 1886): 57–58.

Braude, Ann. *Radical Spirits: Spiritualism and Women's Rights in Nineteenth Century America*. Boston: Beacon, 1989.

Broken Hearts and Broken Lives: Trapped by the Mormons. Pamphlet. February 13, 1922. Church History Library, Salt Lake City, Utah.

Brooks, Joanna. *Mormonism and White Supremacy: American Religion and the Problem of Racial Innocence*. New York: Oxford University Press, 2020.

Brooks, Juanita, ed. *On the Mormon Frontier: The Diary of Hosea Stout*. Salt Lake City: University of Utah Press, 2009.

Brown, Benjamin. *Testimonies for the Truth: A Record of Manifestations of the Power of God*. Liverpool, U.K.: S. W. Richards, 1853.

Brown, Candy Gunther. *The Word in the World: Evangelical Writing, Publishing, and Reading in America, 1789–1880*. Chapel Hill: University of North Carolina Press, 2004.

Brown, Charles Brockden. *Edgar Huntley, or The Sleep Walker*. London: Colburn and Bentley, 1831.

Brown, Gordon S., and Donald P. Campbell. "Control Systems." *Scientific American*, September 1952, 56–67.

Brown, Samuel Morris. *In Heaven as It Is on Earth*. Oxford: Oxford University Press, 2012.

Brown, Samuel Morris, and Kate Holbrook. "Embodiment and Sexuality in Mormon Thought." In *The Oxford Handbook of Mormonism*, edited by Philip Barlow and Terryl L. Givens, 291–306. Oxford, U.K.: Oxford University Press, 2015.

Buckland, Michael K. "Emanuel Goldberg, Electronic Document Retrieval, and Vannevar Bush's Memex." *Journal of the American Society for Information Science* 43 (1992): 284–94.

Buckland, Warren. "A Rational Reconstruction of 'The Cinema of Attractions.'" In *The Cinema of Attractions Reloaded*, edited by Wanda Strauven, 41–56. Amsterdam: Amsterdam University Press, 2006.

Bunker, Gary L., and Davis Bitton. *The Mormon Graphic Image 1834–1914*. Salt Lake City: University of Utah Press, 1983.

Burt, Olive Woolley. "Susa Young Gates." *Westerner*, January 1930, 2–3.

Bush, Vannevar. "As We May Think." *Atlantic*, September 1945, 112–24.

Bushman, Richard. "Joseph Smith and His Visions." In *The Oxford Handbook of Mormonism*, edited by Terryl Givens and Philip Barlow, 109–20. Oxford: Oxford University Press, 2015.

———. *Joseph Smith: Rough Stone Rolling*. New York: Alfred A. Knopf, 2005.

Byerly, Alison. "A Prodigious Map beneath His Feet: Virtual Travel and the Panoramic Perspective." In *Nineteenth-Century Worlds: Global Formations Past and Present*, edited by Keith Hanley and Greg Kucich, 79–96. Abingdon: Routledge, 2008.

Cady, Susan. "Machine Tool of Management: A History of Microfilm Technology." Ph.D. diss., Lehigh University, 1994.

Caldwell, Estelle Neff. "Biographical: Susa Young Gates." In *History of the Young Ladies Mutual Improvement Association: From November 1869 to June 1910*, edited by Susa Young Gates, 121–26. Salt Lake City, Utah: Deseret News, 1911.

Campbell, Mary. *Charles Ellis Johnson and the Erotic Mormon Image*. Chicago: University of Chicago Press, 2016.

———. "Mormonism, Gender, and Art." In *The Routledge Handbook of Mormonism and Gender*, edited by Taylor Petrey and Amy Hoyt, 239–57. New York: Routledge, 2020.

Canning, Kathleen. *Gender History in Practice: Historical Perspectives on Bodies, Class, and Citizenship*. Ithaca, N.Y.: Cornell University Press, 2006.

Cannon, Brian Q., and Jacob Olmstead. "'Scandalous Film': The Campaign to Suppress Anti-Mormon Motion Pictures, 1911–12." *Journal of Mormon History* 29, no. 2 (Fall 2003): 42–76.

Cannon, George Q. "Discourse." *Deseret News* 38, no. 22 (May 25, 1889): 674–78.

———. "The Influence and Sphere of Woman." *Deseret Weekly* 44, no. 3 (January 9, 1892): 66–71.

Cannon, Jeffrey G. "The Image as Text and Context." In *Foundational Texts of Mormonism*, edited by Mark Ashurst-McGee, Robin Scott Jensen, and Sharalyn D. Howcroft, 336–72. Oxford: Oxford University Press, 2018.

Cannon, Sylvester. *One Hundred and Sixth Semi-annual General Conference of the Church of Jesus Christ of Latter-day Saints, October 1935*, 110–13. Salt Lake City, Utah: Church of Jesus Christ of Latter-day Saints, 1935.

Carey, James. *Communication as Culture: Essays on Media and Society*. New York: Routledge, 2009.

Carlyle, Thomas. *The French Revolution*. London: Fraser, 1837.

Carmack, Noel. "'One of the Most Interesting Seeneries That Can Be Found in Zion': Philo Dibble's Museum and Panorama." *Nauvoo Journal* 9 (1997): 25–38.

Carpenter, Lynette, and Wendy Kolmar. *Ghost Stories by British and American Women: A Selected, Annotated Bibliography*. Abingdon: Routledge, 2014.

Carroll, Bret E. *Spiritualism in Antebellum America*. Bloomington: Indiana University Press, 1997.

Castle, Terry. "Phantasmagoria: Spectral Technology and the Metaphorics of Modern Reverie." *Critical Inquiry* 15, no. 1 (Autumn 1988): 26–61.

"Century of 'Mormonism.'" *Deseret Evening News*, February 3, 1913. Historical Department, Journal History of the Church, February 3, 1913, 1.

Chaplin, Tamara. *Turning on the Mind*. Chicago: University of Chicago Press, 2007.

Chen, Chiung Hwang. "Diverse Yet Hegemonic: Expressions of Motherhood in 'I'm a Mormon' Ads." *Journal of Media and Religion* 13 (2014): 31–47.

———. "Internet as Battleground: Challenging and Reasserting Mormon Authority in the Digital Age." *Religion Online: How Digital Technology Is Changing the Way We Worship and Pray*. Vol. 2, *Faith Groups and Digital Media*, edited by August E. Grant, Amanda F. C. Sturgill, Chiung Hwang Chen, and, Daniel Stout, 57–78. Santa Barbara, Calif.: Praeger, 2019.

———. "Marketing Religion Online: The LDS Church's SEO Efforts." *Journal of Media and Religion* 10 (2011): 185–205.

Chevalier, Michel. *Society, Manners, and Politics in the United States.* Boston: Jordan and Weeks, 1839.

Christensen, Jerome. *Romanticism at the End of History.* Baltimore: Johns Hopkins University Press, 2000.

Church Education System. *Eternal Marriage Student Manual.* Salt Lake City, Utah: Church of Jesus Christ of Latter-day Saints, 2003.

"'Church History,' 1 March 1842." Joseph Smith Papers. www.josephsmithpapers.org /paper-summary/church-history-1-march-1842/2.

"Church Microfilm Program." *Genealogical Helper* 1, no. 4 (December 1947): 15.

"Church Publishes First LDS Edition of the Bible." *Ensign,* October 1979. www .churchofjesuschrist.org/study/ensign/1979/10/church-publishes-first-lds-edition -of-the-bible?lang=eng.

Chun, Wendy Hui Kyong. *Updating to Remain the Same: Habitual New Media.* Cambridge, Mass.: MIT Press, 2016.

Clapp, Matthew S. "Mormonism." *Painesville Telegraph,* February 15, 1831.

Clark, Carlos. Carlos Clark Papers, ca. 1901–74. Typescript. Church History Library, Salt Lake City, Utah.

Clark, Cassandra L. "No True Religion without True Science: Science and the Construction of Mormon Whiteness." *Journal of Mormon History* 42 (January 2016): 44–72

Clark, Ezra T. "The Testimony of Ezra T. Clark." July 24, 1901, Farmington, Utah. Heber Don Clark Papers, ca. 1901–74, Church History Library, Salt Lake City, Utah.

Clark, Susie C. *The Round Trip: From the Hub to the Golden Gate.* Boston: Applewood Books, 1890.

Clarke, Alison. *Tupperware: The Promise of Plastic in 1950s America.* Washington, D.C.: Smithsonian Institute, 1999.

Clarke, Carrie. "Man and Woman in the Shorthand World." *Western Stenographer* 1 (January 1894): 8–9.

Clarke, Uriah. *Plain Guide to Spiritualism.* Boston: William White, 1863.

Clawson, Rudger. "The Anti-'Mormon' Moving Pictures and Play." *Millennial Star* 51 (December 21, 1911): 808.

———. Letters to the First Presidency. December 15, 1911, March 5, 1912. Rudger Clawson Papers, Church History Library, Salt Lake City, Utah.

———. *One Hundred Seventh Semi-annual Conference of the Church of Jesus Christ of Latter-day Saints, October 1936,* 115–18. Salt Lake City, Utah: Church of Jesus Christ of Latter-day Saints, 1936.

Clayton, William. *An Intimate Chronicle: The Journals of William Clayton.* Salt Lake City, Utah: Signature Books, 1991.

Cohen, Lizabeth. "A Consumer's Republic: The Politics of Mass Consumption in Postwar America." *Journal of Consumer Research* 31 (June 2004): 236–39.

———. *A Consumers' Republic: The Politics of Mass Consumption in Postwar America.* New York: Vintage, 2003.

Coleridge, Samuel Taylor. *Biographia Literaria.* 1817. New York: Leavitt, 1834.

Commolli, Jean-Louis. "Historical Fiction: A Body Too Much?" In *The History on Film Reader,* edited by Marnie Hughes-Warrington, 65–74. New York: Routledge, 2009.

———. "Machines of the Visible." In *The Cinematic Apparatus*, edited by Teresa de Lauretis and Stephen Heath, 14–22. London: Macmillan, 1985.

"Computerized Scriptures Now Available." *Ensign*, April 1988. www.churchofjesuschrist .org/study/ensign/1988/04/computerized-scriptures-now-available?lang=eng.

"Computerizing Religion, Medicine." *Jewish Telegraphic Agency* 42 (April 4, 1975), 3.

Cooper, J. Fenimore. *The Last of the Mohicans: A Narrative of 1757*. 1826. New York: Stringer and Townsend, 1854.

Coray, Martha Jane Knowlton. Notebook, Church History Library, Salt Lake City, Utah.

Coviello, Peter. *Make Yourself Gods: Mormons and the Unfinished Business of American Secularism*. Chicago: University of Chicago Press, 2019.

Coward, Kevin, and Dagan Wells, eds. *Textbook of Clinical Embryology*. Cambridge: Cambridge University Press, 2013.

Cowley, Matthew. "Miracles." February 8, 1953. Brigham Young University Speeches. speeches.byu.edu/talks/matthew-cowley/miracles/.

Crane, Rhonda J. *The Politics of International Standards*. New Jersey: Ablex, 1979.

Crary, Jonathan. "Gericault, the Panorama, and Sites of Reality in the Early Nineteenth Century." *Grey Room* 9 (Fall 2002): 5–25.

———. *Techniques of the Observer: On Vision and Modernity in the Nineteenth Century*. Cambridge, Mass.: MIT Press, 1999.

Crewdson, Charles N. [Lula Cox Crewdson]. "Mormon Women at Home." *Millennial Star* 66 (1904): 292–95.

Crocheron, Augusta Joyce, ed. *Representative Women of Deseret*. Salt Lake City, Utah: J. C. Graham, 1884.

Crowl, P. L. Letter to Orson Hyde and Orson Pratt, July 15, 1880. Church Historian's Office. Correspondence, Church History Library, Salt Lake City, Utah.

"A Curious Trial—Spirit Photography." *Deseret News*, May 12, 1869, 162.

Dahl, Larry E., and Donald Q. Cannon, eds. *Encyclopedia of Joseph Smith's Teachings*. Salt Lake City, Utah: Deseret, 1997.

Daniels, William. *A Correct Account of the Murder of Generals Joseph and Hyrum Smith*. Nauvoo, Utah: John Taylor for proprietor, 1845.

D'Arc, James. "The Mormon as Vampire: A Comparative Study of Winifred Graham's *The Love Story of a Mormon*, the Film Trapped by the Mormons, and Bram Stoker's *Dracula*." *BYU Studies* 46 (2007): 164–87.

Darley, Felix Octavius Carr. *Ghost Stories: Collected with a Particular View to Counteract the Vulgar Belief in Ghosts and Apparitions*. Philadelphia: Carey and Hart, 1846.

Davidson, Ian Arthur. *Receiving Aerial Systems, for Broadcast and Television*. New York: Philosophical Library, 1957.

Davidson, Karen Lynn, Richard L. Jensen, and David J. Whittaker, eds. *The Joseph Smith Papers: Histories*. Vol. 2, *Assigned Histories, 1831–1847*. Salt Lake City, Utah: Church Historian's Press, 2012.

Davies, Margery. *Woman's Place Is at the Typewriter*. Philadelphia: Temple University Press, 1982.

Davis, Andrew Jackson. *The Present Age and Inner Life*. Boston: William White, 1869.

Davis, Daniel. "Appreciating a Pretty Shoulder: The Risquie Images of Charles Ellis Johnson." *Utah Historical Quarterly* 74 (Spring 2006): 131–46.

Davis, John. *The Landscape of Belief*. Princeton, N.J.: Princeton University Press, 1996.

Daynes, Kathryn M. *More Wives Than One: Transformation of the Mormon Marriage System, 1840–1910*. Champaign: University of Illinois Press, 2001.

Dearinger, Ryan. *The Filth of Progress*. Berkeley: University of California Press, 2016.

Debates of the House of Commons 24 (April 19, 1911).

de Certeau, Michel. "The Gaze: Nicholas of Cusa." Translated by Catherine Porter. *Diacritics* 17, no. 3 (1987): 2–37.

Defoe, Daniel [Andrew Moreton]. *The Secrets of the Invisible World Disclosed*. London: Cecil, 1740.

"Department Store Sees Television." *Salt Lake Telegram*, May 28, 1948, 20.

Derrida, Jacques. "Demeure: Fiction and Testimony." In *The Instant of My Death/Demeure*, edited by Maurice Blanchot and Jacques Derrida, 13–104. Stanford, Calif.: Stanford University Press, 2000.

Derrida, Jacques, and Bernard Stiegler. "Spectographies." In *The Spectralities Studies Reader*, edited by Maria del Pilar Blanco and Esther Peeren, 37–52. London: Bloomsbury, 2013.

Detzer, Karl. "The Rescue of the Books." *Saturday Review* 24 (1941): 10.

Dew, Sheri L. *Ezra Taft Benson, a Biography*. Salt Lake City, Utah: Deseret, 1987.

Dibble, Philo. "Brother Philo Dibble's Sceneries, Museum, &c." *Millennial Star* 11 (January 1, 1849): 11–12.

———. Letter to John Taylor, April 29, 1879. Church History Library, Salt Lake City, Utah.

———. *Philo Dibble's Reminiscences of Early Church History and the Prophet Joseph Smith*. Logan, Utah: M. A. Smith, 1995.

———. Reminiscences. Church History Library, Salt Lake City, Utah.

Dickens, Charles. "In the Name of the Prophet—Smith!" *Household Words* 3, no. 69 (1851): 385–89.

Dienst, Richard. *Still Life in Real Time: Theory after Television*. Durham, N.C.: Duke University Press, 1994.

"Discourse, 1 May 1842, as Reported by Willard Richards." Joseph Smith Papers. www.josephsmithpapers.org/paper-summary/discourse-1-may-1842-as -reported-by-willard-richards/1.

"Discourse, 7 April 1844, as Reported by Wilford Woodruff." Joseph Smith Papers. www.josephsmithpapers.org/paper-summary/discourse-7-april-1844 -as-reported-by-wilford-woodruff/3.

"Discourse, 17 May 1843–B, as Reported by William Clayton." Joseph Smith Papers. www.josephsmithpapers.org/paper-summary/discourse-17-may-1843-b-as -reported-by-william-clayton/1.

"Discourse, between circa 26 June and circa 4 August 1839—A, as Reported by Willard Richards." Joseph Smith Papers. www.josephsmithpapers.org/paper-summary /discourse-between-circa-26-june-and-circa-4-august-1839-a-as-reported-by-willard -richards/9.

The Doctrine and Covenants of the Church of Jesus Christ of Latter-day Saints. Salt Lake City, Utah: Church of Jesus Christ of Latter-day Saints, 2013.

Doleniewski, Lillian. *Telecommunications Essentials*. Boston: Addison-Wesley, 2003.

Dolphijn, Rick, and Iris van der Tuin, eds. *New Materialism: Interviews and Cartographies*. Ann Arbor, Mich.: Open Humanities, 2012.

Duerden, G. C., and Ben Groen. "The History of LDS.org Shows God's hands." May 30, 2014. tech.lds.org/blog/606-the-history-of-ldsorg-shows-gods-hands-part-2.

Dunlap, William. *The Life of Charles Brockden Brown*. Vol. 1. Philadelphia: James P. Parke, 1815.

Edwards, Paul N. "Infrastructure and Modernity: Force, Time, and Social Organization in the History of Technical Systems." In *Modernity and Technology*, edited by Thomas J. Misa, Philip Brey, and Andrew Feenberg, 185–225. Cambridge, Mass.: MIT Press, 2002.

"18th Ward Primary Presents Square Dances on Television." *Deseret News*, January 31, 1951, 36.

"Elders' Journal, July 1838." Joseph Smith Papers. www.josephsmithpapers.org/paper -summary/elders-journal-july-1838/11.

Elsaesser, Thomas. "Media Archaeology as Symptom." *New Review of Film and Television Studies* 14, no. 2 (2016): 181–215.

Embry, Jessie L. "Grain Storage: The Balance of Power between Priesthood Authority and Relief Society Autonomy." *Dialogue: A Journal of Mormon Thought* 15 (Winter 1982): 59–66.

Enns, Anthony. "The Undead Author: Spiritualism, Technology and Authorship." In *The Ashgate Research Companion to Nineteenth-Century Spiritualism and the Occult*, edited by Tatiana Kontou and Sarah Willburn, 59–68. Burlington, Vt.: Ashgate, 2012.

Ernst, Wolfgang. *Chronopoetics: The Temporal Being and Operativity of Technological Media*. New York: Rowman and Littlefield, 2016.

Esplin, Ronald K. "Joseph Smith and the Kirtland Crisis." In *Joseph Smith, the Prophet and Seer*, edited by Richard Neitzel Holzapfel and Kent P. Jackson, 261–90. Salt Lake City, Utah: Deseret Book, 2010.

"The Ethics and Etiquette of Photography." *Independent*, July–December 1907, 107–9.

Evans, Henry Ridgely. *The Spirit World Unmasked*. Chicago: Laird and Lee, 1902.

Evans, John Henry. *One Hundred Years of Mormonism*. Salt Lake City, Utah: Deseret News, 1905.

Evans, Richard L. Philo T. Farnsworth funeral, remarks by Richard L. Evans, March 16, 1971. Church History Library, Salt Lake City, Utah.

———. *One Hundred Thirty-Second Semi-annual Conference*, October 1962, 74–76. Salt Lake City: Church of Jesus Christ of Latter-day Saints, 1962.

Everson, George. *The Story of Television, the Life of Philo T. Farnsworth*. New York: W. W. Norton, 1949.

Fadiman, Clifton. *I Believe: The Personal Philosophies of Certain Eminent Men and Women of Our Time*. New York: Simon and Schuster, 1939.

Falk, Andrew Justin. *Upstaging the Cold War: American Dissent and Cultural Diplomacy, 1940–1960*. Boston: University of Massachusetts Press, 2010.

"Families See Eye-to-Eye on KSL-TV." *Improvement Era* 59 no. 71 (1956): 519.

"Familysearch Digital Records Access Replacing Microfilm." Familysearch.org, June 26, 2017. www.familysearch.org/en/newsroom/familysearch-digital -records-access-replacing-microfilm.

Feller, Gavin. "Media as Compromise: A Cultural History of Mormonism and New Communication Technology in Twentieth-Century America." Ph.D. diss., University of Iowa, 2017.

Fessenden, Tracy. *Culture and Redemption: Religion, the Secular, and American Religion*. Princeton, N.J.: Princeton University Press, 2007.

Fiedler, Leslie A. *Love and Death in the American Novel*. 1960. Champaign, Ill.: Dalkey Archive, 2003.

Fielding, Joseph. Diary of Joseph Fielding, Church History Library, Salt Lake City, Utah.

Fink, Donald G., ed. *Television Standards and Practice: Selected Papers from the Proceedings of the National Television System Committee and Its Panels*. New York: McGraw-Hill, 1943.

Flake, Kathleen. *The Politics of American Religious Identity: The Seating of Senator Reed Smoot, Mormon Apostle*. Chapel Hill: University of North Carolina Press, 2004.

Foster, Gwendolyn Audrey. *Performing Whiteness: Postmodern Re/constructions in the Cinema*. New York: State University of New York Press, 2003.

Foster, Lawrence. *Women, Family, and Utopia: Communal Experiments of the Shakers, the Oneida Community, and the Mormons*. Syracuse, N.Y.: Syracuse University Press, 1991.

Frosh, Paul, and Amit Pinchevski, eds. *Media Witnessing: Testimony in the Age of Mass Communication*. New York: Palgrave Macmillan, 2009.

Fyans, J. Thomas. "Ours Is a Shared Ancestry." In *One Hundred Forty-Eighth Annual Conference of the Church of Jesus Christ of Latter-day Saints, October 1978*, 38–40. Salt Lake City: Church of Jesus Christ of Latter-day Saints, 1978.

Gaboury, Jacob. *Image Objects: An Archaeology of Computer Graphics*. Cambridge, Mass.: MIT Press, 2021.

Gallagher, Catherine. *Practicing New Historicism*. Chicago: University of Chicago Press, 2000.

"Gambling Resumed at Poker Joints." *Salt Lake Herald*, March 8, 1901, 2.

Gates, Susa Young. Autobiographical Sketches. Susa Young Gates Papers, Church History Library, Salt Lake City, Utah.

———. "Boy versus Girl." *Young Woman's Journal* 6, no. 1 (October 1894): 30–32.

———. "Barton, Clara." Susa Young Gates Papers, Church History Library, Salt Lake City, Utah.

———. "Editor's Department." *Young Woman's Journal* 3 (November 1891): 86–88.

———. "From a Mother to Her Babe." Autobiographical Sketches. Susa Young Gates Papers, Church History Library, Salt Lake City, Utah.

———. *History of the Young Ladies' Mutual Improvement Association*. Salt Lake City, Utah: Deseret News, 1911.

———. "The Importance of Record Keeping." *Utah Genealogical Magazine*, January 1914, 16–19.

———. "Lion House Memories of Susa Young Gates." Susa Young Gates Papers, Church History Library, Salt Lake City, Utah.

———. "A Message: From a Woman of the Latter-day Saints to the Women in All the World." *Improvement Era* 10, no. 6 (April 1907): 447–52.

———. Notes on Life History. Susa Young Gates Papers, Church History Library, Salt Lake City, Utah.

———. "The Perfect Woman." *Young Woman's Journal* 12 (September 1890): 451–54.

———. "Relief Society Organized at Nauvoo." Susa Young Gates Papers, Church History Library, Salt Lake City, Utah.

———. "To My Mother's Mothers." *Improvement Era* 20 (July 1917): 777.

———. "To My Mother's Mothers." Susa Young Gates Papers, Church History Library, Salt Lake City, Utah.

———. "Verses about My Sisters." June 1, 1897. Susa Young Gates Papers, Church History Library, Salt Lake City, Utah.

———. "The Vision Beautiful." *Improvement Era* 23 (April 1920): 542–43.

———. "Vision of the Redemption of the Dead." *Relief Society Magazine* 6 (January 1919): 16–21.

———. "Witchcraft." *Young Woman's Journal* 11 (September 1900): 396–403.

———. "Woman's World and Work." *Daily Picayune*, February 2, 1899, 3.

———. "Women's Place in the Plan of Salvation." Susa Young Gates Papers, Church History Library, Salt Lake City, Utah.

Geertz, Clifford. *The Interpretation of Cultures.* New York: Basic Books, 1973.

Genealogical Society of Utah, Temples Archives Record Committee. Minutes of Meeting, December 7, 1938. Church History Library, Salt Lake City, Utah.

———. Minutes of Meeting, February 20, 1940. Church History Library, Salt Lake City, Utah.

———. Minutes of Meeting, February 17, 1941. Church History Library, Salt Lake City, Utah.

———. Minutes of Meeting, September 10, 1941. Church History Library, Salt Lake City, Utah.

Geoghegan, Bernard Dionysius. "Mind the Gap: Spiritualism and the Infrastructural Uncanny." *Critical Inquiry* 42 (July 2016): 899–922.

"Ghost or Shadow Pictures." *Photographic Times* 21 (May 1, 1891): 213.

Giddens, Anthony. *The Consequences of Modernity.* Cambridge, U.K.: Polity, 1990.

"Gift of the Holy Ghost." *Times and Seasons* 3 (June 15, 1842): 823–26.

Ginsburg, Walter. "Electrifying English." *Educational Screen*, June 1939, 187–89.

"The Girl in Business." *Deseret Evening News*, December 11, 1909, 15.

Gitelman, Lisa. *Scripts, Grooves, and Writing Machines.* Stanford, Calif.: Stanford University Press, 1999.

Given, Jock. *Turning of the Television.* Sydney: University of New South Wales Press, 2003.

Givens, Fiona. "Feminism and Heavenly Mother." In *The Routledge Handbook of Mormonism and Gender,* edited by Taylor Petrey and Amy Hoyt, 553–68. New York: Routledge, 2020.

Givens, Terryl, and Matthew Grow. *By the Hand of Mormon.* Oxford: Oxford University Press, 2002.

———. *Parley P. Pratt: The Apostle Paul of Mormonism.* Oxford: Oxford University Press, 2011.

———. *Viper on the Hearth.* Oxford: Oxford University Press, 1997.

———. *Wrestling the Angel.* Oxford: Oxford University Press, 2014.

Glover, Mary Baker [Eddy]. *Science and Health.* Boston: Christian Science Publishing, 1875.

Godfrey, Donald G., and Kenneth W. Godfrey. *The Diaries of Charles Ora Card: The Utah Years, 1871–1886.* Provo, Utah: Religious Studies Center, 2006.

Godfrey, Eliot. *Film and Education.* New York: Philosophical Library, 1948.

Godfrey, Matt, Mark Ashurst-McGee, Grant Underwood, Grant Woodford, and William Hartley. *Joseph Smith Papers: Documents.* Vol. 2. Salt Lake City, Utah: Church Historian's Press, 2013.

Godfrey, Matt, Spencer McBride, Alex Smith, and Christopher James Blythe, eds. *Joseph Smith Papers: Documents.* Vol. 7, *September 1839–January 1841.* Salt Lake City, Utah: Church Historian's Press, 2018.

Goldberg, Robert A. "From New Deal to New Right." In *Thunder from the Right: Ezra Taft Benson in Mormonism and Politics*, edited by Matthew L. Harris, 68–96. Urbana: University of Illinois Press, 2019.

Goodman, Michael. "Correlation: The Early Years." In *A Firm Foundation: Church Organization and Administration*, edited by David J. Whittaker and Arnold K. Garr, 319–38. Salt Lake City, Utah: Deseret, 2011.

Goodstein, Laurie. "Some Mormons Search the Web and Find Doubt." *New York Times*, July 20, 2013. www.nytimes.com/2013/07/21/us/some-mormons-search-the-web-and-find-doubt.html.

Goodwin, Megan. *Abusing Religion: Literary Persecution, Sex Scandals, and American Minority Religions*. New Brunswick, N.J.: Rutgers University Press, 2020.

Gorky, Maxim. "War and Civilization." *Current History* 3 (1916): 1152–53.

"Gospel Topics Essays." churchofjesuschrist.org. www.churchofjesuschrist.org/study/manual/gospel-topics-essays/essays?lang=eng.

Gover, C. Jane. *The Positive Image: Women Photographers in Turn-of-the-Century America*. New York: State University of New York Press, 1988.

Graham, Archie. "A Visit beyond the Veil." 1918. Church History Library, Salt Lake City, Utah.

Graham, Winifred. *That Reminds Me*. London: Skeffington and Son, 1945.

Grant, Heber J. *Ninetieth Annual Conference of the Church of Jesus Christ of Latter-day Saints, April 1920*, 2–16. Salt Lake City, Utah: Church of Jesus Christ of Latter-day Saints, 1920.

Greenblatt, Stephen. *Shakespearian Negotiations: The Circulation of Social Energy in Renaissance England*. Berkeley: University of California Press, 1988.

Grieveson, Lee. *Policing Cinema: Movies and Censorship in Early Twentieth-Century America*. Berkeley: University of California Press, 2004.

Griffiths, Alison. *Shivers Down Your Spine: Cinema, Museums, and the Immersive View*. New York: Columbia University Press, 2008.

Gripsrud, Jostein. "Television, Broadcasting, Flow: Key Metaphors in TV Theory." In *The Television Studies Book*, edited by Christine Geraghty and David Lusted, 17–32. London: Arnold, 1998.

Grover, Roscoe A. Interview. Salt Lake City, Utah, 1979. Church History Library, Salt Lake City, Utah.

Grow, Matthew J., Ronald K. Esplin, Mark Ashurst-McGee, Gerrit J. Dirkmaat, and Jeffrey D. Mahas. *Administrative Records, Council of Fifty, Minutes, March 1844–January 1846*. Joseph Smith Papers. Salt Lake City, Utah: Church Historian's Press, 2016.

Gunning, Tom *D. W. Griffith and the Origins of American Narrative Cinema*. Champaign: University of Illinois Press, 1991.

———. "Now You See It, Now You Don't." In *Silent Film*, edited by Richard Abel, 71–84. New York: Continuum, 1996.

———. "Spirit Photography, Magic Theater, Trick Films, and Photography's Uncanny." In *Cinematic Ghosts: Haunting and Spectrality from Silent Cinema to the Digital Era*, edited by Murray Leeder, 17–38. New York: Bloomsbury Academic, 2015.

———. "To Scan a Ghost: The Ontology of Mediated Vision." In *The Spectralities Reader: Ghosts and Haunting in Contemporary Cultural Theory*, edited by Maria del Pilar Blanco and Esther Peeren, 207–44. New York: Bloomsbury Academic, 2013.

Haight, David B. "Personal Temple Worship." *Ensign*, May 1993, 23–25.

Halbwachs, Maurice. *On Collective Memory*. Chicago: University of Chicago Press, 1992.

"Hana Kaapea's [*sic*] Presentation." *Salt Lake Herald-Republican*, February 26, 1899, 4.

Hanks, Maxine. *Women and Authority*. Salt Lake City, Utah: Signature Books, 1992.

Hansen, Joseph H. "Juniors Visit the Genealogical Society." *Utah Genealogical and Historical Magazine* 30, no. 4 (October 1939): 242–43.

Hansen, Mark. *New Philosophy for New Media*. Cambridge, Mass.: MIT Press, 2004.

Hansen, Miriam. *Babel and Babylon: Spectatorship in American Silent Film*. Cambridge, Mass.: Harvard University Press, 1991.

———. *Cinema and Experience: Siegfried Kracauer, Walter Benjamin, and Theodor W. Adorno*. Berkeley: University of California Press, 2011.

———. "The Mass Production of the Senses: Classical Cinema as Vernacular Modernism." *Modernism/Modernity* 6, no. 2 (1999): 59–77.

Harline, Paula Kelly. *The Polygamous Wives Writing Club*. Oxford: Oxford University Press, 2014.

Harper, Steven. *First Vision: Memory and Mormon Origins*. Oxford: Oxford University Press, 2019.

Harris, Matthew. "Breaching the Wall: Ezra Taft Benson on Church and State." In *Thunder from the Right: Ezra Taft Benson in Mormonism and Politics*, edited by Matthew L. Harris, 1–20. Urbana: University of Illinois Press, 2019.

———. *Watchman on the Tower: Ezra Taft Benson and the Making of the Mormon Right*. Salt Lake City: University of Utah Press, 2020.

Harris, Sharon J., and Peter McMurray. "Sounding Mormonism." *Mormon Studies Review* 5 (2018): 33–45.

Hartley, William G. "Coming to Zion: Saga of the Gathering." *Ensign* 5 (July 1975): 14–18.

Harvey, John. *Photography and Spirit*. London: Reaktion, 2007.

Hatch, Trevan. *Visions, Manifestations, and Miracles of the Restoration*. Orem, Utah: Granite, 2008.

Hauglid, Brian. *Textual History of the Book of Abraham: Manuscripts and Editions*. Orem, Utah: Neal A. Maxwell Institute for Religious Scholarship, 2011.

Hawes, William. *American Television Drama: The Experimental Years*. Tuscaloosa: University of Alabama Press, 1986.

Hawthorne, Nathaniel. *The House of the Seven Gables*. Boston: Ticknor, Reed, and Fields, 1851.

Hazen, Craig James. *The Village Enlightenment in America: Popular Religion and Science in the Nineteenth Century*. Urbana: University of Illinois Press, 2000.

Heaton, Eliza Putnam. "Woman and the Camera." *British Journal of Photography* 11 (1891): 8–9.

"Heber G. Wolsey interview: Salt Lake City, Utah, 1979." Church History Library, Salt Lake City, Utah.

Hedges, Andrew, Alex D. Smith, and Richard Lloyd Anderson, eds. *Journals*. Vol. 2. Joseph Smith Papers. Salt Lake City, Utah: Church Historian's Press, 2011.

Heidegger, Martin. *Basic Writings*. Edited by David Farrell Krell. San Francisco: Harper Collins, 1993.

———. *Vorträge und Aufsätze*. Frankfurt: Vittorio Klostermann, 2000.

Henry, B. C. "Touching Jesus." *Homiletic Review* 20 (1890): 346–48.

Hickman, Jared. "*The Book of Mormon* as Amerindian Apocalypse." *American Literature* 86 (September 2014): 429–61.

Hicks, Stephen. *Mormonism and Music: A History*. Urbana: University of Illinois, 2003.

Hinckley, Gordon B. *One Hundred Thirty-Second Annual Conference of the Church of Jesus Christ of Latter-day Saints, October 1962*, 72–74. Salt Lake City, Utah: Church of Jesus Christ of Latter-day Saints, 1962.

Hines, Richard, Jr. "Women and Photography." *Wilson's Photographic Magazine* 36 (March 1899): 137–41.

Hirsch, Eric. "New Technologies and Domestic Consumption." In *The Television Studies Book*, edited by Christine Geraghty and David Lusted, 158–74. New York: Arnold, 1998.

Historical Department Office Journal, 1844–2012. Church History Department, Salt Lake City, Utah.

History, 1838–1856. Vol. F-1, *1 May 1844–8 August 1844.* Joseph Smith Papers. www .josephsmithpapers.org/paper-summary/history-1838-1856-volume-f-1-1-may -1844-8-august-1844/435.

"History, circa Summer 1832." Joseph Smith Papers. www.josephsmithpapers.org/paper -summary/history-circa-summer-1832/2.

"History of Joseph Smith, Continued." *Millennial Star* 25, no. 16 (April 18, 1863): 248–49.

"History of 'Mormonism' in Picture." *Deseret Evening News* 7 (January 25, 1913).

Hollister-Short, Graham. *History of Technology.* Vol. 20. New York: Bloomsbury Academic, 1999.

Holzapfel, Richard N., and Andrew H. Hedges. *Through the Lens: The Original 1907 Church History Photographs of George Edward Anderson.* Salt Lake City, Utah: Deseret, 2010.

History, 1838–1856. Vol. F-1, *1 May 1844–8 August 1844.* Joseph Smith Papers. www .josephsmithpapers.org/paper-summary/history-1838-1856-volume-f-1-1-may -1844-8-august-1844/435.

Hood, Thomas. *The Comic Annual.* London: Bradbury and Evans, 1839.

Horak, Jan-Christopher. Review of Stephen Oetterman, *The Panorama: History of a Mass Medium. Screening the Past*, no. 6 (1999). www.screeningthepast.com/2014/12 /the-panorama-history-of-a-mass-medium/.

Houghton, Georgiana. *Chronicles of the Photographs of Spiritual Beings and Phenomena Invisible to the Material Eye.* London: Ballantine, 1882.

Howe, Mary. "Professional and Business Opportunities for Women. Stenography and Typewriting." *Young Woman's Journal* 1 (October 1891): 24–25.

Hoyt, Amy, and Sara M. Patterson. "Mormon Masculinity: Changing Gender Expectations in the Era of Transition from Polygamy to Monogamy, 1890–1920." *Gender and History* 23 (April 2011): 72–91.

Huhtamo, Erkki. *Illusions in Motion: Media Archaeology of the Moving Panorama and Related Spectacles.* Cambridge, Mass.: MIT Press, 2013.

———. "Screen Tests: Why Do We Need an Archaeology of the Screen?" *Cinema Journal* 51 (Winter 2012): 144–48.

"A Hundred Years of Genealogical Progress." *Genealogical Helper* 1, no. 1 (September 1947): 3.

Hunter, Milton R. *One Hundred Thirty-Third Annual Conference of the Church of Jesus Christ of Latter-day Saints, April 1963*, 14–18. Salt Lake City, Utah: Church of Jesus Christ of Latter-day Saints, 1963.

Huntington Bagley Collection. L. Tom Perry Special Collections, Brigham Young University, Provo, Utah.

Huntington, Oliver B. *History of the Life of Oliver B. Huntington, Written by Himself, 1878–1900.* N.p.: n.p., n.d.

————. "History of the Life of Oliver B. Huntington." Typescript. L. Tom Perry Special Collections, Brigham Young University, Provo, Utah.

Hyde, Orson. *Ein Ruf aus der Wüste: Eine Stimme aus dem Schoose [Shosse] der Erde.* Frankfurt: Orson Hyde, 1842.

Illinois Copyright Records, vol. 18, August 1821–September 1848.

"Imitation Is Sincerest Flattery." Advertisement. *Moving Picture World* 14, no. 13 (December 28, 1912): 1331.

"Information Retrieval." *Business Automation* 11, part 1 (1964): 20–25.

"Instruction, 2 April 1843, as Reported by William Clayton." Joseph Smith Papers. www .josephsmithpapers.org/paper-summary/instruction-2-april-1843-as-reported-by -william-clayton/4.

"Instruction, 9 February 1843 [D&C 129], as Reported by William Clayton." Joseph Smith Papers. www.josephsmithpapers.org/paper-summary/instruction-9-february-1843 -dc-129-as-reported-by-william-clayton/1.

"An Interesting Meeting." *Territorial Enquirer,* October 30, 1883, 3.

Irigaray, Luce. *The Sex Which Is Not One.* Ithaca, N.Y.: Cornell University Press, 1985.

————. *Speculum of the Other Woman.* Ithaca, N.Y.: Cornell University Press, 1985.

Isaacson, Thorpe. *One Hundred Thirtieth Annual Conference of the Church of Jesus Christ of Latter-day Saints, April 2, 3, 4, and 6, 1960,* 59–62. Salt Lake City, Utah: Church of Jesus Christ of Latter-day Saints, 1960.

Iverson, Heber C. *Seventy-Eighth Annual Conference of the Church of Jesus Christ of Latter-day Saints, April 1908,* 68–72. Salt Lake City, Utah: Church of Jesus Christ of Latter-day Saints, 1908.

Jacobs, Briant S. "Literature—the Literature of England: Lesson 19." *Relief Society Magazine* 39, no. 1 (January 1952): 632–36.

Jantzen, Grace. *Becoming Divine: Towards a Feminist Philosophy of Religion.* Manchester: Manchester University Press, 1998.

Jarvis, T. M. *Accredited Ghost Stories.* London: J. Andrews, 1823.

Jensen, Devan. "Philo Dibble's Dream of 'A Gallery in Zion.'" *Journal of Mormon History* 44 (October 2018): 19–39.

Jensen, Heather Belnap. "Aesthetic Evangelism, Artistic Sisterhood, and the Gospel of Beauty: Mormon Women Artists at Home and Abroad, circa 1890–1920." In *Mormon Women's History: Beyond Biography,* edited by Rachel Cope, 470–84. New York: Oxford University Press, 2017.

Jensen, Richard L. *C. C. A. Christensen, 1831–1912: Mormon Immigrant Artist.* Salt Lake City, Utah: Church of Jesus Christ of Latter-day Saints, 1984.

Jensen, Richard, and William G. Hartley. "Immigration and Emigration." In *Encyclopedia of Mormonism,* vol. 2, edited by Daniel H. Ludlow, 673–76. New York: Macmillan, 1992.

Jensen, Robin Scott. "Archives of the Better World: The Nineteenth-Century Historian's Office and Mormonism's Archival Flexibility." Ph.D. diss., University of Utah, 2019.

Jessee, Dean C. "Return to Carthage: Writing the History of Joseph Smith's Martyrdom." *Journal of Mormon History* (1981): 3–19.

Jessee, Dean C., Mark Ashurst-McGee, and Richard L. Jensen, eds. *Documents.* Vol. 1. Joseph Smith Papers. Salt Lake City, Utah: Church Historian's Press, 2008.

J.M.S. "In Switzerland." *Deseret Weekly* 38, no. 1 (February 1889): 185–86.

Johnson, Alan D. "The Heavens Are Opened: The New Church History Museum Exhibit." *Ensign,* July 2016, 40–47.

Johnson, Benjamin F. *My Life's Review*. Independence, Mo.: Zion's, 1947.

Johnson, Jake. *Mormons, Musical Theater, and Belonging in America*. Urbana: University of Illinois Press, 2019.

Johnson, Kirk. "Mormons on a Mission." *New York Times*, August 20, 2010. www.nytimes .com/2010/08/22/arts/music/22choir.html.

Johnson, Sylvester. *African American Religions, 1500–2000: Colonialism, Democracy, and Freedom*. New York: Cambridge University Press, 2015.

Jones, Carey Stevens. *A Women's View: The Photography of Elfie Huntington*. Springville, Utah: Springville Museum of Art, 1988.

Jones, David J. *Gothic Machines: Textualities, Pre-cinematic Media and Film in Popular Visual Culture*. Cardiff: University of Wales, 2011.

Jones, J. Nelson. *Thaumat—Oahspe*. Melbourne, Australia: J. C. Stephens, 1912.

Jones, Megan Sanborn. *Contemporary Mormon Pageantry: Seeking after the Dead*. Ann Arbor: University of Michigan Press, 2018.

———. *Performing American Identity in Anti-Mormon Melodrama*. New York: Routledge, 2010.

Jorgenson, Lynne Watkins. "The Mantle of the Prophet Joseph Passes to Brother Brigham: A Collective Spiritual Witness." *BYU Studies Quarterly* 36 (1996): 125–204.

Jung, Andrew M. "Twittering Away the Right of Publicity: Personality Rights and Celebrity Impersonation on Social Networking Sites." *Chicago-Kent Law Review* 86, no. 1 (December 2010): 381–417.

Jütte, Robert. *A History of the Senses: From Antiquity to Cyberspace*. Translated by James Lynn. Cambridge, U.K.: Polity, 2005.

Kane, Elizabeth Wood. *Twelve Mormon Homes Visited in Succession on a Journey through Utah to Arizona*. Philadelphia: William Wood, 1874.

Kant, Immanuel. "Dreams of a Spirit-Seer." In *Theoretical Philosophy, 1755–1770*. Translated and edited by David Walford, 301–60. Cambridge: Cambridge University Press, 1992.

Keathley, Christian. *Cinephilia and History, or, The Wind in the Trees*. Bloomington: Indiana University Press, 2006.

Keep, Christopher. "Blinded by the Type: Gender and Information Technology at the Turn of the Century." *Nineteenth Century Contexts* 23 (2001): 149–73.

———. "The Cultural Work of the Type-Writer Girl." *Victorian Studies* 40, no. 3 (Spring 1997): 401–26.

Keil, Charlie, and Shelley Stamp, eds. *American Cinema's Transitional Era: Audiences, Institutions, Practices*. Berkeley: University of California Press, 2004.

Keil, Charlie. *Early American Cinema in Transition*. Madison: University of Wisconsin Press, 2001.

Keller, Catherine, and Mary-Jane Rubenstein. *Entangled Worlds: Religion, Science, and New Materialism*. New York: Fordham University Press, 2017.

Kenneally, Christine. "The Mormon Church Is Building a Family Tree of the Entire Human Race." *New Republic*, October 14, 2014. newrepublic.com/article/119785 /extensive-mormon-genealogy-offers-limited-vision-history.

Kent, Barbara. "Points of the Ideal Woman." *Salt Lake Tribune*, January 20, 1895, 11.

Kern, Stephen. *The Culture of Time and Space, 1880–1918*. Cambridge, Mass.: Harvard University Press, 2003.

Kimball, Heber C. "Knowledge of the Saints . . ." Delivered November 29, 1864. *Journal of Discourses* 10 (Liverpool, U.K.: Latter-day Saints Book Depot, 1865): 365–72.

————. "Obedience—the Priesthood-Spiritual Communication." *Journal of Discourses* 2 (Liverpool, U.K.: Latter-day Saints Book Depot, 1855): 220–25.

Kimball, Mary Ellen. *Journal of Mary Ellen Kimball, Including a Sketch of Our History in This Valley.* Salt Lake City, Utah: Pioneer, 1994.

Kimball, Spencer W. *One Hundred Thirty-Second Annual Conference of the Church of Jesus Christ of Latter-day Saints, April 1962,* 59–64. Salt Lake City, Utah: Church of Jesus Christ of Latter-day Saints, 1962.

————. "Spiritual Communication." In *One Hundred Thirty-Second Annual Conference of the Church of Jesus Christ of Latter-day Saints, April 1962,* 59–64. Salt Lake City, Utah: Church of Jesus Christ of Latter-day Saints, 1962.

————. *A Style of Our Own: Modesty in Dress and Its Relationship to the Church, An Apostle Speaks to Youth.* Provo, Utah: Brigham Young University, 1951.

Kirkham, Francis. Letter to James Kirkham, November 21, 1932. Church of the Air Material, Church History Library, Salt Lake City, Utah.

Kittler, Friedrich. *Discourse Network 1800/1900.* Translated by Michael Metteer and Chris Cullens. Stanford, Calif.: Stanford University Press, 1990.

————. *Gramophone, Film, Typewriter.* Translated by Geoffrey Winthrop-Young and Michael Wutz. Stanford, Calif.: Stanford University Press, 1999.

————. *Literature, Media, Information Systems.* Abingdon: Routledge, 1997.

————. *Optical Media.* Translated by Anthony Enns. Cambridge, U.K.: Polity, 2010.

Kiver, Milton Sol. *Television Receiver Servicing.* New York: Van Nostrand, 1959.

Koehler, Ernst. Letter to the Board of Directors of the Genealogical Society, July 1, 1946. Ernst Koehler Files, Church History Library, Salt Lake City, Utah.

Kontou, Tatiana, and Sarah Willburn, eds. *The Ashgate Research Companion to Nineteenth Century Spiritualism and the Occult.* Burlington, Vt.: Ashgate, 2012.

Kracauer, Siegfried. *The Mass Ornament: Weimar Essays.* Edited and translated by Thomas Y. Levin. Cambridge, Mass.: Harvard University Press, 1995.

————. *Siegfried Kracauer's American Writings: Essays on Film and Popular Culture.* Edited by Johannes von Moltke and Kristy Rawson. Berkeley: University of California Press, 2012.

Kraidy, Marwan. "The Body as Medium in the Digital Age: Challenges and Opportunities." *Communication and Critical/Cultural Studies* 10 (2013): 285–90.

Kuhlman, Augustus Frederick. *Archives and Libraries.* Chicago: American Library Association, 1940.

Lambourne, Alfred. *The Pioneer Trail.* Salt Lake City, Utah: Deseret, 1913.

Landsberg, Alison. *Prosthetic Memory: The Transformation of American Remembrance in the Age of Mass Culture.* New York: Columbia University Press, 2004.

Lang, Daniel J. *One Hundred-Seventh Semi-annual Conference of the Church of Jesus Christ of Latter-day Saints, October 1936,* 119–21. Salt Lake City, Utah: Church of Jesus Christ of Latter-day Saints, 1936.

Laqueur, Thomas. *The Work of the Dead.* Princeton, N.J.: Princeton University Press, 2015.

Larson, Erik. *Thunderstruck.* New York: Random House, 2007.

Larson, Lauren. "The Mormon Church vs. the Internet." *Verge,* July 1, 2019. www.theverge .com/2019/7/1/18759587/mormon-church-quitmormon-exmormon-jesus-christ -internet-seo-lds.

Lassander, Mika, and Peik Ingman. "Exploring the Social without a Separate Domain for Religion." *Scripta Instituti Donneriani Aboensis* 24 (2012): 201–17.

Lasswell, Harold. "The Structure and Function of Communication in Society." In *The Communication of Ideas*, edited by Lyman Bryson, 37-51. New York: Institute for Religious and Social Studies, 1949.

Latour, Bruno. *Reassembling the Social*. Oxford: Oxford University Press, 2005.

"LDS Confab Seen on Video." *Salt Lake Telegram*, September 30, 1949, 8.

Lee, Harold B. *One Hundred Thirty-Second Annual Conference of the Church of Jesus Christ of Latter-day Saints, October 1962*, 19–83. Salt Lake City, Utah: Church of Jesus Christ of Latter-day Saints, 1962.

———. *One Hundred Thirty-second Semi-annual Conference of the Church of Jesus Christ of Latter-day Saints, October 1962*, 71–72. Salt Lake City, Utah: Church of Jesus Christ of Latter-day Saints, 1962.

———. *One Hundred Thirty-eighth Semi-annual Conference of the Church of Jesus Christ of Latter-day Saints, October 1968*, 59–62, Salt Lake City, Utah: Church of Jesus Christ of Latter-day Saints, 1962.

Lee, Harold B., Gordon B. Hinckley, Richard L. Evans, and Marion G. Romney. "Report from the Correlation Committee." *Improvement Era* 65 (December 1962): 936–41.

Lemov, Rebecca. *Database of Dreams: The Lost Quest to Catalog Humanity*. New Haven, Conn.: Yale University Press, 2015.

Letterbook 1. Joseph Smith Papers. www.josephsmithpapers.org/paper-summary /letterbook-1/14?highlight=broken%20scattered.

Letter from First Presidency to Presidents of Manti, St. George, Logan, and Salt Lake Temples, June 8, 1942, Genealogical Society of Utah. Temples Archives Record Committee, Church History Library, Salt Lake City, Utah.

"Letter to Hyrum Smith, 3–4 March 1831." Joseph Smith Papers. www.josephsmithpapers .org/paper-summary/letter-to-hyrum-smith-3-4-march-1831/1.

"Letter to William W. Phelps, 27 November 1832." Joseph Smith Papers. www .josephsmithpapers.org/paper-summary/letter-to-william-w-phelps-27-november -1832/2.

Leventhal, Herbert. *In the Shadow of the Enlightenment: Occultism and Renaissance Science in Eighteenth Century America*. New York: New York University Press, 1976.

Lewis, William Draper, and Miriam McConnell, eds. *Equity Jurisdiction, Bills of Peace: A Collection of Cases with Notes*. Philadelphia: International Printing,1910.

Lieberknecht, George. "Typewriting Extraordinary." *Borderland* 1, no. 1 (1893): 61.

Lieberman, Irving. "A Mathematical Model for Integrated Business Systems." *Management Science* 2, no. 4 (July 1956): 327–36.

The Life and Labors of Eliza R. Snow. Salt Lake City, Utah: Juvenile Instructor, 1888.

Lightner, Mary. *Life and Testimony of Mary Lightner*. Salt Lake City, Utah: Pioneer, 1997.

Lindsey, Rachel McBride. *A Communion of Shadows: Religion and Photography in Nineteenth-Century America*. Chapel Hill: University of North Carolina Press, 2017.

Lindström, Matts. "Drömmar om det minsta: Mikrofilm, överflöd och brist, 1900–1970." Ph.D. diss., Stockholm University, 2017.

Lofton, Kathryn. *Consuming Religion*. Chicago: University of Chicago Press, 2017.

Loughran, Trish. *The Republic in Print*. New York: Columbia University Press, 2007.

"Lucy Mack Smith, History, 1845." Joseph Smith Papers. www.josephsmithpapers.org /paper-summary/lucy-mack-smith-history-1845/102.

Ludlow, Daniel, ed. *Encyclopedia of Mormonism*. New York: Macmillan, 1992.

Lund, Robert. "Proclaiming the Gospel in the Twentieth Century." In *Out of Obscurity: The LDS Church in the Twentieth Century*, 226–34. Salt Lake City, Utah: Deseret Books, 2000.

Lunney, Heather. "Exploring the Cold War through the Twilight Zone." *History in the Making* 3, no. 1 (2014): 39–50.

Lusted, David, and Christine Geraghty, eds. *The Television Studies Book*. New York: Arnold, 1998.

Lyman, Amasa. "A Vision." Related July 19, 1857. *Journal of Discourses* 5 (Liverpool, U.K.: Latter-day Saints Book Depot, 1858): 58–59.

Lyman, Amy Brown. "In Retrospect." *Relief Society Magazine* 29 (January 1942): 5–10.

Lynch, Eugene B. "Germany's Service to Genealogy." *Utah Genealogical and Historical Magazine* 30, no. 1 (January 1939): 8.

Lynott, Patricia A. "Susa Young Gates 1856–1933: Educator, Suffragist, Mormon." Ph.D, diss., Loyola University Chicago, 1996.

Lythgoe, Dennis L. "The Changing Image of Mormonism." *Dialogue: A Journal of Mormon Thought* 3 (1968): 45–58.

MacKay, Michael Hubbard, and Gerrit J. Dirkmaat. *The Joseph Smith Papers: Documents*. Vol. 1, *July 1828–June 1831*. Salt Lake City, Utah: Church Historian's Press, 2013.

Madsen, Arch L., Blaine M. Yorgason, and Richard Peterson. *The Infinite Journey: A Brief Overview of the Earthly Life of Arch L. Madsen*. Orem, Utah: The Author, 1995.

Madsen, Carol Cornwall. "The 'New Woman' and the *Woman's Exponent*: An Editorial Perspective." *BYU Studies Quarterly* 59 (2020): 71–92.

———. "Retrenchment Association." In *Encyclopedia of Mormonism*, edited by Daniel H. Ludlow, 3:1223–25. New York: Macmillan, 1992.

Mahas, Jeffrey. "Remembering the Martyrdom." In *Revelations in Context*, edited by Matthew McBride and James Goldberg, 299–306. Salt Lake City, Utah: Church of Jesus Christ of Latter-day Saints, 2016.

Major, Jill C. "Artworks in the Celestial Room of the First Nauvoo Temple." *BYU Studies* 41 (2002): 47–69.

Mann, Horace. *A Few Thoughts on the Powers and Duties of Woman*. Syracuse, N.Y.: Hall, Mills, 1853.

Manseau, Peter. *The Apparitionists: A Tale of Phantoms, Fraud, Photography, and the Man who Captured Lincoln's Ghost*. New York: Houghton Mifflin Harcourt, 2017.

Marcel, Gabriel. *The Decline of Wisdom*. New York: Philosophical Press, 1955.

Marchand, Philip. *Marshall McLuhan: The Medium and the Messenger*. Cambridge, Mass.: MIT Press, 1989.

Marvin, Frederic. *The Philosophy of Spiritualism and the Pathology and Treatment of Mediomania*. New York: Asa K. Butts, 1874.

Marx, Karl, and Friedrich Engels. *Manifest der kommunistischen Partei*. London: Burghard, 1848.

Maurice, Alice. *The Cinema and its Shadow: Race and Technology in Early Cinema*. Minneapolis: University of Minnesota Press, 2013.

May, Dean L. *Utah: A People's History*. Salt Lake City, Utah: Bonneville, 1987.

McAllister, Stanley, Claude Cornwall, Roscoe Grover, and Dave Paine. Letter to Broadcaster, November 7, 1932. Church of the Air Material, 1932, Church History Library, Salt Lake City, Utah.

McCarthy, Anna. *Citizen Machine: Governing by Television in 1950s America*. New York: New York University Press, 2013.

McConkie, Bruce R. *Official Report of the First Mexico and Central America Area General Conference*. Salt Lake City, Utah: Church of Jesus Christ of Latter-day Saints, 1973.

———. *One Hundred Forty-First Annual Conference of the Church of Jesus Christ of Latter-day Saints, April 1971*, 98–101. Salt Lake City, Utah: Church of Jesus Christ of Latter-day Saints, 1971.

———. *One Hundred Nineteenth Annual Conference of the Church of Jesus Christ of Latter-day Saints, April 1949*, 89–94. Salt Lake City, Utah: Church of Jesus Christ of Latter-day Saints, 1949.

McGarry, Molly. *Ghosts of Futures Past: Spiritualism and the Politics of Nineteenth Century America*. Berkeley: University of California Press, 2012.

McKay, David O. *One Hundred Seventh Semi-annual Conference of the Church of Jesus Christ of Latter-day Saints, October 1936*, 102–6. Salt Lake City, Utah: Church of Jesus Christ of Latter-day Saints, 1936.

———. *One Hundred Thirty-First Annual Conference of the Church of Jesus Christ of Latter-day Saints, April 1961*, 96–97. Salt Lake City, Utah: Church of Jesus Christ of Latter-day Saints, 1961.

———. *One Hundred Thirty-Ninth Semi-annual Conference of the Church of Jesus Christ of Latter-day Saints, October 1969*, 135–38. Salt Lake City, Utah: Church of Jesus Christ of Latter-day Saints, 1969.

———. *One Hundred Thirty-Seventh Semi-annual Conference of the Church of Jesus Christ of Latter-day Saints, September and October 1967*, 135–38. Salt Lake City, Utah: Church of Jesus Christ of Latter-day Saints, 1967.

———. *One Hundred Twenty-Ninth Annual Conference of the Church of Jesus Christ of Latter-day Saints, April 1959*, 69–70, 121–22. Salt Lake City, Utah: Church of Jesus Christ of Latter-day Saints, 1959.

———. *One Hundred Twenty-Sixth Semi-annual Conference, September and October 1955*, 128–30. Salt Lake City, Utah: Church of Jesus Christ of Latter-day Saints, 1955.

McLuhan, Eric, and Frank Zingrone, eds. *Essential McLuhan*. New York: Basic Books, 1995.

McLuhan, Marshall. *Understanding Media*. Cambridge, Mass.: MIT Press, 1994.

M.C.S. "Television in the Home." *Relief Society Magazine* 36 (August 1949): 532.

Mehr, Kahlile. "The Microfilm Mission of Archibald F. Bennett." *Ensign*, April 1982, 69.

Mensel, Robert E. "'Kodakers Lying in Wait': Amateur Photography and the Right of Privacy in New York, 1885–1915." *American Quarterly* 43 (March 1991): 24–45.

Metcalf, Keyes D. "Microphotography for Libraries." *American Library Association Bulletin* 32, no. 1 (January 1939): 59–60.

Meyer, Birgit. "Medium." *Material Religion* 7 (2011): 58–64.

Meyer, Stephenie. *Twilight*. New York: Little Brown, Young Readers, 2005.

Miller, Clinton R., Washington, D.C., to Arch Madsen, Salt Lake City, Utah, July 22, 1969. Church History Library, Salt Lake City, Utah.

"Minutes of Meeting Sep. 10, 1941." Temples Archives Record Committee, Genealogical Society, Church History Library, Salt Lake City, Utah.

Mitchell, W. J. T., and Mark B. N. Hansen, eds. *Critical Terms for Media Studies*. Chicago: University of Chicago Press, 2010.

———. *What Do Pictures Want?* Chicago: University of Chicago Press, 2005.

Mockler, Robert J. "A Systems Approach to Business Organization and Decision Making." *California Management Review* 11, no. 2 (1968): 53–58.

Modern, John Lardas. *Secularism in Antebellum America*. Chicago: University of Chicago Press, 2011.

Moffett, Cleveland. "Doing the Impossible." *American Magazine*, February 1915, 11–15.

Monson, Thomas S. "Correlation Brings Blessings." *Relief Society Magazine* 54 (April 1967): 244–47.

Morgan, David. *The Embodied Eye: Religious Visual Culture and the Social Life*. Berkeley: University of California Press, 2012.

———. *The Forge of Vision*. Berkeley: University of California Press, 2015.

———. "Introduction: The Matter of Belief." In *Religion and Material Culture: The Matter of Belief*, edited by David Morgan, 1–12. London: Routledge, 2010.

———. *The Lure of Images*. New York: Routledge, 2007.

Morimoto, Tomomi, et al. "Habitat Disruption Induces Immune-Suppression and Oxidavite Stress in Honey Bees." *Ecology and Evolution* 1 (October 2011): 201–17.

"'Mormonism' and Spiritism." *Deseret Evening News*, March 22, 1902, 4.

"Mormon Story to Be Told by Film." Historical Department Journal History of the Church, July 12, 1912, Church History Library, Salt Lake City, Utah.

"Motion Pictures to Tell Story of Mormonism." *San Francisco Call*, August 13, 1912, 3.

"Moving Pictures." *Institution Quarterly* 2, no. 1 (June 1911): 11.

Mullin, Katherine. *Working Girls: Fiction, Sexuality, and Modernity*. Oxford: Oxford University Press, 2016.

Mulvey, Laura. *Visual and Other Pleasures*. New York: Palgrave Macmillan, 1989.

Münsterberg, Hugo. *The Photoplay: A Psychological Study*. New York: D. Appleton, 1916.

"The Murder." *Times and Seasons* 5 (July 15, 1844): 584–86.

Murray, Susan. "'Never Twice the Same Colour': Standardizing, Calibrating and Harmonizing NTSC Colour Television in the Early 1950s." *Screen* 56 (2015): 415–35.

Musser, Charles, and Carol Nelson. *High-Class Moving Pictures*. Princeton, N.J.: Princeton University Press, 1991.

Natale, Simone. "A Short History of Superimposition: From Spirit Photography to Early Cinema." *Early Popular Visual Culture* 10 (May 2012): 125–45.

National Archives. *Second Annual Report of the Archivist of the United States*. Washington, D.C.: United States Government Printing Office, 1936.

Nelson, N. L. "Gospel Studies: An Inward Kingdom of God Necessary to Salvation." *Improvement Era* 2 (Salt Lake City, Utah: General Board, 1899): 217–21.

Nelson, Richard Alan. "Commercial Propaganda in the Silent Film: A Case Study of 'A Mormon Maid' (1917)." *Film History* 1, no. 2 (1987): 149–62.

Nelson, William G. "Joseph Smith, the Prophet." *Young Woman's Journal* 17 (December 1906): 537–48.

"The New Microfilm Records." *Genealogical Helper* 1, no. 1 (September 1947): 2.

"New Publications." *Light* 17 (January 9, 1897): 23.

"New Television Outlet for Salt Lake Starts Evening Shows on June 1." *Salt Lake Telegram*, May 31, 1949, 2T.

Nicholas of Cusa. *The Vision of God*. Translated by Emma Gurney Salter. New York: Cosimo Books, 2007.

Nicholson, William. "Narrative and Explanation of the Appearance of Phantoms and Other Figures in the Exhibitions of the Phantasmagoria." *Journal of Natural Philosophy, Chemistry, and the Arts* 1 (February 1802): 147–50.

Nietzsche, Friedrich. *The Gay Science.* Translated by Thomas Common. New York: Dover, 2006.

Noam, Eli. *European Television.* Oxford: Oxford University Press, 1991.

Noble, Safiya Umoja. *Algorithms of Oppression: How Search Engines Reinforce Racism.* New York: New York University Press, 2018.

Nolan, Max. "Materialism and the Mormon Faith." *Dialogue: A Journal of Mormon Thought* 22 (Winter 1989): 62–75.

Noll, Daniel F. "The Maintenance of Microfilm Files." *American Archivist* 13, no. 2 (April 1950): 129–34.

Nord, David Paul. *Faith in Reading: Religious Publishing and the Birth of Mass Media in America.* New York: Oxford University Press, 2004.

"Noted American Writer." *Cinema News and Property Gazette,* February 19, 1913, 39.

Novak, Daniel A. *Realism, Photography, and Nineteenth-Century Fiction.* Cambridge: Cambridge University Press, 2008.

Oaks, Dallin H., and Marvin S. Hill. *Carthage Conspiracy: The Trial of the Accused Assassins of Joseph Smith.* Chicago: University of Illinois Press, 1979.

"Of Interest to Women." *Deseret News,* December 2, 1899, 16.

Ogden, Emily. *Credulity: A Cultural History of US Mesmerism.* Chicago: University of Chicago Press, 2018.

Orlob, C. Letter to Susa Young Gates, August 19, 1890, Salt Lake City, Utah. Susa Young Gates Papers, ca. 1870–1933, Correspondence Files, Church History Library, Salt Lake City, Utah.

Oetterman, Stephen. *Panorama: History of a Mass Medium.* Princeton, N.J.: Zone Books, 1997.

"'100 Years of Mormonism' in Pictures at the Empire." *Bridgeport Evening Farmer,* September 12, 1913, 13.

"100 Years of Mormonism." *Logan Republican,* February 4, 1913, 8.

"100 Years of Mormonism" [advertisement]. *Logan Republican,* February 6, 1912, 4.

"100 years of Mormonism: the Days of '47." *The Evening Standard,* April 12, 1913, 6.

"One of the Biggest Film Epics, District Records 'On Camera.'" *Brantford Expositor,* March 24, 1958. Clipping in Microfilm Department Papers, Church History Library, Salt Lake City, Utah.

Orsi, Robert. *History and Presence.* Cambridge, Mass.: Harvard University Press, 2016.

Orwell, George. *1984.* 1949. New York: Alfred A. Knopf, 1992.

Osterhammel, Jürgen. *The Transformation of the World: A Global History of the Nineteenth Century.* Princeton, N.J.: Princeton University Press, 2014.

Ostwald, Wilhelm. "Ein Weltreich der Wissenschaft." *Berliner Tageblatt,* February 6, 1914, title page.

Otto, Peter. "Artificial Environments, Virtual Realities, and the Cultivation of Propensity in the London Colosseum." In *Virtual Victorians: Networks, Connections, Technologies,* edited by Veronica Alfano, 167–88. Basingstoke: Palgrave Macmillan, 2015.

Otterstrom, Samuel M. "Genealogy as Religious Ritual: The Doctrine and Practice of Family History in the Church of Jesus Christ of Latter-day Saints." In *Geography and*

Genealogy: Locating Personal Pasts, edited by Dallen J. Timothy and Jeanne Kay Guelke, 137–51. New York: Routledge, 2016.

"Our Advertisers." *Western Stenographer* 1, no. 7 (July 1894): 12.

Owen, Alex. *The Darkened Room: Women, Power, and Spiritualism in Late Victorian England*. Chicago: University of Chicago Press, 1989.

Page, John E. "Letter." *Nauvoo Neighbor* 3, no. 13 (July 30, 1845).

Pallasmaa, Juhani. "Hapticity and Time: Notes on Fragile Architecture." *Architectural Review* 207 (2000): 78–84.

Palmquist, Peter E., and Thomas R. Kailbourn, eds. *Pioneer Photographers of the Far West: A Biographical Dictionary, 1840–1865*. Stanford, Calif.: Stanford University Press, 2000.

Parikka, Jussi. "Insects and Canaries: Medianatures and Aesthetics of the Invisible." *Angelaki: Journal of the Theoretical Humanities* 18 (2013): 107–19.

———. *What Is Media Archaeology?* Cambridge, U.K.: Polity Press, 2013.

Park, Benjamin E., and Jordan T. Watkins. "The Riches of Mormon Materialism: Parley P. Pratt's 'Materiality' and Early Mormon Theology." *Mormon Historical Studies* 11 (Fall 2010): 159–72.

Patterson, Zabet. *Peripheral Vision: Bell Labs, the S-C 4020, and the Origins of Computer Art*. Cambridge, Mass.: MIT Press, 2015.

"Patty Sessions." *Woman's Exponent* 13, no. 17 (February 1885): 134–35.

Paulsen, David L., and Martin Pulido. "'A Mother There': A Survey of Historical Teachings about Mother in Heaven." *BYU Studies* 50 (2011), article 7.

Pearson, Roberta E., and Nicola Simpson Khullar. "Reverse Flow: European Media in the United States." In *The Paradox of Global U.S.A.*, edited by Bruce Mazlish, Nayan Chanda, and Kenneth Weisbrode, 103–21. Stanford, Calif.: Stanford University Press, 2007.

Peery, Joseph S. "The Bureau of Information." *Liahona: The Elders' Journal* 14 (October 3, 1916): 215–18.

Peet, V. S. "Anti-Mormon Crusade in England." *Utah Independent* 3 (August 14, 1911): 1–2.

Peloubet, Francis Nathan. *Suggestive Illustrations on the Gospel According to Matthew*. New York: E. R. Herrick, 1897.

Penrose, Charles W. *Eighty-Third Annual Conference of the Church of Jesus Christ of Latter-day Saints, April 1913*, 56–65. Salt Lake City, Utah: Church of Jesus Christ of Latter-day Saints, 1913.

Perry, Seth. "The Many Bibles of Joseph Smith: Textual, Prophetic, and Scholarly Authority in Early-National Bible Culture." *Journal of the American Academy of Religion* 84 (September 2016): 750–75.

Peters, Ben, and John Durham Peters. "Introduction: Small Means, Great Things." *Mormon Studies Review* 5 (2018): 17–25.

———. "Review: Matter Made Graciously Present." *Dialogue* 46, no. 4 (Winter 2013): 190–97.

Peters, John Durham. "Google Wants to Be God's Mind: The Secret Theology of I'm Feeling Lucky." *Salon.com*, July 19, 2015. www.salon.com/2015/07/19/google _wants_to_be_gods_mind_the_secret_theology_of_im_feeling_lucky/.

———. *The Marvelous Clouds: Toward a Philosophy of Elemental Media*. Chicago: University of Chicago Press, 2015.

———. "Mormonism and Media." In *The Oxford Handbook of Mormonism*, edited by Terryl Givens and Philip Barlow, 407–21. Oxford: Oxford University Press, 2015.

———. "Recording beyond the Grave: Joseph Smith's Celestial Bookkeeping." *Critical Inquiry* 42 (Summer 2016): 842–64.

———. *Speaking into the Air: A History of the Idea of Communication*. Chicago: University of Chicago Press, 1999.

Petrey, Taylor. *Tabernacles of Clay: Sexuality and Gender in Modern Mormonism*. Chapel Hill: University of North Carolina Press, 2020.

Petsco, Bela. "My Mother and Genealogy." In *Families Lost and Found*, edited by Lee Nelson and Marylin Brown, 16. Springville, Utah: Cedar Fort, 2005.

Phillips, H. I. "Good or Bad, Television . . ." *Kane County Standard*, June 3, 1949, [6].

Piesing, Mark. "Why We Often View Digital Culture through Insect Metaphors." *Wired.co.uk*, May 3, 2013. www.wired.co.uk/article/insect-technology.

Piner, Howard L. *Werner's Readings and Recitations* 23. New York: Edgar S. Werner, 1899.

Plate, S. Brent. *Key Terms in Material Religion*. London: Bloomsbury, 2015.

Plummer, Louise. "Gates, Susa Young." *Encyclopedia of Mormonism*. Vol. 1, ed. Daniel H. Ludlow, 535–36. New York: Macmillan, 1992.

Polidori, John. *The Vampyre: A Tale*. London: Sherwood, Neely, and Jones, 1819.

Poulsen, Richard C. "Fate and the Persecutors of Josephs Smith: Transmutations of an American Myth." *Dialogue* 11, no. 4 (1978): 63–78.

"Pratt's 'Materiality' and Early Mormon Theology." *Mormon Historical Studies* 11 (Fall 2010): 159–72.

Pratt, Orson. *Absurdities of Immaterialism, or, A Reply to T. W. P. Taylder's Pamphlet, Entitled, "The Materialism of the Mormons or Latter-day Saints, Examined and Exposed."* Liverpool, U.K.: R. James, 1849.

———. "Elijah's Latter-day Mission." Delivered August 28, 1859. *Journal of Discourses* 7 (Liverpool, U.K.: Latter-day Saints Book Depot, 1860): 74–90.

———. "An Interesting Account of Several Remarkable Visions, 1840." In *Histories*. Vol. 1 of *Joseph Smith Papers*, edited by Karen Lynn Davidson, David J. Whittaker, Mark Ashurst-McGee, and Richard L. Jensen, 517–46. Salt Lake City, Utah: Church Historian's Press, 2012.

———. "Preparations for the Second Advent." *Seer* 2, no. 8 (1854): 305–20.

———. "Revelation on the Judgments of the Lord." December 28, 1873. *Journal of Discourses* 16 (Liverpool, U.K.: Latter-day Saints Book Depot, 1874): 326–38.

———. "Temples to Be Built to the Name of the Lord." Delivered October 7, 1873. *Journal of Discourses* 16 (Liverpool, U.K.: Latter-day Saints Book Depot, 1874): 251–62.

Pratt, Parley Parker. *An Autobiography of Parley Parker Pratt*. Chicago: Law, King, and Law, 1888.

Prescott, Cynthia Culver. *Pioneer Mother Monuments: Constructing Cultural Memory*. Norman: University of Oklahoma Press, 2019.

Prescott, Marianne Holman. "Help Build 'Unwavering Faith' in Students' Lives, Elder Ballard Tells CES Teachers." *Church News*, February 29, 2016. www.lds.org/church/news/help-build-unwavering-faith-in-students-lives-elder-ballard-tells-ces-teachers.

Price, Leah, and Pamela Thurschwell, eds. *Literary Secretaries / Secretarial Culture*. New York: Routledge, 2016.

Prince, Gregory. *David O. McKay and the Rise of Modern Mormonism*. Salt Lake City: University of Utah Press, 2005.

"Proceedings of Societies." *Photographic News*, February 20, 1863, 94.

"Progress in Microfilming." *Utah Genealogical and Historical Magazine* 30, no. 2 (April 1939): 100.

Pulsipher, Zera. "History of Zerah Pulsipher as Written by Himself." Zera Pulsipher autobiography, ca. 1872, Church History Library, Salt Lake City, Utah.

Quinn, D. Michael. "Ezra Taft Benson and Mormon Political Conflicts." *Dialogue: A Journal of Mormon Thought* 26 (Summer 1993): 1–87.

———. "The Mormon Succession Crisis of 1844." *BYU Studies Quarterly* 16 (1976): 187–233.

Rank, Otto. *The Double: A Psychoanalytic Study.* Chapel Hill: University of North Carolina Press, 1971.

Raykoff, Ivan. "Piano, Telegraph, Typewriter: Listening to the Language of Touch." In *Media, Technology, and Literature in the Nineteenth Century: Image, Sound, Touch,* edited by Colette Colligan and Margaret Linley, 159–88. Farnham, England: Ashgate, 2011.

Rayward, W. Boyd. "Information Revolutions, the Information Society, and the Future of the History of Information Science." *Library Trends* 62, no. 3 (2014): 681–713.

"Read through a Machine." *Deseret News,* November 23, 1889, 6.

"Recollections of the Prophet Joseph Smith." *Juvenile Instructor* 27, no. 1 (January 1892): 22–24.

"Recovering Identities of Black Latter-day Saints." *Perspectives: The Official Magazine of the University of Utah College of Humanities,* 2018–19. humanities.utah.edu /perspectives/2018-2019/recovering-identities-black-lds.php.

Rector, Connie, and Diane Deputy. *The Celestial Connection.* Salt Lake City, Utah: Bookcraft, 1980.

Reed, Robert, and Maxine Reed. *The Encyclopedia of Television, Cable, and Video.* New York: Van Nostrand Reinhold, 1992.

Reeve, Paul. *Religion of a Different Color: Race and the Mormon Struggle for Whiteness.* Oxford: Oxford University Press, 2015.

Reid, Thomas. *Essays on the Intellectual Power of the Human Mind.* London: Thomas Tegg, 1827.

———. *An Inquiry into the Human Mind on the Principles of Common Sense.* Edinburgh: Bell and Bradfute, 1810.

Reid, William James. *Lectures on the Revelation.* Pittsburg: Stevenson, Foster, 1878.

"Religion to Be Computerized." *Jewish Telegraphic Agency* 38 (September 8, 1971): 3.

Remington Typewriter Company. *How to Become a Successful Stenographer: For the Young Woman Who Wants to Make Good.* New York: Stenographic Efficiency Bureau, 1916.

"Revelation, circa 8 March 1831–A [D&C 46]." Joseph Smith Papers, 76–78. www .josephsmithpapers.org/paper-summary/revelation-circa-8-march-1831-a-dc-46/3.

"Revelation, 9 May 1831 [D&C 50]," 82–85. Joseph Smith Papers. www.josephsmithpapers .org/paper-summary/revelation-9-may-1831-dc-50/1.

Richards, Bradley W. *The Savage View.* Nevada, Calif.: Carl Mautz, 1995.

Richards, Franklin D. "Discourse by Elder Franklin D. Richards." Delivered April 7, 1894. *Millennial Star* 56 (Liverpool, U.K.: Anthon H. Lund, 1894): 401–5.

———. *One Hundred Thirty-First Annual Conference of the Church of Jesus Christ of Latter-day Saints, April 1961,* 83–87. Salt Lake City, Utah: Church of Jesus Christ of Latter-day Saints, 1961.

Riches, Harriet. "Picture Taking and Picture Making: Gender Difference and the Historiography of Photography." In *Photography, History, Difference,* edited by Tanya Sheehan, 128–50. Lebanon, N.H.: Dartmouth College Press, 2015.

Riess, Jana. *The Next Mormons: How Millennials Are Changing the LDS Church.* Oxford: Oxford University Press, 2019.

Riley, Glenda. *Women and Nature: Saving the "Wild" West.* Lincoln: University of Nebraska Press, 1999.

Roberts, B. H. "Comprehensiveness of the Gospel." *Contributor* 13, no. 9 (July 1892): 393–98.

Robinson, Henry Peach. *The Elements of a Pictorial Photograph.* Bradford, U.K.: Percy Lund / Country, 1896.

Rogers, Aurelia Spencer. *Life Sketches of Orson Spencer and Others.* Salt Lake City, Utah: George Q. Cannon and Sons, 1898.

Rogers, Brent M., Mason K. Allred, Gerrit Dirkmaat, and Brett L. Dowdle, eds. *Documents.* Vol. 8, *February-November 1841,* Joseph Smith Papers. Salt Lake City, Utah: Church Historian's Press, 2019.

Romney, Marion G. *One Hundred Thirty-Second Annual Conference of the Church of Jesus Christ of Latter-day Saints, April 1962, 16–20.* Salt Lake City, Utah: Church of Jesus Christ of Latter-day Saints, 1962.

Rose, Jerry. "The Correlation Program of the Church of Jesus Christ of Latter-day Saints during the Twentieth Century." Master's thesis, Brigham Young University, 1973.

Rozmarin, Miri. "Living Politically: An Irigarayan Notion of Agency as a Way of Life." *Hypatia* 28 (Summer 2013): 469–82.

Saints: The Story of the Church of Jesus Christ in the Latter Days. Vol. 1, *The Standard of Truth, 1815–1846.* Salt Lake City, Utah: Church of Jesus Christ of Latter-day Saints, 2018.

Saints: The Story of the Church of Jesus Christ in the Latter Days. Vol. 2, *No Unhallowed Hand, 1846–1893.* Salt Lake City, Utah: Church of Jesus Christ of Latter-day Saints, 2020.

"Salt Lake City 13th to Have Television." *Salt Lake Telegram* 47 (April 21, 1948): 12.

Savoy, Eric. "The Rise of the American Gothic." In *The Cambridge Companion to Gothic Fiction,* edited by Jerrold E. Hogle, 167–88. Cambridge: Cambridge University Press, 2002.

Schiller, Friedrich, and Johann Wolfgang von Goethe. *Correspondence between Schiller and Goethe.* Vol. 1. Translated by Geo H. Calvert. London: Wiley and Putnam, 1845.

Schivelbusch, Wolfgang. *The Railway Journey.* Berkeley: University of California Press, 1986.

Schilpp, Paul Arthur, and Lewis Edwin Hahn, eds. *The Philosophy of Gabriel Marcel.* Chicago: Open Court, 1984.

Schmidt, Leigh Eric. *Hearing Things: Religion, Illusion, and the American Enlightenment.* Cambridge, Mass.: Harvard University Press, 2000.

———. *Heaven's Bride: The Unprintable Life of Ida C. Craddock.* New York: Basic Books, 2010.

———. *Holy Fairs: Scotland and the Making of American Revivalism.* Princeton, N.J.: Princeton University Press, 1989.

Schor, Naomi. "This Essentialism Which Is Not One: Coming to Grips with Irigaray." In *Engaging with Irigaray: Feminist Philosophy and Modern European Thought,* edited by Carolyn Burke, Naomi Schor, and Margaret Whitford, 57–78. New York: Columbia University Press, 1994.

Schüttpelz, Erhard. "Körpertechniken." *Zeitschrift für Medien- und Kulturforschung* 1 (2010): 101–20.

"Scientific News." *English Mechanic and World of Science* 56 (January 27, 1893): 518–19.

Sconce, Jeffrey. *Haunted Media: Electronic Presence from Telegraphy to Television.* Durham, N.C.: Duke University Press, 2000.

Scott, Richard G. "Redemption the Harvest of Love" *Ensign*, November 1990, 5–7.

Sedgwick, Catherine Maria. *Stories for Young Persons.* New York: Harper and Brothers, 1840.

Seeman, Erik R. *Speaking with the Dead in Early America.* Philadelphia: University of Pennsylvania Press, 2019.

Seltzer, Mark. *Bodies and Machines.* New York: Routledge, 1992.

"Sensitive Machines." *Deseret Evening News*, May 26, 1892, 8.

Sewell, Philip. *Television in the Age of Radio.* New Brunswick, N.J.: Rutgers University Press, 2014.

Seymour, Mary. "Type-Writing." *Contributor* 10, no. 11 (September 1889): 425–29.

Shapiro, Gary. *Archaeologies of Vision.* Chicago: University of Chicago Press, 2003.

Shiach, Morag. "Modernity, Labour and the Typewriter." In *Modernist Sexualities*, edited by Hugh Stevens and Caroline Howlett, 114–29. Manchester: Manchester University Press, 2000.

Shipps, Jan. *Mormonism: The Story of a New Religious Tradition.* Urbana: University of Illinois Press, 1985.

———. *Sojourner in the Promised Land: Forty Years among the Mormons.* Urbana: University of Illinois Press, 2000.

Shirts, Kathryn H. "The Role of Susa Young Gates and Leah Dunford Widtsoe in the Historical Development of the Priesthood/Motherhood Model." *Journal of Mormon History* 44 (April 2018): 104–39.

Siegel, Greg. *Forensic Media: Reconstructing Accidents in Accelerated Modernity.* Durham, N.C.: Duke University Press, 2014.

Siegert, Bernhard. *Cultural Techniques: Grids, Filters, Doors, and Other Articulations of the Real.* New York: Fordham University Press, 2015.

Simmel, Georg. "The Metropolis and Mental Life." In *The Urban Sociology Reader*, edited by Jan Lin and Christopher Mele, 23–31. New York: Routledge, 2005.

Simpson, Robert L. *One Hundred Forty-Sixth Annual Conference of the Church of Jesus Christ of Latter-day Saints, April 1976,* 86–89. Salt Lake City, Utah: Church of Jesus Christ of Latter-day Saints, 1976.

Simpson, Thomas W. *The American University and the Birth of Modern Mormonism, 1867–1940.* Chapel Hill: University of North Carolina Press, 2016.

Smith, E. Wesley. *Ninety-Fifth Semi-annual Conference of the Church of Jesus Christ of Latter-day Saints, October 1924,* 113–16. Salt Lake City, Utah: Church of Jesus Christ of Latter-day Saints, 1924.

Smith, Eldred G. *One Hundred Eighteenth Annual Conference of the Church of Jesus Christ of Latter-day Saints, April, 1948,* 97–99. Salt Lake City, Utah: Church of Jesus Christ of Latter-day Saints, 1948.

———. *One Hundred Twenty-Seventh Semi-annual Conference of the Church of Jesus Christ of Latter-day Saints, October 1956,* 75–76. Salt Lake City, Utah: Church of Jesus Christ of Latter-day Saints, 1956.

Smith, George A. "History of George Albert Smith." June 9, 1841, George A. Smith Auto-biography and Journals, 1839–1875, Church History Library, Salt Lake City, Utah.

———. "Sacrament—Self-Examination—Recollections of Early Life." *Journal of Discourses* 15 (Liverpool, U.K.: Latter-day Saints Book Depot, 1873): 92–98.

Smith, John Henry. "Remarks." *Deseret Weekly* 53, no. 15 (September 26, 1896): 449–50.

Smith, Joseph. *The Book of Mormon: An Account Written by the Hand of Mormon, upon Plates Taken from the Plates of Nephi.* Palmyra, New York: E. B. Grandin, 1830.

Smith, Joseph Fielding. *One Hundred Eighteenth Annual Conference of the Church of Jesus Christ of Latter-day Saints, April 1948,* 131–36. Salt Lake City, Utah: Church of Jesus Christ of Latter-day Saints, 1948.

Smith, Joseph F. Letter to John Taylor and the Council of the Twelve (draft). September 17, 1878. Joseph F. Smith Papers, Church History Library, Salt Lake City, Utah.

Smith, Lizzie. "Equality of the Sexes." *Young Woman's Journal* 1 (March 1890): 175–76.

Smith, Lucy. *Biographical Sketches of Joseph Smith the Prophet and His Progenitors for Many Generations.* Liverpool, U.K.: Orson Pratt and S. W. Richards, 1853.

Smith, Robert Ellis. *The Law of Privacy Explained.* Providence, R.I.: Privacy Journal, 1993.

Smith, Woodrow, and Ray Dawley. *Better Television Reception in Fringe and Low-Signal Areas.* Santa Barbara, Calif.: Editors and Engineers, 1952.

Smoot, Stephen. "Reports of the Death of the Church Are Greatly Exaggerated." Faithful Answers, Informed Response (website), January 15, 2013. www.fairmormon.org /blog/2013/01/15/reports-of-the-death-of-the-church-are-greatly-exaggerated.

Snow, Erastus. "Remarks by Elder Erastus Snow." Delivered February 28, 1869. *Journal of Discourses* 13 (Liverpool, U.K.: Latter-day Saints Book Depot, 1871): 5–11.

———. "Discourse by Apostle Erastus Snow." Delivered June 24, 1883. *Journal of Discourses* 24 (Liverpool, U.K.: Latter-day Saints Book Depot, 1884): 158–66.

Snow, Lorenzo. "The Iowa Journal of Lorenzo Snow." Edited by Maureen Ursenbach Beecher. *BYU Studies* 24, no. 3 (1984): 261–73.

Snow, Steven E. "Balancing Church History." *New Era,* June 2013, 21–22.

Snyder, Katherine. *Bachelors, Manhood, and the Novel, 1850–1925.* Cambridge, U.K.: Cambridge University Press, 2009.

Sobchack, Vivian. *Carnal Thoughts: Embodiment and Moving Image Culture.* Berkeley: University of California Press, 2004.

Solomon, Matthew. *Disappearing Tricks: Silent Film, Houdini, and the New Magic of the Twentieth Century.* Urbana: University of Illinois Press, 2010.

Speek, Vickie Cleverley. *"God Has Made Us a Kingdom": James Strang and the Midwest Mormons.* Salt Lake City, Utah: Signature Books, 2006.

Spencer, Stan. "Seers and Stones: The Translation of the Book of Mormon as Divine Visions of an Old-Time Seer." *Interpreter* 24 (2017): 27–98.

Sperry, M. E. "Women and Photography." Excerpted from *Pacific Coast Photographer. Photography* 7 (April 18, 1895): 251.

Spigel, Lynn. *Welcome to the Dreamhouse: Popular Media and Postwar Suburbs.* Durham, N.C.: Duke University Press, 2001.

"Spiritism on Trial." *Deseret Evening News,* November 14, 1901, 4.

"Springville Celebrates." *Salt Lake Herald-Republican,* July 5, 1900, 5.

"Springville Notes." *Salt Lake Herald-Republican,* December 23, 1897, 6.

Stapley, Jonathan, A. "Women and Priesthood." In *The Routledge Handbook of Mormonism and Gender,* edited by Taylor Petrey and Amy Hoyt, 569–79. New York: Routledge, 2020.

Steinberg, Avi. *The Lost Book of Mormon: A Quest for the Book That Just Might Be the Great American Novel.* New York: Anchor Books, 2014.

Stegner, Wallace. *Mormon Country.* Lincoln: University of Nebraska Press, 1996.

Sternberger, Dolf. *Panorama, oder Ansichten vom 19. Jahrhundert.* Hamburg: Claasen Verlag, 1955.

Stevenson, Robert Louis. *A Child's Garden of Verses.* New York: Dover, 1992.

Steward, William Juke. *The Vision of Aorangi, and Other Poems.* Timaru, New Zealand: Timaru Post Newspaper Company, 1906.

Stoker, Bram. *Dracula.* New York: Grosset and Dunlap, 1897.

Stolow, Jeremy, ed. *Deus in Machina: Religion, Technology, and the Things in Between.* New York: Fordham University Press, 2013.

———. "Salvation by Electricity." In *Religion: Beyond a Concept,* edited by Hendt de Vries, 668–86. New York: Fordham University Press, 2008.

Stout, Hosea. Journal. Church History Library, Salt Lake City, Utah.

Strom, Sharon H. *Beyond the Typewriter: Gender, Class, and the Origins of Modern American Office Work, 1900–1930.* Champaign: University of Illinois Press, 1992.

Sullivan, Winnifred Fallers. *The Impossibility of Religious Freedom.* Princeton, N.J.: Princeton University Press, 2005.

Tait, Lisa Olsen. "Susa Young Gates and the Vision of the Redemption of the Dead." In *Revelations in Context: Stories behind the Sections of the Doctrine and Covenants,* 315–22. Salt Lake City, Utah: Church of Jesus Christ of Latter-day Saints, 2016.

———. "The 'Young Woman's Journal' and Its Stories: Gender and Generations in 1890s Mormondom." Ph.D. diss., University of Houston, 2010.

———. "The 'Young Woman's Journal'": Gender and Generations in a Mormon Women's Magazine. *American Periodicals* 22 (2012): 51–71.

"Take Time to Safeguard Children." *Relief Society Magazine* 42, no. 1 (January 1955): 99.

Talbot, Frederick A. *Moving Pictures and How They Are Made.* Philadelphia: Lippincott, 1912.

"Talented Uncle Roscoe." *Deseret News,* June 22, 1977, C3.

Talmage, James E. "Genealogy and Work for the Dead." *Utah Genealogical and Historical Magazine* 10 (April 1919): 49–61.

Tanner, N. Eldon. *One Hundred Thirty-First Annual Conference of the Church of Jesus Christ of Latter-day Saints, April 1961,* 106–10. Salt Lake City, Utah: Church of Jesus Christ of Latter-day Saints, 1961.

Tate, George S. "'The Great World of the Spirits of the Dead': Death, the Great War, and the 1918 Influenza Pandemic as Context for Doctrine and Covenants 138." *BYU Studies* 46, no. 1 (2007): 4–40.

Taves, Ann. *Fits, Trances, and Visions: Experiencing Religion and Explaining Experience from Wesley to James.* Princeton, N.J.: Princeton University Press, 1999.

———. "History and the Claims of Revelation: Joseph Smith and the Materialization of the Golden Plates." *Numen* 61 (2014): 182–207.

Taylor, Charles. *A Secular Age.* Cambridge, Mass.: Harvard University Press, 2007.

Taylor, Gregory. *Shut Off: The Canadian Digital Television Transition.* Montreal: McGill-Queen's University Press, 2013.

Taylor, Henry D. "When the Lord Commands, Do It." *Improvement Era* 69 (June 1966): 529–30.

Taylor, John. "Discourse." Delivered December 14, 1884. *Journal of Discourses* 26 (Liverpool, U.K.: Latter-day Saints Book Depot, 1886): 30–39.

———. "God the Source of All Intelligence and Wisdom." February 5, 1865. *Journal of Discourses* 11 (Liverpool, U.K.: Latter-day Saints Book Depot, 1867): 76–77.

———. "Gospel Preached to the Antediluvians." Delivered February 12, 1882. *Journal of Discourses* 26 (Liverpool, U.K.: Latter-day Saints Book Depot, 1882): 87–97.

———. "Honesty of Purpose Should Actuate All True Believers." *Journal of Discourses* 26 (Liverpool, U.K.: Latter-day Saints Book Depot, 1874): 284–301.

———. "Revelation from God, True Knowledge." Delivered October 7, 1865. *Journal of Discourses* 11 (Liverpool, U.K.: Latter-day Saints Book Depot, 1867): 157–66.

Thayne, Mirla Greenwood. "Heaven's Radio." *Improvement Era* 54 (March 1951): 162.

Thomas, Sophie. *Romanticism and Visuality*. New York: Routledge, 2008.

Thurschwell, Pamela. "The Typist's Remains: Theodora Bosanquet in Recent Fiction." *Henry James Review* 32 (Winter 2011): 1–11.

Timms, Howard L., and Michael F. Pohlen. *The Production Function in Business*. Madison: University of Wisconsin Press, 1970.

Timothy, Dallen J., and Jeanne Kay Guelke, eds. *Geography and Genealogy: Locating Personal Pasts*. Hampshire, England: Ashgate, 2008.

Tingey, Mattie Horn. "The School of Experience." In *At the Pulpit: 185 Years of Discourses by Latter-day Saint Women*, edited by Jennifer Reeder and Kate Holbrook, 83–87. Salt Lake City, Utah: Church Historian's Press, 2017.

Törneman, Mira Stolpe. "Queering Media Archaeology." *Communication +1* 7 (2019): 1–17.

Tourist's Handbook: Descriptive of Colorado, New Mexico and Utah. Denver: Passengers Department of Denver and Rio Grande Railroad, 1901.

"Try the Spirits." *Times and Seasons* 3 (April 1, 1842): 743–48.

Tucker, Jennifer. *Nature Exposed: Photography as Eyewitness in Victorian Science*. Baltimore: Johns Hopkins University Press, 2005.

Tybjerg, Casper. "Seeing through Spirits: Superimposition, Cognition, and the Phantom Carriage." *Film History* 28, no. 2 (2016): 114–41.

"The Typewriter Girl." *Salt Lake Tribune*, September 11, 1887, 4.

"The Typewriter—Only 75 Years Old." *Rotarian* 73, no. 5 (November 1948): 30.

Ursenbach, Octave. "The Awakening, ca. 1930." Church History Library, Salt Lake City, Utah.

Utah Agricultural College Bulletin, no. 33 (June 1894).

Vance, Laura. *Women in New Religions*. New York: New York University Press, 2015.

Van Wagoner, Richard S. "The Making of a Mormon Myth: The 1844 Transfiguration of Brigham Young." *Dialogue: A Journal of Mormon Thought* 34 (2001): 159–82.

Villela, Khristaan D. "Beyond Stephens and Catherwood." In *Past Presented: Archaeological Illustration and the Ancient Americas*, edited by Joanne Pillsbury, 143–71. Washington, D.C.: Dumbarton Oaks Research Library and Collection, 2012.

Vismann, Cornelia. "Cultural Techniques and Sovereignty." *Theory, Culture, and Society* 30 (2013): 83–93.

Wade, Joseph M. *Posthumous Memoirs of Helena Petrona Blavatsky*. Boston: Joseph M. Wade, 1896.

Wadsworth, Nelson B. *Set in Stone, Fixed in Glass: The Great Mormon Temple and its Photographers*. Salt Lake City, Utah: Signature Books, 1996.

———. "Zion's Cameramen: Early Photographers of Utah and the Mormons." *Utah Historical Quarterly* 40 (Winter 1972): 26–56.

Wagoner, Richard S. Van, ed. *Complete Discourses of Brigham Young*. Salt Lake City, Utah: Smith-Pettit Foundation, 2009.

Wajcman, Judith. *TechnoFeminism*. Cambridge, U.K.: Polity, 2004.

Walker, Charles Lowell. *Diary of Charles Lowell Walker*. Edited by Karl Larson and Katharine Miles Larson. Logan: Utah State University Press, 1980.

Walker, David. "The Humbug in American Religion Ritual Theories of Nineteenth-Century Spiritualism." *Religion and American Culture* 23 (Winter 2013): 30–74.

———. "Mormon Melodrama and the Syndication of Satire, from *Brigham Young* (1940) to *South Park* (2003)." *Journal of American Culture* 40 (September 2017): 259–75.

———. "Railroading Independence: Pulpit Rock and the Work of Mormon Imagination." *John Whitmer Historical Association Journal* 37 (2017): 29–50.

———. *Railroading Religion: Mormons, Tourists, and the Corporate Spirit of the West.* Chapel Hill: University of North Carolina Press, 2019.

Walker, Ronald. "Six Days in August: Brigham Young and the Succession Crisis of 1844." In *A Firm Foundation: Church Organization and Administration*, edited by Arnold K. Garr and David J. Whittaker, 161–96. Provo, Utah: Religious Studies Center, 2011.

———. *Wayward Saints: The Godbeites and Brigham Young*. Champaign: University of Illinois Press, 1998.

Walkowitz, Judith, R. "Science and the Séance: Transgressions of Gender and Genre in Late Victorian London." *Representations* 22 (Spring, 1988): 3–29.

Warner, Marina. *Phantasmagoria: Spirit Visions, Metaphors, and the Media into the Twenty-First Century*. Oxford: Oxford University Press, 2006.

Warren, Samuel, and Louis Brandeis. "The Right to Privacy." *Harvard Law Review* 4, no. 5 (1890): 193–220.

Waterman, Bryan. "Ernest Wilkinson and the Transformation of BYU's Honor Code, 1965–71." *Dialogue* 31, no. 4 (Winter 1998): 85–112.

Watson, Elden Jay, ed. *Manuscript History of Brigham Young, 1801–1844*. Salt Lake City, Utah: Smith Secretarial Service, 1968.

Webb, Stephen H. *Mormon Christianity: What Other Christians Can Learn from the Latter-day Saints*. Oxford: Oxford University Press, 2013.

Weber, Brenda R. *Latter-day Screens: Gender, Sexuality, and Mediated Mormonism*. Durham, N.C.: Duke University Press, 2019.

Wegenstein, Bernadette. "Body." In *Critical Terms for Media Studies*, edited by W. J. T. Mitchell and Mark B. N. Hansen, 19–34. Chicago: University of Chicago Press, 2010.

———. *Getting under the Skin: Body and Media Theory*. Cambridge, Mass.: MIT Press, 2006.

Weisenfeld, Judith. "Framing the Nation: Religion, Film, and American Belonging." *Journal of Mormon History* 45 (April 2019): 23–48.

Welch, Rosalynde. "The New Mormon Theology of Matter." *Mormon Studies Review* 4 (January 2017): 64–79.

Wells, Emmeline B. "The New Civilization." *Woman's Exponent*, October 1, 1904, 28.

———. "A Recent Monograph." *Woman's Exponent*, October 15, 1896, 63.

Wells, H. G. *Science and the World Mind*. London: New Europe, 1942.

———. *World Brain*. Garden City, N.Y.: Doubleday, Doran, 1938.

Wershler-Henry, Darren. *The Iron Whim: A Fragmented History of Typewriting*. Ithaca, N.Y.: Cornell University Press, 2005.

Wesemann, Margot, and Wolfgang Wesemann, eds. *Arthur Clemens Ernst Koehler: A 1928 German Immigrant Who Introduced Microfilming to the LDS Church*. Self-published, Wesemann, 2002.

"What Moving Pictures Teach." In *Nickelodeon* 3 (March 5, 1910): 154.

"What Young People Have Accomplished in Research." *Utah Genealogical Society Magazine* 31 (January 1940): 124–25.

Whissell, Kristen. *Picturing American Modernity: Traffic, Technology, and the Silent Cinema*. Durham, N.C.: Duke University Press, 2008.

Whitaker, John M. Daily Journal. Church History Library, Salt Lake City, Utah.

Whitaker, John M., and Franklin D. Richards. "Correspondence." Salt Lake City, July 7, 1884. John Mills Whitaker Papers, University of Utah Archive.

White, Hayden. *Figural Realism: Studies in the Mimesis Effect*. Baltimore: Johns Hopkins University Press, 1999.

Whitmer, David. *An Address to All Believers in Christ*. Richmond, Mo.: David Whitmer, 1887.

Whitney, Orson F. "Discourse by Bishop Orson F. Whitney." Delivered June 21, 1885. *Journal of Discourses* 26 (Liverpool, U.K.: Latter-day Saints Book Depot, 1885): 260–68.

———. *Elias: An Epic of the Ages*. 1904. Salt Lake City, Utah: O. F. Whitney, 1914.

———. *History of Utah*. Vol. 2. Salt Lake City, Utah: George Q. Cannon and Sons, 1893.

Whittaker, David J., and Arnold K. Garr, eds. *A Firm Foundation: Church Organization and Administration*. Provo, Utah: Religious Studies Center, Brigham Young University; Salt Lake City, Utah: Deseret, 2011.

Wicke, Jennifer. "Vampiric Typewriting: *Dracula* and Its Media." *ELH* 59 (Summer 1992): 467–93.

Widtsoe, John A. *One Hundred and Sixth Semi-annual Conference of the Church of Jesus Christ of Latter-day Saints, April 1936*, 69–72. Salt Lake City, Utah: Church of Jesus Christ of Latter-day Saints, 1936.

Wiener, Norbert. *Cybernetics, or Control and Communication in the Animal and the Machine*. 1948. Cambridge, Mass.: MIT Press, 1985.

Wilcox, Miranda. "Sacralizing the Secular in Latter-day Saint Salvation Histories (1890–1930)." *Journal of Mormon History* 46 (2020): 23–59.

Willard, Francis E. *Occupations for Women*. Copper Union, N.Y.: Success, 1897.

Williams, Linda. "Film Bodies: Gender, Genre, and Excess." *Film Quarterly* 44, no. 4 (Summer 1991): 2–13.

———. "Motion and E-motion: Lust and the 'Frenzy of the Visible.'" *Journal of Visual Culture* 18 (2019): 97–129.

Williams, Raymond. *Television: Technology and Cultural Form*. New York: Schocken Books, 1975.

Wind, Edgar. "Warburg's Concept of *Kulturwissenschaft* and Its Meaning for Aesthetics." In *Art of Art History*, edited by Donald Preziosi, 207–14. Oxford: Oxford University Press, 1998.

Winthrop-Young, Geoffrey. "Cultural Techniques: Preliminary Remarks." *Theory, Culture, and Society* 30 (2013): 3–19.

———. *Kittler and the Media*. Cambridge, U.K.: Polity, 2011.

Wirthlin, LeRoy A. "Evil Designs . . . of Conspiring Men in the Last Days." *Relief Society Magazine* 39, no. 1 (January 1952): 647.

Woman's Exponent 15, no. 8 (September 15, 1886): 57–58.

Wood, Henry. *Ideal Suggestion through Mental Photography*. Boston: Lee and Shepard, 1890.

Woodger, Mary Jane. "From Obscurity to Scripture: Joseph F. Smith's Vision of the Redemption of the Dead." In *You Shall Have My Word: Exploring the Text of the Doctrine and Covenants*, edited by Scott C. Esplin, Richard O. Cowan, and Rachel Cope, 234–54. Salt Lake City, Utah: Brigham Young University, 2012.

Woodruff, Wilford. "The Church and Kingdom of God, and the Churches and Kingdoms of Men." Delivered February 25, 1855. *Journal of Discourses* 2 (Liverpool, U.K.: Latter-day Saints Book Depot, 1855): 191–202.

———. *The Discourses of Wilford Woodruff*. Edited by G. Homer Durham. Salt Lake City, Utah: Bookcraft, 1990.

———. "Necessity of a Temple, and Works in Behalf of the Dead." Delivered April 6, 1876. *Journal of Discourses* 18 (Liverpool, U.K.: Latter-day Saints Book Depot, 1877): 186–93.

———. "Priesthood and the Right of Succession." *Deseret News Semi-weekly*, March 15, 1892, 3.

———. "To the Officers and Members of the Church of Jesus Christ of Latter-day Saints in the British Islands." *Millennial Star* 5 (February 1845): 134–42.

———. "Unchangeableness of the Gospel." *Journal of Discourses* 16 (Liverpool, U.K.: Latter-day Saints Book Depot, 1874): 263–72.

———. *Wilford Woodruff's Journal: Typescript*. Vols. 2, 3, 7, 8. Edited by Scott G. Kenney. Salt Lake City, Utah: Signature Books, 1983–85.

———. Wilford Woodruff's Journals and Papers, 1828–1898. Church History Library, Salt Lake City, Utah.

"The World Congress of Universal Documentation." *Science* 86 (October 1, 1937): 303–4.

Wright, Carole M. Bethke. "A Clue in an Obituary." In *Families Lost and Found*, edited by Lee Nelson and Marylin Brown, 20–22. Springville, Utah: Cedar Fort, 2005.

Yorgason, Ethan R. *Transformation of the Mormon Culture Region*. Champaign: University of Illinois Press, 2003.

Young, Brigham. "Increase of Saints since Joseph Smith's Death." *Journal of Discourses* 15 (Liverpool, U.K.: Latter-day Saints Book Depot, 1877): 135–39.

———. "Our Relatives . . . the Prophet Joseph Not Yet Resurrected." Delivered March 15, 1857. *Journal of Discourses* 4 (Liverpool, U.K.: S. W. Richards, 1857): 279–91.

———. "Remarks by President Brigham Young." Delivered August 24, 1872. *Journal of Discourses* 15 (Liverpool, U.K.: Latter-day Saints Book Depot, 1873): 135–39.

Young, Clifford E. *One Hundred Eighteenth Annual Conference of the Church of Jesus Christ of Latter-day Saints, April 1948*, 37–40. Salt Lake City, Utah: Church of Jesus Christ of Latter-day Saints, 1948.

Young, Levi. "Mormonism in Picture." *Young Woman's Journal* 24 (1913): 75–80.

Young, S. Dilworth. *One Hundred Twenty-Fifth Annual Conference of the Church of Jesus Christ of Latter-day Saints, April 1955*, 98–100. Salt Lake City, Utah: Church of Jesus Christ of Latter-day Saints, 1955.

Zante, Helen J. Van. *Household Equipment Principles*. Hoboken, N.J.: Prentice-Hall, 1964.

INDEX

death: Latter-day Saint beliefs about, 3, 16, 90; and media, 15, 16, 22, 105, 135; and print, 24. *See also* Smith, Joseph: death of

deception: as modern issue, 24–25; and optical media, 24, 30; and phantasmagoria, 27–28; techniques to avoid, 33–36, 40, 42–44, 185; spiritual, 39, 40–42

demons, 17, 23, 42. *See also* spirits

Deseret, 187

Deseret Alphabet, 94

determinism, 4, 14, 190

devices: and popular culture, 17, 27, 30; effect of, 31, 82, 118; and spiritualism, 84, 101; Latter-day Saint use of, 137, 141, 158, 184, 188; and patriotism, 170–71

Dibble, Philo: use of panorama, 18, 46–48; and Joseph Smith, 40, 46; visions of, 46, 47, 51–52; and Brigham Young, 59; and C. C. A. Christensen, 65

digital age, 151, 184–85, 187–88

discourse: entanglement with materiality, 5–8, 10–11, 38; and media, 11–12, 145, 174; and gender, 74; and class, 129

discourse network, 6–7, 9, 16, 34, 116, 189

distant vision, 156, 158–60

distraction, 30, 49, 56, 166, 167

Doctrine and Covenants, 42

domesticity, 109, 122, 123, 161, 165, 166, 168

doppelgänger: and technology, 16; in photography, 87; in film, 105, 106, 110, 114, 116–18, 120

double. *See* doppelgänger

double exposure, 21, 86–88, 99, 103, 125, 131

doubt, 29, 84, 187

Dracula, 19, 89

dreams: and deception 39, 41; as revelation, 141, 147, 148, 149; and technology, 158, 160, 185. *See also* Bachelor's Dream (trope); visions

dress and grooming, 22, 173. *See also* modesty

Dupin, C. Auguste, 33

duplication: and microfilm, 21, 141, 143, 145, 152, 153; and public image, 119, 132–34

earth: in Latter-day Saint theology, 3, 134–35, 139, 141–42, 144, 149–50,

189; and spirit world, 42, 117, 181; and maternity, 73, 91; and broadcasting, 155

Eddy, Mary Baker, 97

electricity, 37, 64, 111, 170–71

Enemy Hath Done This, An (Benson), 170

Ensign, 174

eternity, 91, 135, 172

eugenics, 121, 140

Evans, John Henry, 125

Evans, Richard L., 181

eyes: in Latter-day Saint belief, 3; natural vs. spiritual, 4, 21, 24–25, 37; of Joseph Smith, 23–24, 99; reliability of, 23, 25, 28, 35, 40–41, 43; disciplining of, 30, 50; to discern visions, 43–44, 53, 180, 185, 188; interacting with media, 48, 53, 55, 62, 82, 96, 147, 166; in representations of Mormons, 112, 114

faces: of the Lord, 63; of Joseph Smith's assassins, 68, 130; of Elfie Huntington, 79, 83; of Joseph Smith, 126. *See also* whiteface

Facebook, 184

faith: in sight, 30; in technology, 86; crisis of, 187–88

Family History Center, 153

Familysearch.org, 153

Farnsworth, Philo, 158–59, 181

fear: media experience of, 37, 93; of media effects, 89, 180; of Mormons, 107, 111, 115; of losing records, 135; of communism, 170

femininity, 74, 79, 93, 102

feminism, 99. *See also* women's rights

Fielding, Joseph, 41

film. *See* cinema

first vision: written accounts of, 17, 23–24, 31, 98–99; visual representations of, 69, 183–84; familiarity of, 99, 160; and Philo Farnsworth, 158; and mobile phones, 184–85

Fiskoscope, 136

focus. *See* attention

For the Strength of Youth (pamphlet), 173

Gates, Susa Young: and typewriter, 19–20, 88; upbringing, 88–89; and spiritualism, 93–94; and gender roles, 96–102, 189–90. *See also* typewriters; "Vision Beautiful"

gaze: Mormon, 50, 69, 157, 187; male, 77–80

gender: coconstruction with technology, 19–20, 74, 88, 101–2; and visions, 41, 57, 147–48; in Latter-Day Saint beliefs, 73–75, 175, 179; and photography, 79–80; norms, 82–83, 85, 165–66; norms of Latter-day Saints, 92–93, 96, 100; roles, 90, 97; and polygamy, 108, 112

Genealogical Helper, 137

Genealogical Society of Utah, 133–34, 136, 141, 143, 146, 151

genealogy: and duplication, 135; and visions, 135, 148–50; and technology, 137, 146, 151–52; Latter-day Saint practice of, 139, 142–44, 186, 188; and race, 140, 190; national interest in, 141

German media theory, 6–8, 14

Ghost-Seer (Schiller), 29

ghost stories, 17, 25, 28–29, 31, 34, 36–39, 43

Ginsburg, Walter, 146

glitches, 109, 190

Goodwin, Megan, 115

gothic film, 117, 118. *See also* ghost stories; gothic literature

gothic literature, 17, 25, 27–29, 34–37, 43, 90. *See also* ghost stories; gothic film

governance, 22, 43, 72, 102, 143, 181, 189

Graham, Winifred, 114, 120

Granger, Oliver, 39

Grant, Heber J., 120, 160, 175

Griffith, D. W., 112, 130

Grover, Roscoe, 174, 175

Halbwachs, Maurice, 55

hands: as media, 3, 15; in Latter-day Saint theology, 42–43; and interaction with other media, 53, 81–82, 92, 96, 98, 181

Haraway, Donna, 8

harmony, 22, 168, 174, 175, 177, 181

Harper, Steven, 68

Harris, Sharon, 13

haunting: ghosts, 16, 56; and print media, 24, 37–38, 48; and phantasmagoria, 27;

and gothic literature, 34–35, 38; and photography, 87–88; and film, 105, 116; and Latter-day Saint history, 186–87

hauntology, 16

Hawaii, 89

Hawthorne, Nathaniel, 28, 93

health, 80, 89, 121, 179; mental, 96; Latter-day Saint code of, 109, 172

heavenly mother, 90, 99

Hegel, Georg Wilhelm Friedrich, 29

Hickman, Jared, 10, 35

Hinckley, Gordon B., 176

hippies, 161, 173

Hitchcock, Alfred, 80

Holmes, Sherlock, 33

Holy Ghost, 15–16, 101, 172

"Homefront" ads, 161

Hood, Thomas, 76

Howe, Mary, 95

Hoyt, Amy, 100, 108

human trafficking: by Latter-day Saints in film, 20, 105–8, 111, 114–16; and modernity, 107; and film, 108, 115

Huntington, Elfie: and gender, 19–20, 101–2, 189; upbringing, 76; and photography, 75, 76–83, 87–88, 99; and Mormon culture, 85, 189

Hyde, Orson, 50, 81

hypnotism, 112, 114

image dissector, 158

immigrants, 49, 120, 134

Improvement Era, 99, 100

Indians. *See* Native Americans

infrastructure: in media theory, 7–8; and spiritualism, 84; Latter-day Saint, 106, 111, 115, 157, 173, 178; and modernity, 108, 116; and genealogy, 135, 141, 144; and television, 156–57; and patriotism, 170

inscription, 19, 73, 90, 97

internet, 13, 184, 187–88

Ivins, Anthony, 143, 144

Jensen, Marlin K., 187, 188

Jensen, Richard, 178

Jesus, 17, 97, 99, 149, 160; images of, 26, 59, 62

and photography, 81, 85; and women's
  roles, 95–96
postsecularism, 10
Pratt, Orson, 64, 81, 135, 140, 141, 159
Price, Leah, 91
priesthood: and spirit communication,
  93–94, 101; and gender, 100, 102; and
  Correlation, 174–75, 177–81
print media: and visions of the dead 5, 17,
  24–25, 33, 37–38, 44; and community,
  18, 35, 39, 53; and optical media, 28–32;
  private consumption of, 47, 53, 62. *See
  also* media
privacy rights, 105, 117–19
psychical research, 125, 158
Pulsipher, Zera, 39

quantum mechanics, 3, 8

race: and Mormon belonging, 19, 21,
  106, 121, 128–29; in American gothic
  literature, 34–35; and film, 111–12, 121–
  22; and genealogy, 140; and Latter-day
  Saint practice, 186–87, 190
radio: and genealogy, 137; influence on
  television, 167; as threat, 170–71,
  173; and revelation, 171–72; and
  standardization, 174–76
railroad. *See* railway
railway: and experience of panorama, 47,
  49, 66–67; and stereograms, 55; in Utah,
  65–66, 111, 124; and modernity, 115
rapping. *See* spiritualism
reading, 25, 37, 38, 63, 93; and Latter-day
  Saint visions 5, 18, 29, 39; American
  Christian practices, 29, 39, 63; passive
  vs. active, 31; and deception, 37–38, 40;
  community, 53; and microfilm, 136–38,
  142, 146, 151
receiver, 171, 186
records, 12, 21, 24, 59, 64; preservation of,
  134; in Latter-day Saint theology, 135,
  138–39; and labor, 137, 142–43; and race,
  140; spiritual help with, 141, 146–50;
  and technology, 143–44, 151–52; and
  world brain, 144–46
rectigraph, 153

Reeve, Paul, 128, 140
Reid, Thomas, 31, 36
Reid, William James, 63
Rejlander, Oscar, 77
religion: study of, 3, 4, 6, 7, 8, 9–11, 22;
  Latter-day Saint performance of, 4–5,
  9–11, 12–13; and media, 13, 49, 62, 86, 138,
  185–87, 190; and the body, 15–16; and
  gender, 74–75; and modernity, 106; and
  film, 123–24
reproduction: with typewriters, 19, 88; with
  print, 24–25, 28, 34, 38; of visions, 32,
  37–38; and gender, 73–75, 92, 97–98,
  102; and polygamy, 106–8, 110; and
  privacy, 116–18. *See also* childbirth;
  motherhood
resurrection, 1, 26, 62, 116, 159
Reveries of a Bachelor (Mitchell), 76
Rigdon, Sidney, 51, 56–58, 67
Robinson, Henry Peach, 86
Rogers, Aurelia Spencer, 58
romanticism, 25, 29

Schmidt, Leigh Eric, 13, 25
screens: different types of, 20, 142; use with
  phantasmagoria, 26; and panorama,
  48, 183; and television, 163, 166, 182; in
  digital age, 184–85, 187–88
scripture: production of, 2, 56, 92; reading
  of, 24, 188; and ghosts, 34; and
  panorama, 64; and photography, 86. *See
  also* Bible; Book of Mormon; Doctrine
  and Covenants
séance, 35, 74, 83, 92, 183
secretaries, 19, 74, 91, 94, 134, 155, 168. *See
  also* amanuenses; assistants
seers: Joseph Smith as, 2, 27, 31; of spirits,
  26–27; and print, 38
seer stones: Joseph Smith's use of, 2, 27,
  31, 184; Hiram Page's use of, 41; and
  photography, 86; and genealogy, 141;
  and smartphones, 184–85, 187
Seltzer, Mark, 96
sender, 171, 186
sensitivity: and visionary abilities, 27,
  86–87; and women, 74–75, 96, 99; and
  spiritualism, 84–85

Sessions, Patty, 60
sexuality: of bachelors, 76–77, 80; and
 photography, 80–82; normative, 87, 156,
 186, 190; media depictions of Mormon,
 106–7, 115. See also courtship
Sharp, Thomas, 53
Shipman, Nell, 123
Shipps, Jan, 127, 161
Siegel, Greg, 33
Siegert, Bernhard, 7, 8
signal, 86, 115, 150, 160
slavery: and polygamy, 76, 81, 94, 114–15;
 and human trafficking, 107, 108, 112,
 114–15
Smith, Eldred G., 180
Smith, George Albert, 140
Smith, Joseph F., 80, 93, 100, 123, 159
Smith, Joseph Fielding, 41, 142
Smith, Joseph, 85, 94, 112, 152, 173, 187; and
 materialism, 3, 16; appearances of, 17, 18,
 45–48, 56–58, 60, 61, 72; death of, 17, 45,
 67, 189; and money-digging, 27
—images and memory of: in panorama,
 50–51, 56, 60–61, 65, 68–69; in film,
 103–4, 126, 129–30
—teachings of: about language, 12; about
 visions, 31, 40–41, 42–43, 44; about
 baptism for the dead, 138, 150–51, 189;
 about records, 139
—visions of: in translating Book of
 Mormon, 1–2; and seer stones, 2, 27, 31,
 41, 44, 141–42, 184; first vision, 17, 23–25,
 98–99
Smith, Lizzie, 57, 95
Smoot, Reed, 106, 116, 119, 120, 128
Snow, Steven E., 188
Sobchack, Vivian, 14, 182
sound: in Mormon culture, 12–13, 171; and
 Deseret Alphabet, 94. See also music
spectators, 31–32. See also audiences;
 observers
specters. See spirits
Spigel, Lynn, 156, 160
spirit photography, 86–88, 104, 125
spirits: and materiality 3, 8, 181; in Latter-
 day Saint theology, 15–17, 142–44, 147;
 and childbirth, 19, 73, 90–91; and use of

microfilm, 21; visitations of, 21, 34, 35,
 37–38, 190; ability to discern types of,
 24, 31, 40, 41–43; and phantasmagoria,
 26–27; and gothic fiction, 35, 38;
 communication with, 64, 84, 86, 92–93;
 in films, 123, 125–26, 132, 171. See also
 demons
spiritualism, 4, 75, 83–84, 92–94, 96, 101
spiritualist mediums, 58, 74, 83–84, 88, 92
spirit world: relation to physical world,
 15, 73, 142, 146; and print, 29; efforts
 to behold, 32, 84–85, 101, 159;
 communication with, 92–93, 147–50
standards, 21–22: in Mormon culture, 88,
 156–57, 172–74, 180–81; of American
 living, 162, 164–65; of television
 technology, 163
standard works. See scripture
Stapley, Jonathan, 100
Stead, William Thomas, 92
stenography, 19, 94
Stevenson, Robert Louis, 66
Stolow, Jeremy, 7, 85
Stout, Hosea, 51, 57, 58
Strang, James, 51, 56
succession: Latter-day Saint crisis of, 18,
 55; and panorama 46–47; and Brigham
 Young, 56–59; and Sidney Rigdon, 67
switchboard, 74, 147
systems: for temple work, 21–22,
 133, 143, 150–52; and gender, 102;
 media representations of Mormon
 underground, 107, 108–11, 114, 131; and
 modernity, 132; and microfilm, 135. See
 also Correlation; cybernetics; world
 brain

Talmage, James, 146
Taves, Ann, 20, 25, 32
Taylor, John, 52, 65, 122
technofeminism, 74–75
technologies: of stones, 2; study of 4–7, 9;
 relationship of Mormonism with,12–13;
 and the human body, 14–15; and spirits,
 16–17; for broadcast, 21, 137, 157, 162, 170,
 186; of deception, 36; and polygamy,
 107, 109–10; and privacy, 118; and

genealogy, 136–37, 141–43; and gender, 20, 75, 97; in spiritualism, 75, 83, 84–85, 92, 96, 101. *See also* discourse network; inscription; media

telephones, 115, 147, 151

television: Latter-day Saint use of, 21–22, 155–57, 179–81; and Philo Farnsworth, 158–59; in American culture, 160-61; and consumerism, 165–67; and patriotism, 168–71. *See also* standards

temples: rituals in, 21, 42, 86, 139; destruction of, 68–69; media representations of, 112; and work for the dead, 140–44, 153

theophany, 23, 99

Thurschwell, Pamela, 91

traffic, 20–21; and modernity, 105, 107–8; and polygamy, 108, 110–11; and white slave trade, 115–16

Traffic in Souls (film), 115

train. *See* railway

Trapped by the Mormons (film), 112–14, 125

Trip to Salt Lake City, A (film), 110

Twain, Mark, 100

Twilight Zone, The (TV show), 170–71

typewriters, 19–20; and gender, 74–75, 91, 100; and Susa Young Gates, 88–89, 96–99; cultural effect of, 89–90, 96, 99; and spiritualism, 92–93; Latter-day Saint adoption of, 94–95

Uchtdorf, Dieter F., 184

undead, 59, 105, 188

unity. *See* harmony

unseen. *See* matter: invisible to the eye

uranium, 180

Urim and Thummim, 2, 44, 141. *See also* seer stones

vampires, 37, 108, 112, 114, 120

V-mail, 145

veil of the living, 15, 21, 24, 60, 63. *See also* spirit world

Vertigo (film), 80

victims: Latter-day Saints as, 120, 129, 130, 132; of delusion, 40, 44; of Mormons in cinema, 105, 110–12

Victim of the Mormons (film), 20, 114–16, 118–20, 125

violence, 34, 53, 189

"Vision Beautiful" (Gates), 99–100

visions: of Joseph Smith, 1–2, 23–25; evolution of Latter-day Saint visions, 4, 16, 185, 189–90; and media, 17–19, 20–22, 27, 29, 147, 172; different modes of, 32–34; of early Latter-day Saint converts, 37–41, 46, 57; and the senses, 42 43; and succession crisis, 45–47, 55, 58, 72; and gender, 74–75, 83, 88, 101–2; and authority, 94, 101. *See also* first vision; Smith, Joseph: visions of; panorama; phantasmagoria; photography; optical media; television

Vismann, Cornelia, 9

Wade, Joseph M., 92

Walker, David, 53, 84, 125

Warburg, Aby, 55

Warren, Samuel, 118–19

Watt, George, 60, 94

Weber, Brenda, 130

Weber, Max, 56

Weisenfeld, Judith, 111–12

Wells, Emmeline, 90

Wells, H. G., 145

Whissell, Kristen, 107, 115

whiteface, 129

whiteness, 19, 21, 115, 121–22, 128, 129, 132. *See also* race

Whitmer, John, 39–40

Whitney, Orson, 63

Wiener, Norbert, 142, 150

Wilkinson, Ernest, 173

women: and technology, 19–20, 81–82, 166–67; and visions, 41, 57, 98–99, 147–50; and maternity, 42–43, 88, 98; and labor, 74–75, 89, 91–93, 95–96; and spiritualism, 84–85, 93–94; absence of, in archives, 92; and human trafficking in cinema, 109, 112, 114–15

women's rights: and spiritualism, 84, 101; and Susa Young Gates, 89; in Mormonism, 98–99

Woodruff, Wilford: and succession crisis, 58–61, 67; and panorama 64; and work for the dead, 139, 141–42

world brain, 21, 134, 136, 144–45, 152

Young, Brigham: and succession crisis, 18, 57–59, 67; visions of, 18, 58; and polygamy, 85; as father, 98; and work for the dead, 134, 139

Young, Clifford E., 159

Young, Levi, 124, 129

Young Woman's Journal, 89, 93, 100

youth, 61, 90, 95, 173

ZCMI (Zion's Co-operative Mercantile Institution), 165–66

Zion: and media, 13; and gathering, 157, 174; and Correlation, 177–78

Zion's Co-operative Mercantile Institution (ZCMI), 165–66

CPSIA information can be obtained
at www.ICGtesting.com
Printed in the USA
LVHW031628310323
742522LV00040B/174